ANIMAL BIODIVERSITY AND FISHERIES

S.N.	Species Name	Reported by	Geographical Distribution at Different Protected Areas					
			AWLS	BWLS	CTR	GL(GNP/GWLS)	NDBR	RNP
114.	*Oniticellus cinctus* Fabricius	Chandra *et al.*, 2012 & Uniyal *et al.*, 2013	-	-	-	+	-	-
115.	*Onitis excavatus* Arrow	Chandra *et al.*, 2012	-	-	-	+	-	-
116.	*Onitis falcatus* Wulfen	Chandra *et al.*, 2012 & Dayakrishna, 2017	-	-	+	+	-	-
117.	*Onitis philemon* Fabricius	Chandra *et al.*, 2012	-	-	-	+	-	-
118.	*Onitis subopacus* Arrow	Chandra *et al.*, 2012	-	-	-	+	-	-
119.	*Onitis virens* Lansberge	Chandra *et al.*, 2012	-	-	-	+	-	-
120.	*Onthophagus abreui* Arrow	Chandra *et al.*, 2012	-	-	-	+	-	-
121.	*Onthophagus aenescens* Wiedmann	Chandra *et al.*, 2012	-	-	-	+	-	-
122.	*Onthophagus amplexus* Sharp	Chandra *et al.*, 2012	-	-	-	+	-	-
123.	*Onthophagus atropolitus* d'Orb	Chandra *et al.*, 2012	-	-	-	+	-	-
124.	*Onthophagus bengalensis* Harold	Chandra *et al.*, 2012	-	-	-	+	-	-
125.	*Onthophagus bifasciatus* (Fabricius)	Chandra *et al.*, 2012 & Uniyal *et al.*, 2013	-	-	-	+	-	-
126.	*Onthophagus bonasus* (Fabricius)	Chandra *et al.*, 2012	-	-	-	+	-	-
127.	*Onthophagus centricornis* (Fabricius)	Chandra *et al.*, 2012	-	-	-	+	-	-
128.	*Onthophagus cervus* Fabricius	Uniyal *et al.*, 2013	-	-	-	+	-	-
129.	*Onthophagus circulifer* Arrow	Chandra *et al.*, 2012	-	-	-	+	-	-
130.	*Onthophagus compactus* Arrow	Chandra *et al.*, 2012	-	-	-	+	-	-
131.	*Onthophagus dama* (Fabricius)	Chandra *et al.*, 2012 & Uniyal *et al.*, 2013	-	-	-	+	-	-
132.	*Onthophagus duporti* Boucomont	Chandra *et al.*, 2012	-	-	-	+	-	-
133.	*Onthophagus expansicornis* Bates	Chandra *et al.*, 2012	-	-	-	+	-	-

(Table Contd...)

S.N.	Species Name	Reported by	Geographical Distribution at Different Protected Areas					
			AWLS	BWLS	CTR	GL(GNP/GWLS)	NDBR	RNP
134.	*Onthophagus falsus* Gill.	Chandra *et al.*, 2012	-	-	-	+	-	-
135.	*Onthophagus furcicollis* Arrow	Chandra *et al.*, 2012	-	-	-	+	-	-
136.	*Onthophagus furcillifer* Bates	Chandra *et al.*, 2012	-	-	-	+	-	-
137.	*Onthophagus gagates* Hope Arya *et al.*, 2016	Chandra *et al.*, 2012,	-	+	-	+	-	-
138.	*Onthophagus gazelle* Fabricius Uniyal *et al.*, 2013	Chandra *et al.*, 2012 &	-	-	-	+	-	-
139.	*Onthophagus gratus* Arrow	Chandra *et al.*, 2012	-	-	-	+	-	-
140.	*Onthophagus gravis* Walker	Uniyal *et al.*, 2013	-	-	-	+	-	-
141.	*Onthophagus griseosetosus* Arrow	Chandra *et al.*, 2012	-	-	-	+	-	-
142.	*Onthophagus hystrix* Boucomont	Chandra *et al.*, 2012	-	-	-	+	-	-
143.	*Onthophagus kuluensis* Bates	Chandra *et al.*, 2012	-	-	-	+	-	-
144.	*Onthophagus marginalis* Gebler	Chandra *et al.*, 2012	-	-	-	+	-	-
145.	*Onthophagus nasalis* Arrow	Chandra *et al.*, 2012	-	-	-	+	-	-
146.	*Onthophagus orientalis* Harold	Chandra *et al.*, 2012	-	-	-	+	-	-
147.	*Onthophagus pactolus* Fabricius	Chandra *et al.*, 2012	-	-	-	+	-	+
148.	*Onthophagus politus* Fabricius	Uniyal *et al.*, 2013	-	-	-	+	-	-
149.	*Onthophagus productus* Arrow	Chandra *et al.*, 2012	-	-	-	+	-	-
150.	*Onthophagus quadridentatus* (Fabricius)	Chandra *et al.*, 2012	-	-	-	+	-	-
151.	*Onthophagus questus* Sharp	Chandra *et al.*, 2012	-	-	-	+	-	-
152.	*Onthophagus ramoselus* Bates Uniyal *et al.*, 2013	Chandra *et al.*, 2012 &	-	-	-	+	-	-
153.	*Onthophagus ramosus* (Wiedmann)	Chandra *et al.*, 2012	-	-	-	+	-	-
154.	*Onthophagus recticornutus* Fabricius	Uniyal *et al.*, 2013	-	-	-	+	-	-

(Table Contd...)

S.N.	Species Name	Reported by	Geographical Distribution at Different Protected Areas					
			AWLS	BWLS	CTR	GL(GNP/GWLS)	NDBR	RNP
155.	*Onthophagus rubricollis* Hope	Arya *et al.*, 2016	-	+	-	-	-	-
156.	*Onthophagus* sp.	Arya & Joshi, 2014	-	-	-	-	+	+
157.	*Onthophagus spinifex* (Fabricius)	Chandra *et al.*, 2012	-	-	-	+	-	-
158.	*Onthophagus sternalis* Arrow	Chandra *et al.*, 2012	-	-	-	+	-	-
159.	*Onthophagus tarandus* (Fabricius)	Chandra *et al.*, 2012	-	-	-	+	-	-
160.	*Onthophagus tibetanus* Arrow	Chandra *et al.*, 2012	-	-	-	+	-	-
161.	*Onthophagus tragus* (Fabricius)	Chandra *et al.*, 2012	-	-	-	+	-	-
162.	*Onthophagus troglodyta* (Wiedemann)	Chandra *et al.*, 2012	-	-	-	+	-	-
163.	*Onthophagus unifasciatus* (Schall.)	Chandra *et al.*, 2012	-	-	-	+	-	-
164.	*Orphus impressus* Westwood	Chandra *et al.*, 2012	-	-	-	+	-	-
165.	*Orphus mysoriensis* Westwood	Chandra *et al.*, 2012	-	-	-	+	-	-
166.	*Oryctes nasicornis* Linnaeus Uniyal *et al.*, 2013	Chandra *et al.*, 2012 &	-	-	-	+	-	-
167.	*Oxycetonia albopunctata* (Fabricius)	Chandra *et al.*, 2012	-	-	-	+	-	+
168.	*Oxycetonia jucunda* (Foldermann)	Chandra *et al.*, 2012	-	-	-	+	-	-
169.	*Oxycetonia versicolor* Fabricius	Pandey *et al.*, 2013	+	-	-	-	-	-
170.	*P. pretiosa* Nonfried	Arya *et al.*, 2016	-	+	-	-	-	-
171.	*Paragymnopleurus sinuatus* (Olivier)	Chandra *et al.*, 2012	-	-	-	+	-	-
172.	*Phaechrous emarginatus* Lap.	Uniyal *et al.*, 2013	-	-	-	+	-	-
173.	*Phalops divisus* (Wiedmann)	Chandra *et al.*, 2012	-	-	-	+	-	-
174.	*Phyllognathus dionysius* (Fabricius)	Chandra *et al.*, 2012	-	-	-	+	-	-
175.	*Popillia impressipyga* Ohars.	Uniyal *et al.*, 2013	-	-	-	+	-	-

(Table Contd...)

S.N.	Species Name	Reported by	Geographical Distribution at Different Protected Areas					
			AWLS	BWLS	CTR	GL(GNP/GWLS)	NDBR	RNP
176.	*Popillia cupricollis* Hope	Chandra *et al.*, 2012 & Pandey *et al.*, 2013	+	-	-	+	-	-
177.	*Popillia cyanea* Hope	Chandra *et al.*, 2012 & Uniyal *et al.*, 2013	-	-	-	+	-	-
178.	*Popillia laevicollis* Kraatz	Chandra *et al.*, 2012	-	-	-	+	-	-
179.	*Popillia lucida* Newmann	Chandra *et al.*, 2012	-	-	-	+	-	-
180.	*Popillia nasuta* Newman	Chandra *et al.*, 2012	-	-	-	+	-	-
181.	*Popillia pilosa* Arrow	Chandra *et al.*, 2012 & Arya & Joshi, 2014	-	-	-	+	+	-
182.	*Popillia* sp.	Pandey *et al.*, 2013	+	-	-	-	-	-
183.	*Popillia sulcata* Redtenbacher	Chandra *et al.*, 2012	-	-	-	+	-	-
184.	*Protaetia alboguttata* (Vigors)	Chandra *et al.*, 2012	-	-	-	+	-	-
185.	*Protaetia coenosa* (Westwood)	Chandra *et al.*, 2012	-	-	-	+	-	-
186.	*Protaetia confusa* (Gory & Percheron)	Chandra *et al.*, 2012	-	-	-	+	-	-
187.	*Protaetia neglacta* Hope	Joshi *et al.*, 2004, Chandra *et al.*, 2012, Arya & Joshi, 2014 & Arya *et al.*, 2016	-	+	-	+	+	-
188.	*Protaetia pretiosa* Nonfried	Dayakrishna, 2017	-	-	+	-	-	-
189.	*Pseudolucanus cantor* Hope	Arya *et al.*, 2016	-	+	-	-	-	-
190.	*Rhinyptia meridionalis* Arrow	Chandra *et al.*, 2012	-	-	-	+	-	-
191.	*Rhomborrhina glaberrima* (Westwood)	Chandra *et al.*, 2012	-	-	-	+	-	-
192.	*Rhyssemus germanus* (Linnaeus)	Chandra *et al.*, 2012	-	-	-	+	-	-
193.	*Scarites sulcatus* Olivier	Arya *et al.*, 2016	-	+	-	-	-	-

(Table Contd...)

S.N.	Species Name	Reported by	Geographical Distribution at Different Protected Areas					
			AWLS	BWLS	CTR	GL(GNP/GWLS)	NDBR	RNP
194.	*Sisyphus hirtus* Weid.	Joshi *et al.*, 2004 and Pandey *et al.*, 2013	+	-	-	-	+	-
195.	*Sisyphus neglectus* Gory	Chandra *et al.*, 2012	-	-	-	+	-	-
196.	*Tinicellus spinipes* (Roth)	Chandra *et al.*, 2012	-	-	-	+	-	-
197.	*Torynorrhina opalina* (Hope)	Chandra *et al.*, 2012, Pandey *et al.*, 2013	+	-	-	+	-	-
198.	*Trichanomala fimbriata* (Newmann)	Chandra *et al.*, 2012	-	-	-	+	-	-
199.	*Xylotrupes gideon* (Linnaeus)	Chandra *et al.*, 2012	-	-	-	+	-	-
	FAMILY: Staphylinidae							
200.	*Bolitobius spinipes* Champ.	Bhargava, 1979	-	-	+	-	-	-
201.	*Creophilus maxillosus* L.	Bhargava, 1979	-	-	+	-	-	-
202.	*Dianous distigma* Champ.	Bhargava, 1979	-	-	+	-	-	-
203.	*Megarthus septumpunctatus* Champ.	Bhargava, 1979	-	-	+	-	-	-
204.	*Philonthus aeneipennis* Boh.	Bhargava, 1979	-	-	+	-	-	-
205.	*Phlonemos pincola* Champ.	Bhargava, 1979	-	-	+	-	-	-
206.	*Phyllodrea almorensis* Champ.	Bhargava, 1979	-	-	+	-	-	-
207.	*Phyllorhinum florivagnum* Champ.	Bhargava, 1979	-	-	+	-	-	-
208.	*Poderus sondaicus* Ful.	Uniyal *et al.*, 2013	-	-	-	+	-	-
209.	*Sternus kratzi* Bernh	Bhargava, 1979	-	-	+	-	-	-
210.	*Tregophloeus indicus* Kr.	Bhargava, 1979	-	-	+	-	-	-
	FAMILY: Chrysomelidae							
211.	*Altica corulea* Al.	Uniyal *et al.*, 2013	-	-	-	+	-	-
212.	*Altica cyanea* Weber	Uniyal *et al.*, 2013	-	-	-	+	-	-

(Table Contd…)

S.N.	Species Name	Reported by	Geographical Distribution at Different Protected Areas					
			AWLS	BWLS	CTR	GL(GNP/GWLS)	NDBR	RNP
213.	*Altica himensis* Shukla	Joshi *et al.*, 2004, Arya & Joshi, 2014 & Arya *et al.*, 2016	-	+	-	-	+	-
214.	*Altica* sp.	Pandey *et al.*, 2013	+	-	-	-	-	-
215.	*Aphthona nigrilabris* Duvivins	Uniyal *et al.*, 2013	-	-	-	+	-	-
216.	*Aphthona* sp.	Uniyal *et al.*, 2013	-	-	-	+	-	-
217.	*Apophylea crotchi*	Uniyal *et al.*, 2013	-	-	-	+	-	-
218.	*Aulacophora abdominalis* Fabricius	Uniyal *et al.*, 2013	-	-	-	+	-	-
219.	*Aulacophora* sp.	Arya & Joshi, 2014	-	-	-	-	+	-
220.	*Auleris tibialis* Jac	Uniyal *et al.*, 2013	-	-	-	+	-	-
221.	*Cassida* sp.	Joshi *et al.*, 2004	-	-	-	-	+	-
222.	*Colaspasoma semicostatum* Jac	Uniyal *et al.*, 2013	-	-	-	+	-	-
223.	*Colasposoma metallicum* (Clark)	Uniyal *et al.*, 2013 & Dayakrishna, 2017	-	-	+	+	-	-
224.	*Colasposoma splendidum* Fabricius	Dayakrishna, 2017	-	-	+	-	-	-
225.	*Corynodes peregrinus* Fuessly	Dayakrishna, 2017	-	-	+	-	-	-
226.	*Cryplocephalus triangularis* Hope	Arya & Joshi, 2014	-	-	-	-	+	-
227.	*Gallerucida rutilans* Hope	Arya *et al.*, 2016	-	+	-	-	-	-
228.	*Hoplasoma unicolor* Tellig.		-	-	-	-	-	+
229.	*Meristata sexmaculata* (Kollar & Redtenbacher)	Arya *et al.*, 2016 & Arya & Joshi, 2014	-	+	-	-	+	-
230.	*Meristata trifasciata* Hope	Arya *et al.*, 2016 & Arya & Joshi, 2014	-	+	-	-	+	-

(Table Contd...)

S.N.	Species Name	Reported by	Geographical Distribution at Different Protected Areas					
			AWLS	BWLS	CTR	GL(GNP/GWLS)	NDBR	RNP
231.	*Mimastra* sp.	Joshi *et al.*, 2004, Arya *et al.*, 2016 & Arya & Joshi, 2014	-	+	-	-	+	-
232.	*Paridea* sp.	Joshi *et al.*, 2004	-	-	-	-	+	-
233.	*Zygogramma bicolorata* Pallister	Dayakrishna, 2017	-	-	+	-	-	-
	FAMILY: Elateridae							
234.	*Adelocera* sp.	Dayakrishna, 2017	-	-	+	-	-	-
235.	*Agrypnus censobrines* (Candeze)	Uniyal *et al.*, 2013	-	-	-	+	-	-
236.	*Agrypnus costicollis* (Candeze)	Uniyal *et al.*, 2013	-	-	-	+	-	-
237.	*Agrypnus fuscipes* Fabricius	Uniyal *et al.*, 2013	-	-	-	+	-	-
238.	*Agrypnus moestus* Caud.	Uniyal *et al.*, 2013	-	-	-	+	-	-
239.	*Agrypnus* sp.	Joshi *et al.*, 2004	-	-	-	-	+	-
240.	*Agrypnus tuberosus* Eshr.	Uniyal *et al.*, 2013	-	-	-	+	-	-
241.	*Aphanobius cylindricus* Esch.	Uniyal *et al.*, 2013	-	-	-	+	-	-
242.	*Argypnus tostanus* (Candeze)	Uniyal *et al.*, 2013	-	-	-	+	-	-
243.	*Camsosternus splendidus* Hrbst.	Uniyal *et al.*, 2013	-	-	-	+	-	-
244.	*Heteroderes leris* Caud.	Uniyal *et al.*, 2013	-	-	-	+	-	-
245.	*Heteroderes macroderes* Candeze	Dayakrishna, 2017	-	-	+	-	-	-
246.	*Heteroderus* sp.	Uniyal *et al.*, 2013	-	-	-	+	-	-
247.	*Lacon costicollis* Caud.	Uniyal *et al.*, 2013	-	-	-	+	-	-
248.	*Melanotus hirticornis*	Uniyal *et al.*, 2013	-	-	-	+	-	-
249.	*Petocera cantorii,* Hope	Uniyal *et al.*, 2013	-	-	-	+	-	-
250.	*Singhalinus* sp.	Uniyal *et al.*, 2013	-	-	-	+	-	-

(Table Contd...)

S.N.	Species Name	Reported by	Geographical Distribution at Different Protected Areas					
			AWLS	BWLS	CTR	GL(GNP/GWLS)	NDBR	RNP
		FAMILY: Meloidae						
251.	*Cylindrothorax pictus* (Laporte)	Uniyal *et al.*, 2013	-	-	-	+	-	-
252.	*Epicanta* sp.	Uniyal *et al.*, 2013	-	-	-	+	-	-
253.	*Epicauta mannerheimi* (Maklin)	Uniyal *et al.*, 2013 & Dayakrishna, 2017	-	-	+	+	-	-
254.	*Meloe violaceus* Mars.	Joshi *et al.*, 2004 and Arya & Joshi, 2014	-	-	-	-	+	-
255.	*Mylabris cichonni* Linnaeus	Joshi *et al.*, 2004, Pandey *et al.*, 2013 & Arya & Joshi, 2014	+	-	-	-	+	-
256.	*Mylabris cichorii* Linnaeus	Arya *et al.*, 2016 & Dayakrishna, 2017	-	+	+	-	-	-
257.	*Mylabris pustulatus* Thun.	Uniyal *et al.*, 2013	-	-	-	+	-	-
258.	*Mylabris* sp.	Arya *et al.*, 2016	-	+	-	-	-	-
259.	*Sybaris praeustus* (Kollar & Redtb.)	Uniyal *et al.*, 2013	-	-	-	+	-	-
260.	*Sybaris testaceus* (Fabricius)	Uniyal *et al.*, 2013	-	-	-	+	-	-
		FAMILY: Curculionidae						
261.	*Alcides* sp.	Dayakrishna, 2017	-	-	+	-	-	-
262.	*Amblyrrhinus poricollis* Bohem.	Uniyal *et al.*, 2013	-	-	-	+	-	-
263.	*Amblyrrhinus subrocticollis* Marshall	Uniyal *et al.*, 2013	-	-	-	+	-	-
264.	*Apion* sp.	Uniyal *et al.*, 2013	-	-	-	+	-	-
265.	*Cryptorrhynchus brandisi* Stebb.	Uniyal *et al.*, 2013	-	-	-	+	-	-
266.	*Curculio calbum* (Fabricius)	Uniyal *et al.*, 2013	-	-	-	+	-	-
267.	*Lepropus indicus*	Uniyal *et al.*, 2013	-	-	-	+	-	-
268.	*Mecirtocenus fossatifrons* Marshall	Uniyal *et al.*, 2013	-	-	-	+	-	-

(Table Contd...)

S.N.	Species Name	Reported by	Geographical Distribution at Different Protected Areas					
			AWLS	BWLS	CTR	GL(GNP/GWLS)	NDBR	RNP
269.	*Myllocerus discolor* Bohem.	Uniyal *et al.*, 2013	-	-	-	+	-	+
270.	*Myllocerus subfasciatus* Geer	Uniyal *et al.*, 2013	-	-	-	+	-	-
271.	*Peltotrachelus himalayensis* Marshall	Uniyal *et al.*, 2013	-	-	-	+	-	-
272.	*Peltotrachelus sjöstedti* Marshall	Uniyal *et al.*, 2013	-	-	-	+	-	-
273.	*Pycnodactylus hypocrites* Cher.	Uniyal *et al.*, 2013	-	-	-	+	-	-
274.	*Sympiezomias cretaceus* Fst.	Joshi *et al.*, 2004	-	-	-	-	+	-
275.	*Tanymecus circumdatus*	Uniyal *et al.*, 2013	-	-	-	+	-	-
276.	*Tanymecus hirticeps* Marshall	Uniyal *et al.*, 2013	-	-	-	+	-	-
277.	*Tanymecus indicus* Faustus	Uniyal *et al.*, 2013	-	-	-	+	-	-
278.	*Tanymecus simplex* Marshall	Uniyal *et al.*, 2013	-	-	-	+	-	-
		FAMILY: Coccinelidae						
279.	*Cheilomenes sexmaculata* (Fabricius)	Arya & Joshi, 2014	-	-	-	-	+	-
280.	*Chilocorus nigritus* F.	Uniyal *et al.*, 2013,	-	-	-	+	-	-
281.	*Coccinella septumpunctata* Linnaeus	Joshi *et al.*, 2004, Pandey *et al.*, 2013, Arya & Joshi, 2014, Arya *et al.*, 2016 & Dayakrishna, 2017	+	+	+	-	+	-
282.	*Coccinella septumpunctata vardivericata* Olivier	Pandey *et al.*, 2013	+	-	-	-	-	-
283.	*Haluzia sanscrieta* Muls.	Joshi *et al.*, 2004, Arya *et al.*, 2016 & Arya & Joshi, 2014	-	+	-	-	+	-
284.	*Hippodamia variegata* (Goeze)	Pandey *et al.*, 2013 & Arya & Joshi, 2014	+	-	-	-	+	-

(Table Contd…)

S.N.	Species Name	Reported by	Geographical Distribution at Different Protected Areas					
			AWLS	BWLS	CTR	GL(GNP/GWLS)	NDBR	RNP
285.	*Leis dimidiata* Fabricius	Dayakrishna, 2017	-	-	+	-	-	-
286.	*Menochilus sexmaculatus* Fabricius	Pandey *et al.*, 2013	+	-	-	-	-	-
287.	*Neocollyris crassicornis* Deg.		-	-	-	-	-	+
288.	*Oenopia kirbyi* Mulsant	Pandey *et al.*, 2013	+	-	-	-	-	-
289.	*Thea cincta*	Uniyal *et al.*, 2013	-	-	-	+	-	-
290.	*Veronia* sp.	Uniyal *et al.*, 2013	-	-	-	+	-	-
FAMILY: Cicindelidae								
291.	*Calochroa bicolor* Fabricius	Bhardwaj *et al.*, 2008	-	-	-	-	-	+
292.	*Calomera angulata* Fabricius	Bhardwaj *et al.*, 2008	-	-	-	-	-	+
293.	*Calomera chloris* Hope	Bhardwaj *et al.*, 2008 & Dayakrishna, 2017	-	-	+	-	-	+
294.	*Calomera plumigera* Horn	Bhardwaj *et al.*, 2008	-	-	-	-	-	+
295.	*Cicindela aurulenta* Fabricius		-	-	-	-	-	+
296.	*Cicindela fastidiosa* Dejean	Bhardwaj *et al.*, 2008	-	-	-	-	-	+
297.	*Cicindela multiguttata* Dejean	Bhardwaj *et al.*, 2008	-	-	-	-	-	+
298.	*Cicindela* sp.	Dayakrishna, 2017	-	-	+	-	-	-
299.	*Cicindela parvomaculata*	Bhargav *et al.*, 2009	-	-	-	-	-	+
300.	*Cicindela vigintiguttata* Herbst	Bhardwaj *et al.*, 2008	-	-	-	-	-	+
301.	*Cosmodela intermedia* Chaudoir	Bhardwaj *et al.*, 2008 & Dayakrishna, 2017	-	-	+	-	-	+
302.	*Cylindera venosa* Kollar	Bhardwaj *et al.*, 2008	-	-	-	-	-	+
303.	*Jansenia chloropleura* Chaudoir	Bhardwaj *et al.*, 2008	-	-	-	-	-	+
304.	*Lophyra parvimaculata* Fowler	Bhardwaj *et al.*, 2008	-	-	-	-	-	+
305.	*Myriochila undulata* Dejean	Bhardwaj *et al.*, 2008	-	-	-	-	-	+

(Table Contd…)

S.N.	Species Name	Reported by	Geographical Distribution at Different Protected Areas					
			AWLS	BWLS	CTR	GL(GNP/GWLS)	NDBR	RNP
FAMILY: Cerambycidae								
306.	*Glena* sp.	Uniyal *et al.*, 2013	-	-	-	+	-	-
307.	*Lophosterus hugeli* Redtnb	Uniyal *et al.*, 2013	-	-	-	+	-	-
308.	*Macrotoma creneta* Fabricius	Uniyal *et al.*, 2013	-	-	-	+	-	-
309.	*Monochamus bimaculatus* Geb.		-	-	-	-	-	+
310.	*Rhytidodera boweinia* White	Uniyal *et al.*, 2013	-	-	-	+	-	-
311.	*Stromatium barbatum* Fabricius	Uniyal *et al.*, 2013	-	-	-	+	-	-
312.	*Xylotrechus smei*	Uniyal *et al.*, 2013	-	-	-	+	-	-
313.	*Xystocera globosa* Oliv.	Uniyal *et al.*, 2013	-	-	-	+	-	-
FAMILY: Carabidae								
314.	*Catascopus whithilli* Hope	Uniyal *et al.*, 2013	-	-	-	+	-	-
315.	*Chlaenius hamifer* Chaud.	Uniyal *et al.*, 2013	-	-	-	+	-	-
316.	*Chlaenius laetiusculus* Chaud.	Uniyal *et al.*, 2013	-	-	-	+	-	-
317.	*Chlaenius vividus* Chaud.	Uniyal *et al.*, 2013	-	-	-	+	-	-
318.	*Dioryche* sp.	Uniyal *et al.*, 2013	-	-	-	+	-	-
319.	*Macrochitus trimaculatus* Al.	Uniyal *et al.*, 2013	-	-	-	+	-	-
320.	*Omphora duplicatus* Weid.	Uniyal *et al.*, 2013	-	-	-	+	-	-
321.	*Omphora pilosa*	Uniyal *et al.*, 2013	-	-	-	+	-	-
322.	*Ophonus indicus* Bates	Dayakrishna, 2017	-	-	+	-	-	-
323.	*Oxycentris parallelus* Chaud.	Uniyal *et al.*, 2013	-	-	-	+	-	-
324.	*Pharaopsopus cantorei* Dejan	Uniyal *et al.*, 2013	-	-	-	+	-	-
325.	*Pheropsophus* sp.	Pandey *et al.*, 2013	+	-	-	-	-	-
326.	*Scarites indicus,*	Uniyal *et al.*, 2013	-	-	-	+	-	-

(Table Contd...)

S.N.	Species Name	Reported by	Geographical Distribution at Different Protected Areas					
			AWLS	BWLS	CTR	GL(GNP/GWLS)	NDBR	RNP
327.	*Scarites* sp.	Pandey *et al.*, 2013	+	-	-	-	-	-
328.	*Stenolophus* sp.	Uniyal *et al.*, 2013	-	-	-	+	-	-
329.	*Triganatoma indica* Beritt.	Uniyal *et al.*, 2013	-	-	-	+	-	-
330.	*Trigonetama* sp.	Uniyal *et al.*, 2013	-	-	-	+	-	-
331.	*Xenodus diabreeri* Anderson	Uniyal *et al.*, 2013	-	-	-	+	-	-
FAMILY: Lucanidae								
332.	*Serrognathus titanus,* Boisduval	Uniyal *et al.*, 2013	-	-	-	+	-	-
333.	*Titanus* sp.	Uniyal *et al.*, 2013	-	-	-	+	-	-
FAMILY: Tenebrionidae								
334.	*Alphitobius piceus*	Uniyal *et al.*, 2013	-	-	-	+	-	-
335.	*Caedius induta* Weid.	Uniyal *et al.*, 2013	-	-	-	+	-	-
336.	*Calathus pallipes,* Anderson	Uniyal *et al.*, 2013	-	-	-	+	-	-
337.	*Cistelomorpha* sp.	Arya *et al.*, 2016	-	+	-	-	-	-
338.	*Egaploa crenulata* Dejan	Uniyal *et al.*, 2013	-	-	-	+	-	-
339.	*Gonocephalum* sp.	Dayakrishna, 2017	-	-	+	-	-	-
340.	*Seleron retteri* Gebien	Uniyal *et al.*, 2013	-	-	-	+	-	-
FAMILY: Lagriidae								
341.	*Cerogria nepalensis* Hope	Arya *et al.*, 2016	-	+	-	-	-	-
FAMILY: Hybosoridae								
342.	*Hybosorus illigeri* Reiche	Chandra *et al.*, 2012	-	-	-	+	-	-
343.	*Hybosorus orientalis* Westwood	Chandra *et al.*, 2012 & Uniyal *et al.*, 2013	-	-	-	+	-	-
344.	*Phaeochrous emarginatus* (Castelnau)	Chandra *et al.*, 2012	-	-	-	+	-	-

(Table Contd...)

S.N.	Species Name	Reported by	Geographical Distribution at Different Protected Areas					
			AWLS	BWLS	CTR	GL(GNP/GWLS)	NDBR	RNP
		FAMILY: Melolonthidae						
345.	*Apogonia blanchardi* Rit.	Uniyal *et al.*, 2013	-	-	-	+	-	-
346.	*Autoserica* sp.	Uniyal *et al.*, 2013	-	-	-	+	-	-
347.	*Brahminia* sp.	Uniyal *et al.*, 2013	-	-	-	+	-	-
		FAMILY: Geotrupidae						
348.	*Bolboceras quadridens* Fabricius	Chandra *et al.*, 2012	-	-	-	+	-	-
349.	*Bolboceras transversale* Westwood	Chandra *et al.*, 2012	-	-	-	+	-	-
		FAMILY: Dysticidae						
350.	*Caccophils parvulus* Aube.	Uniyal *et al.*, 2013	-	-	-	+	-	-
		FAMILY: Hydrophilidae						
351.	*Hydrophilus* sp.	Dayakrishna, 2017	-	-	+	-	-	-

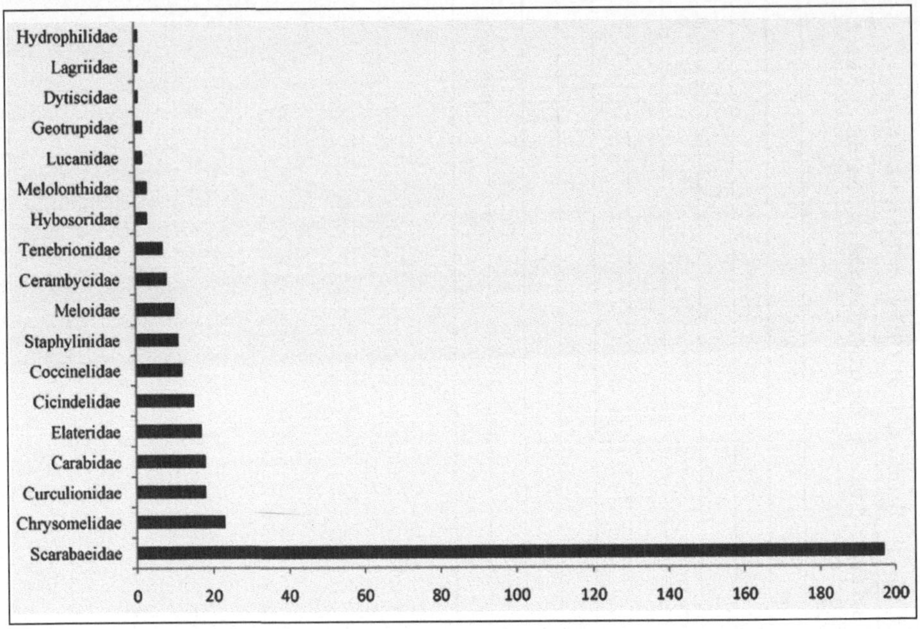

Fig. 1.1: Graph showing number of species belonging to different families of order Coleoptera as compiled from different protected areas of state Uttarakhand

The protected areas of Gangotri Landscape are the most hyper diverse regions in relation to beetle fauna comprising 263 species under 15 families while only 37 species under 10 families have been reported till so far from Corbett tiger reserve. Nanda Devi Biosphere Reserve holds 25 species of beetles under 6 families and similarly, 19 species belonging to five families from Askot Wildlife Sanctuary have been compiled in the present checklist. The total number of 23 species each belonging to six different families of order Coleoptera have also been compiled from two protected areas *viz.*, Binsar Wildlife Sanctuary and Rajaji National Park. Based on the presence or absence of each species in different protected areas, a large proportion of species i.e. 304 species found to be reported from one particular protected area of Uttarakhand. Most of the species were confined to Gangotri landscape with 242 species of the total beetles which have been listed in present checklist which is followed by Corbett tiger reserve (26 species), Rajaji National Park (16 species), Askot Wildlife Sanctuary (11 species), Binsar Wildlife Sanctuary (11 species), while the minimum number of species were restricted to Nanda Devi Biosphere Reserve (nine species). Many species have specialized requirements of their environment, which make them truly specific and sensitive to changes in habitat and its management. Thus, such species with specificity to particular habitat are of prime importance as these taxa can be used as indicators of environmental and ecological health.

However, merely based on its presence and absence in the present checklist, none of the species should be considered truly specific as discrepancies and inconsistency in the exploration of those regions might be attributed for such results. In addition, this is the first comprehensive checklist on Coleopteran fauna protected areas of Uttarakhand based on published information therefore, present study may yield information on not only gap areas at the macro level for all the protected areas but also gaps relating to taxa at the micro level.

REFERENCES

Arya, M.K. and Joshi, P.C. (2014): Studies on the Beetles (Insecta: Coleoptera) in the Nanda Devi Biosphere Reserve, Western Himalayas, Uttarakhand, India. *New York Science Journal*, 7(1): 25-32.

Arya, M.K., Joshi, P.C. and Agarwal, A. (2014): Species Diversity and Fluctuation in Population Density of Coleopteran Insects of Shyampur Forest Range in the Shivalik Foothills, Haridwar, India. *Journal of Environment and Biosciences*, 28(1): 85-91.

Arya, M.K., Tamta, P. and Dayakrishna (2016): Study on Distribution and Diversity of Beetles (Insecta: Coleoptera) in Different Elevational Zones of Binsar Wildlife Sanctuary, Almora, Uttarakhand, India. *Journal of Entomology and Zoology Studies*, 4(4): 311-316.

Bhardwaj, M., Bhargav, V.P. and Uniyal, V.P. (2008): Occurrence of Tiger Beetles (Cicindelidae: Coleoptera) in Chilla Wildlife Sanctuary, Rajaji National Park, Uttarakhand. *Indian Foester*, 1636-1645.

Bhargav, V., Uniyal, V.P. and Sivakumar, K. (2009): Distinctive Patterns in Habitat Association and Distribution of Tiger Beetles in the Shivalik Landscape of North Western India. *Journal of Insect Conservation*, 13: 459-473.

Biswas, S.C. (1995): Coleoptera: Fauna of Western Himalaya (U.P.), Himalayan Ecosystem Series: Part I. Zoological Survey of India, 1: 55-60.

Chandra, K. (2011): Insect Fauna of States and Union Territories in India. ENVIS Bulletin: Wildlife & Protected Areas, 14(1): 189-218.

Chandra, K., Gupta, D., Uniyal V.P., Bhardwaj, M. and Sanyal A.K. (2012): Studies on Scarabaeid Beetles (Coleoptera) of Govind Wildlife Sanctuary, Garhwal, Uttarakhand, India. *Biological forum - An International Journal*, 4(1): 48-54.

Dayakrishna (2017): Ecodynamics and Taxonomic Composition of Insect Fauna in and around Corbett Tiger Reserve, Uttarakhand, India. *Ph.D Thesis, Kumaun University, Nainital*. 254pp.

Fauna of British India Series, (1906-1984): General Introduction of Coleoptera, Cicindelidae, Rhysodidae, Paussidae (by Flower, 1912), Carabidae (by Andrews, 1929, 1935), Staphylinidae (by Cameron, 1930-1939), Scarabaeidae (by Arrow 1910, 1917, 1931), Lucanidae and Passalidae (by Arrow, 1940), Erotylidae, Languriidae and Endomychidae (by Arrow, 1925), Chrysomelidae (by Jacoby, 1908; Maulik, 1919, 1926, 1936), Cerambycidae (by Gahan, 1906), Curculionidae (by Marshall, 1916), Gyrinidae and Haliplidae (by Vazirani, 1984).

Joshi, P.C., Kothari, K., Badoni, V. and Singh, A. (1999): Study of above Ground Entomofauna of Nanda Devi Biosphere Reserve. *Himalayan Biosphere Reserves*, 1(1&2): 29-37.

Joshi, P.C., Kumar, K. and Arya, M. (2008): Assessment of Insect Diversity along an Altitudinal Gradient in Pindari Forests of Western Himalaya, India. *Journal of Asia-Pacific Entomology*, 11: 5-11.

Joshi, P.C., Kothari, K., Badoni, V.P., Arya, M. and Agarwal, A. (2004): Species Composition and Density of Entomofauna *vis a vis* Altitudinal Variations and Disturbances in Nanda Devi Biosphere Reserve, Uttaranchal, India. *Asian Jr. Microbiol. Biotech. Env. Sc.*, 6(2): 301-308.

Kapur, A.P. (1951): Expedition to South-West Arabia 1937-8. 18. Coleoptera: Coccinellidae. Bulletin of the British Museum (Natural History), *Entomology*, 1: 275-297.

Kapur, A.P. (1963): The Coccinellidae of the Third Mount Everest Expedition, 1924 (Coleoptera). Bulletin of the British Museum (Natural History), *Entomology*, 14: 1-48.

Kapur, A.P. (1966): The Coccinellidae (Coleoptera) of the Andamans. *Proceedings of the National Institute of Sciences of India*, 32(B): 148-189.

Kazmi, S.I., Ramamurthy, V.V. (2004): Coleoptera (Insecta) Fauna from the Indian Thar Desert, Rajasthan. *Zoos' Print Journal*, 19(4): 1447-1448.

Kumar, K., Oli, B.P., Joshi. B.M. and Samant, S.S. (2001): The Faunal Diversity of Nanda Devi Biosphere Reserve in West Himalaya. *Himalayan Biosphere Reserve*, 3(182): 18-57.

Kumar, K., Joshi, P.C., Joshi, R. and Arya, M. (2015): Seasonal Variation in Density and Biomass of Insects in Nanda Devi Biosphere Reserve, India. *Journal of Environment and Bio-Sciences*, 29(2): 289-296.

Losey, J.E. and Vaughan, M. (2006): The Economic Value of Ecological Services provided by Insects. *BioScience*, 56: 311-323.

Losey, J.E. and Vaughan, M. (2008): Conserving the Ecological Services provided by Insects. *American Entomologist*, 54: 113-115.

Pajni, H.R. (1990): Fauna of India, Coleoptera: Curculionidae: Eremninae. Zoological Survey of India, Kolkata. 1-568.

Pandey, P., Joshi, P.C. and Kaushal, B.R. (2013). Role of Insects in Sustaining a Forest Ecosystem in Western Himalaya, India. *Journal of Applied Biosciences*, 39(1): 1-22.

Ramakrishna and Alfred, J.R.B. (2006): An Overview: Editor Director. Fauna of Sikkim, State Fauna Series, 9 (Part-1): 1-32. (Published by the Director, Zool. Surv. India, Kolkata)

Rodgers W.A. and Panwar H.S. (1988): Planning a Wildlife Protected Area Network in India. Vols. I & II.Wildlife Institute of India, Dehradun.

Sengupta, T. and Pal, T.K. (1996): Fauna of India, Sylvanidae (Clavicornia: Coleoptera). Zoological Survey of India, Calcutta. 262 pp.

Slipi´nski, S.A., Leschen, R.A.B. and Lawrence, J.F. (2011): Order Coleoptera Linnaeus, 1758. *Animal Biodiversity: An Outline of Higher-Level Classification and Survey of Taxonomic Richness* (ed. by Z.-Q. Zhang). *Zootaxa*, 3148, 203-208.

Supare, N.R., Ghai, S. and Ramamurthy V.V. (1990): A Revision of Tanymecus from India and Adjacent Countries (Coleoptera: Curculionidae). *Oriental Insects*, 24: 1-126.

Uniyal, V.P., Bhardwaj, M. and Sanyal, A.K. (2013): An Assessment of Entomofauna for Management and Conservation of Biodiversity in the Gangotri Landscape. *Annual Progress Report, Wildlife Institute of India, Dehradun*, 237 pp.

Vazirani, T.G. (1977): Catalogue of Indian or Oriental Dytiscidae. Rec. zool. Surv. India, Occ. Paper No. 6: 1-101.

Vazirani, T.G. (1984): The Fauna of India. Coleoptera: Gyrinidae and Haliplidae. Zoological Survey of India, Calcutta. 324 pp.

Zhang, Z.Q. (2011): Animal Biodiversity: An Introduction to Higher-level Classification and Taxonomic Richness. Zootaxa, 3148: 7-12.

Pages: 27-43

Animal Biodiversity and Fisheries

Edited by: **Dr. Rashmi Tripathi; Dr. Vijay Sharma & Dr. Pawan Kumar 'Bharti'**

ISBN: 978-93-88854-06-1

Edition: **2019**

Published by: **Discovery Publishing House Pvt. Ltd., New Delhi (India)**

2

Ameliorating Potency of Vitamin E on Hematological Parameters against Toxicity Induced by Chromium in Laboratory Chicks

Dharmendra Kumar

Vandita Kandpal

ABSTRACT

Since the Industrial Revolution, contamination by heavy metals has become an increasingly serious threat in many regions of the world. It is well-known that chronic exposure to heavy metals and metalloids at relatively low levels can cause adverse effects to humans and animals. Therefore, there has been increasing concern, about exposures, intakes and absorption of heavy metals. In general, blood examination is performed for several reasons as a screening procedure to assess general health.

The determination of blood components by laboratory tests is an important procedure to assist the diagnosis of various poultry diseases and disorders. Considering the importance of this subject, this study gives an overview of toxicity of chromium, its adverse effects on hematological parameters and its amelioration by vitamin E in laboratory chicks.

Developing chicks (2-3 weeks old, body weight 100±20 gm) were used as experimental animals. Total Red Blood Cell count (RBC), total White Blood Cell count (WBC), Hemoglobin concentration (Hb), Packed cell volume (PCV), Mean corpuscular hemoglobin concentration (MCHC), Mean corpuscular volume (MCV) and mean corpuscular hemoglobin (MCH) were assessed. RBC, WBC, Hb, PCV and MCHC showed significant decrease in chromium treated group as compared to vitamin E administered and normal control group.

Department of Zoology, S. V. Govt. P.G. College, Lohaghat, Champawat, Uttarakhand, India

*** Corresponding Author**

The treatment of vitamin E normalized these hematological values up to the control level. MCV and MCH slightly increased in chromium intoxicated chicks as compared to vitamin E treated group. Thus present findings suggest that supplementation of vitamin E has significant effect on hematological values, signifying its protective effect in hexavalent chromium induced toxicity.

Keywords: Chromium, vitamin E, heavy metals, hematological parameters, biological observation.

INTRODUCTION

Hematological profile in animals is an important indicator of physiological or pathophysiological status of the body (Khan and Zafar, 2005). The values of blood parameters vary by race, age, gender, stress, bacterial and viral infections, poisoning (Avram and Cuca, 2004, Khan and Zafar, 2005 and Lanzarot *et al.*, 2001). Thus, it is important to know these variations when assessing clinical blood parameters in birds. Studies on the evaluation of hematologic response after inoculation in chicken with potassium dichromate revealed a highly significant difference between control and experimental group as decline in the number of erythrocytes, leucocytes and hemoglobin %. Among chickens between 40 days and 50 days old there were differences in the values of RBC count, hemoglobin and hematocrit (Khan and Zafar, 2005).

Chromium is the essential element helping the body to use sugar, protein and fat at the same time excessive amount is carcinogenic for organisms. Chromium occurs in several oxidation states in environment ranging from Cr2+ to Cr6+ (Rodriguez *et al.*, 2007) commonly occurring forms are trivalent Cr3+ to Cr6+ with both states toxic to humans and plants (Mohanty and Kumar Patra, 2013). Anthrapogenically chromium is released into the environment through sewage and fertilizers (Ghani, 2011). In India, the chromium level in underground water has been witnessed to be more than 12mg/l. The discharge of industrial wastes and ground water contamination has drastically increased the concentration of chromium ion in soil (Bielicka *et al.*, 2005). Cr III and Cr IV are the most stable form and only their relation to human exposure is of high interest (Zhitkovich, 2005). Cr IV compounds such as calcium chromate, Zinc chromate, Strontium chromate, potassium dichromate and lead chromate are highly toxic and carcinogenic in nature.

In humans exposure to higher amounts can lead to inhibition of erythrocyte glutathione reductase, which in turn lowers the capacity to reduce methemoglobin and hemoglobin (Koutras *et al.*,1965). Once the chromium reaches blood stream it damages blood cells by oxidation reactions leading to hemolysis and subsequently liver and kidney failure. Different experiments have proved that chromate compounds can induce

DNA damage in many different ways and lead to formation of DNA adducts chromosomal aberrations, sister chromatic exchanges, alterations in replication and transcription of DNA (O'Brien *et al.*, 2001 and Matsumato *et al.*, 2006). Because of its mutagenic properties, Cr VI is categorized as a Group 1 human carcinogen by the International Agency for Research on Cancer (Dayan and Paine, 2001 and Zhang, 2011).

Chromium (Cr), a naturally occurring heavy metal, exists in many states, but the trivalent Cr(III) and hexavalent Cr(VI) forms are the most common in the environment (O'Brien *et al.*, 2003). Cr(III) act as essential trace element of body in animal and human and has nutraceutical importance while Cr(VI) present in the environment is mostly man made through industrial emission. Acute and chronic toxicity in both animal and man are mainly caused by Cr(VI) compounds (Ducros, 1992).

The soluble hexavalent chromium Cr(VI) is an environmental contaminant widely recognized as carcinogen, mutagen, and teratogen toward humans and animals. The wide distribution of this contaminant in the environment is the result of its extensive exploitation to produce stainless steel, wood treatment products, tanning of leather or pigments (Barceloux, 1999, Xu *et al.*, 2004). The fate of chromium in the environment is dependent on its oxidation state. The reduction of Cr(VI) to Cr(III) results in the formation of reactive intermediates leading to oxidative tissue damage and cellular injury (Patlolla *et al.*, 2009).

Exposure of rats at different concentration of aerosol of chromium trioxide decreased total erythrocyte count, hematocrit value, hemoglobin% (Kim *et al.*, 2004). Feeding of Cr(VI) in drinking water led to reduction in lymphocyte, hematocrit value, and hemoglobin value in mice. However, studies on hematological parameters in sub-acute toxicity of potassium chromate in broiler chicks are limited.

In general, hexavalent chromium compounds penetrate biological membranes much more readily than trivalent compounds. Based on review of available literature, estimates of the proportion of trivalent chromium that is absorbed from the gastrointestinal tract range up to about 3%, while up to about 10% of ingested hexavalent chromium is estimated to be absorbed; organic complexes are even more readily absorbed. Much of ingested hexavalent chromium is reduced to trivalent chromium before absorption. Absorption of inhaled chromium is believed to be greater, with estimated proportions of up to 12% and 30% for trivalent and hexavalent compounds, respectively; some hexavalent chromium is reduced to the trivalent species by the epithelial lining of the lung.

Absorption is also dependent on the physical/chemical properties of the specific compound. Absorbed chromium is widely distributed throughout the body, including to the fetus, via the bloodstream. After crossing cellular membranes, hexavalent chromium may be reduced to trivalent forms, via a number of hypothesized intermediates. Absorbed chromium is eliminated from the body largely in the urine, while most of the unabsorbed portion is excreted in the feces.

The toxicity of chromium compounds depends principally on valency, as well as physical/chemical properties of the specific compounds. To the extent possible, data on the effects of trivalent and hexavalent chromium have been addressed separately. More detailed information on the effects of specific hexavalent and trivalent chromium compounds is included in the supporting documentation.

In general, the acute toxicity of chromium compounds in experimental animals increases with water solubility; oral LD_{50}s for trivalent compounds have been reported to range from 140 to 522 mg of Cr(III) / kg body weight , while reported LD50 values for hexavalent compounds ranged from 13 to 795 mg of Cr(VI) / kg body wieight. Skin sensitization has been induced in animals by both trivalent and hexavalent chromium.

Most short-term or subchronic studies in which animals have been administered chromium by ingestion have involved hexavalent chromium. The observed effects in these predominantly limited investigations were restricted largely to those on the liver and kidney (histological effects as well as alterations in biochemical parameters), and alterations in hematological parameters; the lowest effect levels were in the range of 50 to 100 mg of Cr(VI)/[kg(b.w.)] (Diaz-Mayans *et al.*, 1986; Coogan *et al.*, 1991; Kumar and Barthwal, 1991; Kumar and Rana, 1982; 1984; Kumar *et al.*, 1985; Laborda *et al.*, 1987; Kennedy *et al.*, 1976; Christofano *et al.*, 1976).

In short-term or subchronic investigations, the effects of inhaled hexavalent chromium on the lung or immunological parameters have been examined. Observed effects included inflammatory changes in the respiratory tract and alterations in response and morphology of macrophages at 180 µg of Cr(VI)/m^3 and above, although some effects on macrophage function and immunological response (not necessarily adverse) have been reported at 25 µg/m^3 (Glaser *et al.*, 1985; Johansson *et al.*, 1986a;b; 1987; Popper *et al.*, 1992).

Hexavalent chromium compounds have been consistently positive in several genotoxicity assays in nonmammalian systems and *in vitro* and *in vivo* mammalian systems, inducing DNA damage, gene mutation, sister chromatid exchange, chromosomal aberrations, aneuploidy, cell transformation, and dominant lethal mutations (IARC, 1990; De Flora *et al.*, 1990). While a variety of genetic effects have been induced by trivalent chromium in subcellular or acellular Systems, in general, trivalent compounds have not been genotoxic in cultured animal or human cells (IARC, 1990; De Flora *et al.*, 1990). Intracellular reduction of hexavalent chromium to Cr(V), Cr(IV), and Cr(III) is believed to be required for genotoxicity.

It has been proposed (Jones, 1990; De Flora *et al.*, 1989) that there may be a threshold for the carcinogenicity of hexavalent chromium, based on the hypothesis that the administered dose must exceed the extracellular capacity to reduce (i.e., by gastric juices or in the mucosal lining) hexavalent chromium to the trivalent species (the form usually found associated with the DNA), which has a lesser ability to cross cellular membranes. Similarly, the ability of trivalent chromium that is produced intracellularly to cross the nuclear membrane is limited.

However, as cellular uptake of trivalent chromium has been demonstrated (Alcedo and Wetterhahn, 1990), although to a lesser degree than the hexavalent species, and since the entry of hexavalent chromium into cells is rapid and extracellular reduction in the mucosal lining is incomplete (Witmer, 1991), currently available data are insufficient to support the hypothesis of a threshold for the interaction of chromium with genetic material.

Vitamin E is found naturally in some foods, added to others, and available as a dietary supplement. "Vitamin E" is the collective name for a group of fat-soluble compounds with distinctive antioxidant activities (Traber *et al.*, 2006). Naturally occurring vitamin E exists in eight chemical forms (alpha-, beta-, gamma-, and delta-tocopherol and alpha-, beta-, gamma-, and delta-tocotrienol) that have varying levels of biological activity (Traber *et al.*, 2006).

Alpha- (or α-) tocopherol is the only form that is recognized to meet human requirements. Serum concentrations of vitamin E (alpha-tocopherol) depend on the liver, which takes up the nutrient after the various forms are absorbed from the small intestine. The liver preferentially resecretes only alpha-tocopherol via the hepatic alpha-tocopherol transfer protein (Traber *et al.*, 2006); the liver metabolizes and excretes the other vitamin E forms (Traber, 2007). As a result, blood and cellular concentrations of other forms of vitamin E are lower than those of alpha-tocopherol and have been the subjects of less research (Sen *et al.*, 2006 and Dietrich *et al.*, 2006).

Free radical injury is responsible for many pathological conditions. Free radicals can exist independently and they bear one or two unpaired electrons in valance shell. They are highly reactive to cell organelles e.g. polyunsaturated fatty acids, proteins and nucleic acid (Sánchez-Mendoza *et al.*, 2015). Metals like Cr are very reactive and induce oxidative damage by generating reactive oxygen species (ROS) (Zhang *et al.*, 2014). It interferes with metabolic process and biological reactions i.e. change in enzyme activity, membrane fluidity, ion transport and protein synthesis (Javed, 2015). Chromium (Cr^{6+}) once entered in a cell is converted into its lower oxidation states i.e. Cr^{3+}, which is a reactive intermediate of Cr^{6+} responsible for the generation of ROS (Shati, 2014).

Antioxidants protect cells from the damaging effects of free radicals, which are molecules that contain an unshared electron. Free radicals damage cells and might contribute to the development of cardiovascular disease and cancer (Verhagen *et al.*, 2006). Unshared electrons are highly energetic and react rapidly with oxygen to form reactive oxygen species (ROS). The body forms ROS endogenously when it converts food to energy, and antioxidants might protect cells from the damaging effects of ROS. The body is also exposed to free radicals from environmental exposures, such as cigarette smoke, air pollution, and ultraviolet radiation from the sun. ROS are part of signaling mechanisms among cells.

Vitamin E is a fat-soluble antioxidant that stops the production of ROS formed when fat undergoes oxidation. Scientists are investigating whether, by limiting free-radical production and possibly through other mechanisms, vitamin E might help prevent or delay the chronic diseases associated with free radicals. In addition to its activities as an antioxidant, vitamin E is involved in immune function and, as shown primarily by *in vitro* studies of cells, cell signaling, regulation of gene expression, and other metabolic processes (Traber *et al.*, 2006). Alpha-tocopherol inhibits the activity of protein kinase C, an enzyme involved in cell proliferation and differentiation in smooth muscle cells, platelets, and monocytes (Institute of Medicine.

Food and Nutrition Board, 2000). Vitamin-E–replete endothelial cells lining the interior surface of blood vessels are better able to resist blood-cell components adhering to this surface. Vitamin E also increases the expression of two enzymes that suppress arachidonic acid metabolism, thereby increasing the release of prostacyclin from the endothelium, which, in turn, dilates blood vessels and inhibits platelet aggregation (Institute of Medicine. Food and Nutrition Board, 2000)

Although much research investigating the effects of high levels of vitamin E on the metabolism of humans (Herman , 1982 and Herbert, 1991) and various animals (Levander *et al.*, 1977, Hawkey 1984 and Aksakal, 1996) has been done, little work has been attempted on animals undergoing rapid growth, such as broilers (Franchini, 1988). It is essential to draw blood profile from birds in different experimental situations. Therefore, in this study, we aimed to investigate the effects of vitamin E supplementation against hexavalent chromium toxicity on a number of blood parameters.

MATERIALS AND METHODS

Developing chicks Crioler - Chabro, (*Gallus gallus domesticus*) were used as experimental animals. 18 Newly hatched domestic chicks (one day old) were purchased from the Uttarakhand Village Poultry Project (State Govt. Poultry Farm), Bin, Pithoragarh (Uttarakhand). Selected all chicks were maintained and acclimatized according to the laboratory conditions. The animals were housed in battery cages under laboratory conditions at existing room temperature and relative humidity. They were fed on commercial food (Starter, Grower and Finisher) purchased from the local market and tap water *ad libitum*.

Healthy male and female chicks (approximately 2-3 weeks old, body weight 100±20 gm) were used in present study. Three groups of animals were used for each experimental set and six animals were included in each group. Each experiment was repeated three times. The experiment was started two weeks old chick onward. The selected chicks were divided into three groups (A, B and C) randomly, each containing at least 6 chicks.

Chromium intoxicated group: Chicks of group A were administered with sublethal dose of potassium dichromate ($K_2Cr_2O_7$) (5 mg/100 gm body weight) was administered orally on each alternate day for 30 days.

Therapeutic group: Chicks of group B were treated with potassium dichromate ($K_2Cr_2O_7$) as chicks of group A but also administered with vitamin-E (intramuscularly) (0.5 IU/100 gm body weight) on each alternate day for 30 days. Vitamin E was dissolved in olive oil and the injections were given intramuscularly in the morning hours.

Control group: Chicks of Group C were administered with saline only to serve as purely control.

Blood Analysis: Blood samples were collected from the wing vein using 3ml disposable syringe than directly transferred into a labeled test tube containing anticoagulant (EDTA). All blood samples for hematological indices were collected into bottles containing EDTA, as anti – coagulant, kept in an ice box, using icepacks and transferred to the laboratory for measuring the hematological parameters.

The hematological indices determined included packed cell volume (PCV), Hemoglobin concentration (Hb), White blood cell count (WBC), Red blood cell count (RBC), Mean corpuscular volume (MCV), Mean corpuscular hemoglobin concentration (MCHC) and mean corpuscular hemoglobin (MCH). Differential WBC counts were made on monolayer blood films, fixed and stained with Giemsa-Wright's stain.

Total red blood cell (TRBC) and total white blood cell count (TWBC) were determined by a manual method using hemacytometer (Campbell, 1995). PCV and MCHC were determined by Wintrobe's hematocrit tube method. Hemoglobin concentration (Hb) was measured by Cyanmethemoglobin method. Erythrocyte indices mean corpuscular volume (MCV) and mean corpuscular hemoglobin (MCH) were calculated from TRBC, PCV and Hb (Ritchie *et al.*, 1994), as:

$$\text{MCV} = \frac{\text{Hematocrite value} \times 10}{\text{Erythrocyte count}}$$

$$MCH = \frac{\text{Hemoglobing } L^{-1} \times 10}{\text{Erythrocyte count}}$$

Statistical Analysis: Mean and standard error were calculated and data were analyzed using standard methods. Parameters of all treatments were compared using Student's "t" test. Data were subjected to one way ANOVA for calculating the significance difference between the treatments. P-values less than 0.05 were considered statistically significant.

RESULTS

Table 2.1 shows the hematological values of different parameters as obtained in present study. Hematological parameters RBC, WBC, Hb, PCV and MCHC showed significant ($p<0.05$) decrease in chromium supplemented chicks as compared to control group. While, in the group co-treated with chromium and vitamin E, the value of these parameters increased. These values were found nearest to control level in comparison to chromium treated chicks.

Table 2.1: Mean values of different hematological parameters in chicks of different groups administered chromium, chromium + vitamin E and control group

Parameters	Group A (Chromium)	Group B (Chromium+ Vitamin E)	Group C (Control)	F- ratio	Level of Significance
Hb(g/dl)	6.27±0.37	8.32±0.55	9.32±0.15	48.33	**
WBC(10^3/mm^3)	13.73±1.44	19.77±0.49	21.40±0.53	38.44	**
RBC(10^6/mm^3)	2.08±0.13	2.77±0.18	3.10±0.05	47.64	**
PCV(%)	15.67±0.93	20.79±1.38	23.31±0.38	46.86	**
MCHC(mg/dl)	39.18±0.26	40.56±0.51	40.54±0.65	1.79	NS
MCV	76.66±0.59	73.43±1.11	74.12±1.12	8.03	**
MCH	30.04±0.04	30.0±0.05	30.05±0.01	1.23	NS

Results are expressed as mean ± SE. ** indicates significant at $p< 0.05$ Hb – Hemoglobin, WBC – White blood cell, RBC – Red blood cell, , PCV – Packed cell volume, MCHC - Mean corpuscular hemoglobin concentration, MCV - Mean corpuscular volume and MCH - mean corpuscular hemoglobin. Analysis of variance (ANOVA) was significant among all these groups.

MCV and MCH shows slightly increase in chromium intoxicated chicks as compared to vitamin E therapeutic group. The study reveals that the white blood cells, hemoglobin, PCV and MCHC values were considerably increased and MCV and MCH were slightly decreased in chromium and vitamin E treated chicks as compared to chromium treated chicks. RBCs count slightly increase in co-treated group. Hence, maximum protection by vitamin E was observed in this study.

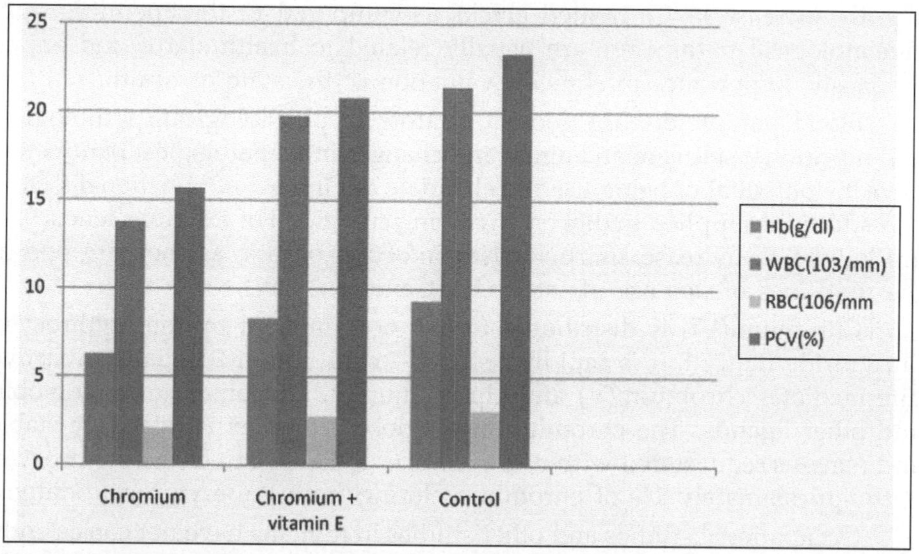

Fig. 2.1: Protective effect of Vitamin E on Hb, WBC, RBC and PCV in Chromium treated chicks

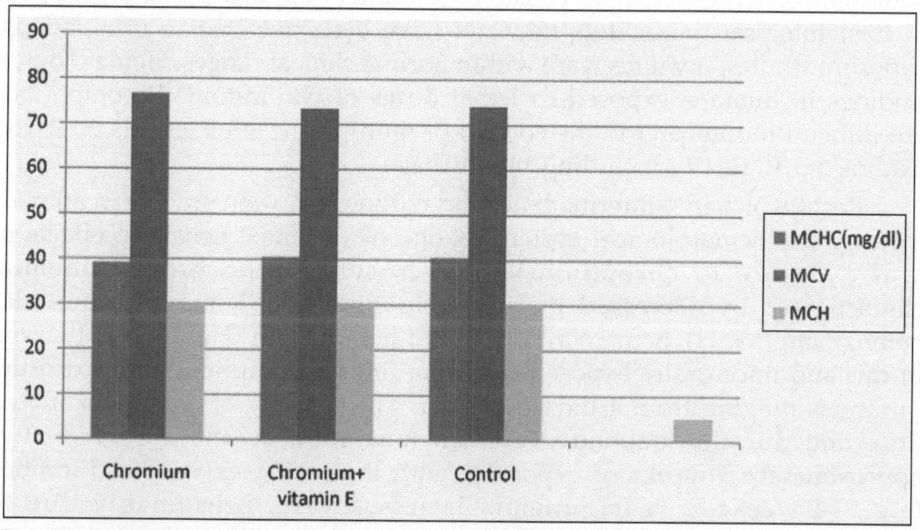

Fig. 2.2: Protective effect of Vitamin E on MCHC, MCV and MCH in Chromium treated chicks

DISCUSSION

The hematological parameters tested in current study include red and white blood cell counts, hemoglobin concentration, hematocrit percentage and Mean corpuscular hemoglobin concentration showed significant ($p<0.05$) decrease in Cr treated chicks as compared to vitamin E and control group, while Mean corpuscular volume and Mean corpuscular hemoglobin showed slightly increase in Cr treated chicks as compared to therapeutic group. Hematological parameters are usually related to health status and are of diagnostic importance in clinical evaluation of the state of health.

Blood parameters are good indicators of physiological, pathological and nutritional status of an animal and changes in hematological parameters have the potential of being used to elucidate the impact of nutritional factors and additives supplied in diet on any living creature. For example, leucocytes are known to increase sharply when infection occurs, as they are one of the first lines of defense of the body (Ganong, 1999).

Chromium(VI) is distributed to and accumulated by the erythrocyte; once inside the cell, it is rapidly reduced to chromium(III) via the reactive intermediates chromium(V) and chromium(IV), and binds to hemoglobin and other ligands. The chromium-hemoglobin complex is relatively stable and remains sequestered within the cell over the life-span of the erythrocyte, with approximately 1% of chromium eluting from the erythrocyte daily.

Occupational studies and other studies in humans have not consistently reported hematological effects, although microcytic, hypochromic anemia has been reported in several recent animals studies on chromium(VI) compounds. However, it is possible that small, exposure-related changes in hematological parameters may not have been detected in occupational exposure studies, if values were within normal clinical ranges. Hematological findings in humans exposed to lethal doses of chromium(VI) compounds are difficult to interpret in the context of multiple systemic effects observed leading up to death, including hemorrhage.

Results of acute, intermediate, and chronic-duration studies in animals identify the hematological system as one of the most sensitive effects of oral exposure to chromium(VI). Microcytic, hypochromic anemia, characterized by decreased mean cell volume (MCV), mean corpuscular hemoglobin (MCH), hematocrit (Hct), and hemoglobin (Hgb), was observed in rats and mice orally exposed to chromium(VI) compounds for exposure durations ranging from 4 days to 1 year. The severity of anemia exhibited dose and duration-dependence, with maximum effects observed after approximately 3 weeks of exposure; with increasing exposures durations (e.g., 14 weeks–1 year), anemia is less severe, presumably due to compensatory hematopoietic responses. In general, effects observed in rats were more severe than those in mice.

In general hematological parameters are affected by diurnal fluctuations or changes in daily physical and metabolic activities (Sanni *et al.*, 2000; Piccione *et al.*, 2001, 2005). The mean hematological values RBC and Hb vary among species. Other factors, which affect the RBC counts, include breed, sex and the nutrition supplied to the bird (Sturkie, 1965). Packed cell volume, hemoglobin concentration and red blood cell count had been reported to increase with age in chickens (Islam *et al.*, 2004).

Result shows that potassium dichromate Cr(VI) produced toxic effect on hematological parameters such as total erythrocyte count, total leucocyte count, haematocrit value, hemoglobin%, mean corpuscular hemoglobin concentration in chicks in dose dependent manner after 30 day of consecutive oral treatment. The exposure of rats at different concentrations of aerosol of chromium trioxide Cr(VI) decreased TEC, PCV value and Hb% (Kim *et al.*, 2004), which is in consonance with the present findings.

Feeding of Cr(VI) in drinking water led to reduction in lymphocyte, PCV value, Hb value in mice (Shrivastava *et al.*, 2005). A series of *in vitro* and *in vivo* studies have demonstrated that Cr(VI) induces an oxidative stress through enhanced production of reactive oxygen species (ROS) leading to genomic DNA damage and oxidative deterioration of lipids and proteins. A cascade of cellular events occur following Cr(VI) induced oxidative stress including enhanced production of superoxide anion and hydroxyl radicals, increased lipid peroxidation and genomic DNA fragmentation, modulation of intracellular oxidized states, activation of protein kinase C, apoptotic cell death and altered gene expression (Bagchi *et al.*, 2001).

Vitamin E is involved in removal of free radical and prevents their peroxidative effect on unsaturated lipid of membrane and thus help in maintaining integrity of membrane. Chromanol ring of tocopherols donates its phenolic hydrogen to reduce the free radical and is itself oxidised to the quinone form. In the Vitamin E treated group TEC, TLC, PCV, Hb value and PCV were preserved, suggesting that oxidative damage is a participating mechanism in Cr (VI) toxicity on these functions.

Present observations showed significant decrease in the number of RBC, WBC, PCV, Hb and MCHC contents in chromium treated chicks. Treatment with vitamin E increases the number of RBC, WBC, PCV, Hb and MCHC contents. Previous studies noted decrease in hematological parameters following Cr administration i.e. in broiler (Kumari, *et al.*, 2013), in rats (Kim, *et al.*, 2004; Balakrishnan, *et al.*, 2013) and fish (Shaheen and Akhtar, 2012).

Reduced hemoglobin concentration and PCV values in chromium treated group were due to the intestinal haemorrhage resulting from the liberation of second generation merozoites which caused sloughing of intestinal mucosa with discharge of large amount of blood (Nayak and Rai, 1985). Decrease in RBC, Hb and PCV level indicate anemia resulting due to iron deficiency and its decreased utilization for Hb synthesis, so Hb concentration also decreases.

When Cr(VI) was inhaled or administered intratracheally, intraperitoneally, or intravenously, much of the chromium in the blood (25 to 70%) was taken up by RBCs (Sayato, *et al.*, 1980; Weber, 1983; Wiegand, *et al.*, 1984; Edel and Sabbioni, 1985; Minoia and Cavalleri, 1988; Gao, *et al.*,

1993). As the erythrocyte to plasma ratio of total chromium increases with increasing hexavalent chromium concentration, Corbett, *et al.*, (1998) proposed that the reductive capacity of erythrocytes was much greater than that of plasma and that the reduction rate of hexavalent chromium in erythrocytes was greater than the rate of uptake from plasma.

Another possible reason could be that the Cr can cross the red blood cell membrane easily and accumulate in it, thereby leading to DNA protein cross linking and thus occurrence of anemia. Another reason could be that Cr has ability to bind to beta chain of hemoglobin so no hemoglobin available for heme synthesis leading to anemia (Adjroud, 2010).

In the present study, leukocyte count was also decreased in chromium treated birds compared to control group. Previous studies report decreases in leukocyte count following Cr administration in the rats (Balakrishnan, *et al.*, 2013). Decrease in leukocyte count could be due to in activation of immune response by chromium. Another opinion could be that leucopenia could be due to ability of chromium to cross membrane through active transport and remain there till the life of the cell leading to depletion of leukocytes.

Cr administration leads to apoptosis of leukocytes leading to leucopenia. Chromium when comes in contact with leukocytes causes peroxidation and inhibits trans membrane potential of mitochondria of lymphocytes (Adjroud, 2010). The MCV and MCH of chromium treated chicks were slightly increased in chromium treated chicks in comparison to chromium and vitamin E treated chicks.

Present study showed decrease in RBC, WBC, Hb, PCV and MCHC after chromium treatment. Co-treatment with vitamin E increased all these hematological parameters nearest to control level. This might be due to the supplemented vitamin E increase in oxygen carrying capacity of hemoglobin. Therefore, vitamin E is an important antioxidant which protects the organs from harmful effects of heavy metals.

CONCLUSION

The toxic effects of Cr and its amelioration with vitamin E on hematological parameters were profiled in this study. It may be concluded that chromium caused the formation of free radicals in the blood by reducing the antioxidant indices. Vitamin E has administration ameliorated hexavalent chromium induced toxicity efficiently in hematological parameters. The results of the present study show that dietary vitamin E has synergistic effects, and as evidences from the results of the blood parameters.

REFERENCES

Adjroud, O. (2010). Protective Effects of Selenium against Potassium Dichromate-induced Hematotoxicity in Female and Male Wistar albino Rats. *Ann. Toxicol. Anal.* 22: 165-172.

Aksakal, M., Naziroglu, M. and Çay, M. (1996): Kuzularda selenyum-E vitamininin bazi hematolojik ve biyokimyasal degerlere etkisi. *Tr. J. of Vet. and Anim. Sci.* 20: 185-190.

Alcedo, J.A. and Wetterhahn, K.E. (1990): "Chromium Toxicity and Carcinogenesis", *Int. Rev. Exp. Pathol.* 31: 85-108.

Avram, N. and Cuca, D. (2004): Explorari Paraclinice. Lucrari Aplicative. Editura FundaÞiei Barceloux, D.G. (1999): Chromium. *J. Toxicol. Clin. Toxicol.* 37: 173-94.Romania de Maine, Bucuresti.

Balakrishnan, R., Kumar, C.S.S., Rani, M.U., Srikanth, M.K., Boobalan, G. and Reddy, A. G. (2013). An Evaluation of the Protective Role of α-tocopherol on free radical induced hepatotoxicity and nephrotoxicity due to chromium in rats. *Ind. J. Pharmacol.*, 45: 490-495.

Bagchi, D., Bagchi, M. and Stohs, S.J. (2001): Chromium (VI)-induced Oxidative Stress, Apoptotic Cell Death and Modulation of p53 Tumor Suppressor Gene. *Mol. Cell Biochem.* 222: 149-158.

Bielicka, A. and Bojonowska wisniewski a.(2005):Two faces of Chromium Pollutant and Bioelement. *Pol J. Environ Stud.* 149 (10): 5-10.

Campbell, T.W. (1995): Avian Hematology and Cytology, *Iowa State University Press.* Ames, Iowa.

Christofano, E.D., Kennedy, G.L., Gordon, D.E., Keplinger, M.L. and Calandra, J.C. (1976): "Toxicity of Lead Chromate Pigments and Tissue Residues following 90 days Feeding to Beagle Dogs", *Toxicol. Appl. Pharmacol.* 37: 161.

Coogan, T.P., Motz, J., Snyder, C.A., Squibb, K.S. and Costa, M. (1991): "Differential DNA-protein Crosslinking in Lymphocytes and Liver following Chronic Drinking Water Exposure of Rats to Potassium Chromate", *Toxicol. Appl. Pharmacol.* 109: 60-72.

Corbett, G.E., Dodge, D.G., O'Flaherty, E., Liang, J., Throop, L., Finley, B.L. and Kerger, B. D. (1998): In vitro Reduction Kinetics of Hexavalent Chromium in Human Blood. *Environ Res.* 78(1): 7-11.

Dayan, A.D. and Paine, A.J. (2001): Mechanisms of Chromium Toxicity, Carcinogenicity and Allergenicity. *Human and Experimental Toxicology.* 20 (9): 439-451.

De Flora, S., Bagnasco, M., Serra, D. and Zanacchi, P. (1990): "Genotoxicity of Chromium Compounds. A Review", *Mut. Res.*, 238: 99-172.

De Flora, S., Serra, D., Basso, C. and Zanacchi, P. (1989): "Mechanistic Aspects of Chromium Carcinogenicity", *Arch. Toxicol. Suppl.* 13: 28-39.

Dietrich, M., Traber, M.G., Jacques, P.F., Cross, C.E., Hu, Y. and Block, G. (2006): Does γ-tocopherol play a role in the primary prevention of heart disease and cancer? A review. *Am. J. Coll. Nutr.* 25: 292-9.

Diaz-Mayans, J., Laborda, R. and Nunez, A. (1966): "Hexavalent Chromium Effects on Motor Activity and Some Metabolic Aspects of Wistar Albino Rats", *Comp. Biochem. Physiol.*, 83C: 191-195.

Ducros, V. (1992): Chromium Metabolism, A Literature Review. *Biological Trace Element Research.* 32: 65-77.

Edel, J. and Sabbioni, E. (1985): Pathways of Cr (III) and Cr (VI) in the Rat after Intratracheal Administration. *Hum. Toxicol,* 4: 409-416.

Franchini, A., Meluzzi, A., Bertuzzi, S. and Giordani, G. (1988): High Doses of Vitamin E in the Broilers Diets. *Arch. Gefugelk.* 52 (1): 1216.

Ganong, W.F. (1999): *Review of Medical Physiology*. 19th ed. Stanford, Connecticut, Appleton and Lange, p. 353.

Gao, M., Levy, L.S., Braithwaite, R.A. and Brown, S. S. (1993): Monitoring of Total Chromium in Rat Fluids and Lymphocytes following Intratracheal Administration of Soluble Trivalent or Hexavalent Chromium Compounds. *Human Exp. Toxicol.* 12: 377-382.

Ghani. (2011): Effect of Chromium Toxicity on Growth, Chlorophyll and some micronutrients of *Brassica juncea L. Egyptian Acad J. Biol Sci.* 2 (1): 9-15.

Glaser, U., Hochrainer, D., Kloppel, H. and Kuhnen, H. (1985): "Low Level Chromium (VI) Inhalation Effects on Alveolar Macrophages and Immune Function in Wistar Rats", *Arch. Toxicol.* 57: 250-256.

Hawkey, C.M., Harty, M.G. and Fitzgerald, A.K. (1984): Haematological Values in Mouflon (ovis Musimon) Influence of Age Sex, Season and Vitamin E Status. *Res. Vet. Sci.* 36(1): 37-42.

Herbert, V. (1991): Vitamin E Supplementation of Elderly people. *Am. J. Clin. Nutr.* 53: 976-978.

Herman, W.J. Jr. (1982): The Effect of Vitamin E on Lipoprotein Cholesterol Distribution. In Vitamin E: Bioch. Haem. Clin. Aspects. *Annals New York Academy of Sciences.* 467-471.

Institute of Medicine. (2000): Food and Nutrition Board. Dietary Reference Intakes: Vitamin C, Vitamin E, Selenium, and Carotenoids. Washington, DC: National Academy Press.

IARC (1990): (International Agency for Research on Cancer), "IARC Monographs on the Evaluation of Carcinogenic Risks to Humans", Volume 49- Chromium, Nickel and Welding, Lyon, France.

Islam, M.S., Lucky, N.S., Islam, M.R., Ahad, A. and Das, B.R. (2004): Hematological Parameter of Fayoumi, Assil and Local Chicken Reared in Sylhet Region in Bangladesh. *Int. J. Poult. Sci.* 3: 144-147.

Javed, M. (2015): Chronic dual Exposure (waterborne+dietary) Effects of Cadmium, Zinc and Copper on Growth and their Bioaccumulation in *Cirrhina mrigala. Pak. Vet. J.* 35: 143-146.

Johansson, A., Robertson, B., Curstedt, T. and Camner, P. (1986a): "Rabbit Lung after Inhalation of Hexa- and Trivalent Chromium", *Environ. Res.,* 41: 110-119.

Johansson, A., Wiernik, A., Jarstrand, C. and Camner, P. (1986b): "Rabbit Alveolar Macrophages After Inhalation of Hexa- and Trivalent Chromium", *Environ. Res.* 39: 372-385.

Jones, R.E. (1990): "Hexavalent Chrome: Threshold Concept for Carcinogenicity", *Biomed. Environ. Sci.* 3: 20-34.

Kennedy, G.L., Keplinger, M.L., Wingender, R.J., Christofano, E.E. and Calandra, J.C. (1976): "Toxicity of Lead Chromate Pigments and Tissue Residues following 90 Days Feeding to Albino Rats", *Toxicol. Appl. Pharmacol,* 37: 160.

Khan, A.T. and Zafar F. (2005): Haematological Study in Response of Varying Doses of Estrogen in Broiler Chicken. *International Journal of Poultry Science,* 4, (10): 748-751.

Kim, H.Y., Lee, S.B. and Jang, B.S. (2004): Subchronic Inhalation Toxicity of Soluble Hexavalent Chromium Trioxide in Rats. *Arch. Toxicol.* 78: 363-368.

Kim, H., Lee, S. and Jang, B. (2004): Subchronic Inhalation Toxicity of Soluble Hexavalent Chromium Trioxide in Rats. *Archiv. Toxicol.* 78: 363-368.

Koutras, G.A., Schneider, A.S., Hattori, M. and Valentine W.N. (1965): Studies on Chromated Erythrocytes. Mechanisms of Chromate Inhibition of Glutathione Reductase. *Br. J. Heamatol.* 11 (3): 360-369.

Kumar, A. and Barthwal, R. (1991): "Hexavalent Chromium Effects on Hematological Indices in Rats", *Bull. Environ. Contam. Toxicol.*, 46: 761-768.

Kumar, A. and Rana, S.V.S. (1982): "Lipid Accumulation in Chromium Poisoned Rats", *Int. J. Tiss. Reac.* IV (4): 291-295.

Kumar, A. and Rana, S.V.S. (1984): "Enzymological Effects of Hexavalent Chromium in the Rat Kidney", *Int. J. Tiss. Reac.* VI (2): 135-139.

Kumar, A., Rana, S.V.S. and Prakash, R. (1985): "Dysenzymia Induced by Hexavalent Chromium in Rat Liver", *Int. J. Tiss. Reac.* VII (4): 333-338.

Kumari, R.R., Kumar P. and Mondal, T.K. (2013): Effect of Vitamin E and Selenium on Haematological Parameters in Sub-acute Toxicity of Hexavalent Chromium in Broiler Chick. *Nat. J. Physiol. Pharm. Pharmacol.* 3: 158-161.

Laborda, R., Diaz-Mayans, J. and Nunez, A. (1987): "Effects of Chromium (VI) in Drinking Water on Liver and Kidney of Albino Rats", *Revista Espanola de Fisiologia,* 43: 275-280.

Lanzarot Maria del Pilar, Motesinos, A., San Andres, M.I., Casilda Rodriguez and Maria Victoria Barahona. (2001): Hematological, Protein Electrophoresis and Cholinesterase Values of Free Living Nestling Peregrine Falcon in Spain. *Journal of Wildlife Diseases,* 37 (1): 172-177.

Levander, O.A., Morris, V.C. and Ferretti, R.J. (1997): Comparative Effects of Selenium and Vitamin E in lead-poisoned Rats. *J. Nutr.* 107: 378-382.

Matsumoto, S.T., Mantovani, M.S., Malaguttii, M.I.A., Dias, A.L., Fonseca, I.C. and Marin-Morales, M.A. (2006): Genotoxicity and Mutagenicity of Water Contaminated with Tannery Effluents as Evaluated by the Micronucleus Test and Commet Essay using the Fish *oreochromis niloticus* Test and Chromosome Aberrations inonion Root Tips. *Genet. Mol. Biol.* 29 (1): 148-158.

Minoia, C. and Cavalleri, A. (1988): Chromium in Urine, Serum and Red Blood Cells in the Biological Monitoring of Workers Exposed to different Chromium Valency States. *Sci. Total Environ.* 71: 323-327.

Mohanty, M. and Kumar Patra, H. (2013): Effect of Iconic and Chelate Assisted Hexavalent Chromium on Mung Bean Seedlings [Vigna radiate (L.) Wilczeck,] Vark-851) during Seedling Growth. JSPB. 9 (2): 232-241.

Nayak, D.C. and Rai, P. (1985): Hemogram of Chickens Experimentally Infected with Eimeria species. *Indian Journal of Veterinary Medicine,* 5: 42-43.

O'Brien, T., Xu, J. and Patierno, S.R. (2001): Effects of Glutathione on Chromium induced Crosslinking and DNA Polymerase Arrest. In Molecular Mechanisms of Metal Toxicity and Carcinogenesis. Springer US. 173-182.

O'Brien, T.J., Ceryak, S. and Patierno, S.R. (2003): Complexities of Chromium Carcinogenesis: Role of Cellular Response, Repair and Recovery Mechanisms. *Mutat. Res.* 533: 3-36.

Patlolla, A.K., Barnes, C., Yedjou, C., Velma, V.R. and Tchounwou, P.B. (2009): Oxidative Stress, DNA Damage, and Antioxidant Enzyme Activity Induced by Hexavalent Chromium in Sprague-Dawley Rats. *Environ. Toxicol.* 24: 66-73.

Piccione, G., Assenza, A., Fazio, F., Giudice, E. and Caola, G. (2001): Different Periodicity of some Hematological Parameters in Exercise-loaded and Sedentary Horses. *J. Equine Sci.* 12: 17-23.

Piccione, G., Fazio, F., Giudice, E., Grasso, F. and Morgante, M. (2005): Nycthemeral Change of some Hematological Parameters in Horses. *J. Applied Biomed.* 3: 123-128.

Popper, H.H., Wiespainer, E., Leingartner, W., Weybora, and Ratschek, M. (1992): "Short-term Chromate Inhalation in a Computer-assisted Inhalation Chamber: Immediate Toxicity and Late Cancer Development", *Environ. Hyg.* III: 127-131.

Ritchie, B.W., Harrison, J.G. and Harrison, R.L. (1994): Avian Medicine, *Winger's Publishing, Inc*, Florida.

Rodriguez, M.C., Barsanti, L., Pasarelli, V., Evangelista, V. and Gualtieri, P. (2007): Effects of Chromium on Photosynthetic and Photoreceptive Apparatus of the Alga *Chlamydomonos reinhardtii*. Environ Res. 105 (2): 234-239.

Sanchez-Mendoza, B.,Aguilar-Hernandez, A., Lopez-Soto, M.A., Barreras, A., Estrada-Angulo, A., Monge-Navarro, F.J., Torrentera, N.G., Zinn R.A. and Plascencia, A. (2015): Effects of High-level Chromium Methionine Supplementation in Lambs Fed a Corn-based Diet on the Carcass Characteristics and Chemical Composition of the Longissimus Muscle. *Turk. J. Vet. Anim. Sci.*, 39: 376-379.

Sayato, Y., Nakamuro, K., Matsui, S. and Ando, M. (1980): Metabolic Fate of Chromium Compounds. I. Comparative behavior of Chromium in Rat Administered with Na251Cr04 and 51CrCl3. *J. Pharm. Dyn.* 3: 17-23.

Shaheen, T. and Akhtar, T. (2012): Assesment of Chromium Toxicity in *Cyprinus carpio* through Hematological and Biochemical Blood markers. *Turk. J. Zool.* 36: 682-690.

Sanni, A.A., Oyedokun O.R. and Alaka, O.O. (2000): Preliminary Observations on Diurnal Rhythm in the Hematological Parameters of Male African Giant Rats (*Cricetomys gambianus,* Waterhouse). *Afr. J. Biomed. Res.* 3: 117-120.

Sen, C.K., Khanna, S, Roy, S. (2006): Tocotrienols: Vitamin E beyond Tocopherols. *Life Sci* 78: 2088-2098.

Shati, A.A. (2014): Ameliorative Effect of Vitamin E on Potassium dichromateinduced Hepatotoxicity in Rats. *J. King Saud. Uni-Sci.* 26: 181-189.

Shrivastava, R., Srivastava, S., Upreti, R.K. and Chaturvedi, U.C. (2005): Effect of Dengue virus Infection on Peripheral Blood Cells of Mice Exposed to Hexavalent Chromium with Drinking Water. *Indian J. Medical Res.*122: 111-119.

Sturkie, P.D., (1965): Avain Physiology. 2nd Edn., Comstock Publishing Associates, *Cornel University Press,* New York, pp: 766.

Traber, M.G. Vitamin E. In: Shils, M.E., Shike, M., Ross, A.C., Caballero, B. and Cousins, R. (2006): eds. *Modern Nutrition in Health and Disease*. 10th ed. Baltimore, MD: Lippincott Williams & Wilkins, 396-411.

Traber, M.G. (2007): Vitamin E Regulatory Mechanisms. *Annu. Rev.* 27: 347-362.

Verhagen, H., Buijsse, B., Jansen, E. and Bueno-de-Mesquita, B. (2006): The State of Antioxidant Affairs. *Nutr. Today.*41: 244-50.

Weber, H. (1983): Long-term Study of the Distribution of Soluble chromate-51 in the Rat after a Single Intratracheal Administration. *J. Toxicol. Environ. Health.* 11: 749-764.

Witmer, C. (1991): "Panel Discussion: Mechanisms and Health Effects of Chromium", *Environ. Health Perspect.,* 92: 87-89.

Wiegand, H.J., Ottenwalder, H. and Bolt, H.M. (1984): Disposition of Intratracheally Administered Chromium (III) and Chromium (VI) in Rabbits. *Toxicol. Lett.* 22(2): 273-6.

Xu, X.R., Li, H.B., Li. X.Y. and Gu, J.D. (2004): Reduction of Hexavalent Chromium by Ascorbic Acid Inaqueous Solutions. Chemosphere. 57: 609-613.

Zhitkovich, A. (2005): Importance of Chromium DNA Adducts in Mutagenicity and Toxicity of Chromium (VI). *Chem. Res. Toxicol.* 18 (1): 3-11.

Zhang,Y.W., Robert Thompson, Han Zhang, and Huaxi Xu. (2011): APP Processing in Alzeihmers Disease. Molecular Brain 4:3.

Zhang, W.Q., Liu, Y., Ge, M., Yao, C.Y., Xue, J.D. and Zhang, Z.G. (2014): Resveratrol Reduces Oxidative Stress and Improves Arsenic Efflux in Rats Exposed to Arsenic Trioxide. *Pak. Vet. J.*, 34: 251 253.

Pages: 44-55

Animal Biodiversity and Fisheries
Edited by: **Dr. Rashmi Tripathi; Dr. Vijay Sharma & Dr. Pawan Kumar 'Bharti'**
ISBN: 978-93-88854-06-1
Edition: **2019**
Published by: **Discovery Publishing House Pvt. Ltd., New Delhi (India)**

3

Antibiotic Residues in Farm Animal and a Food of Animal Origin with Emphasis on Bacterial Resistance (Review)

Abdel Mohsen M. Hammam[1]
Mona S. Zaki[2]**; Mohammad M.N. Authman**[2]
Zeinab M.S. Amin Girh[3]

ABSTRACT

World populations increased dramatically yearly and consequently increase the demand for foods of animal origin, from different species (cattle, sheep, caprines, birds, pigs, fish and seafood/shellfish), milk and eggs, to cover their nutritional needs. Antibiotics drugs are used widely in the animal livestock for the purposes of treatment, or as prophylactive and growth promoters. The misuse or sub-therapeutic doses of antibiotics initiate the microorganisms for inducing resistance to the action of antibacterial drugs. Therefore, the animals and animal by-products my exposed to chemical or biological pollutants during their production cycle which could come from drugs and growth promoters, in addition, biologically-derived toxins (mycotoxins, phycotoxins, phytotoxins) and/or environmental contaminants linked to atmospheric pollution, from the soil and/or water are sources of pollution of foods of animal origin, which have harmful effects on animals and consumers and generate high numbers of microorganisms resistant to the traditionally used antibiotics.

Keywords: Antibiotics-Drugs-Residues-Microorganisms resistance.

ANTIBIOTICS DRUGS RESIDUES

There are many types and generations of antibiotics or antibacterial agents (e.g. aminoglycosides, tetracyclines, macrolides and sulphonamides)

1 Animal Reproduction Department, Veterinary Research Division, National Research Centre, Egypt
2 Hydrobiology Department, National Research Centre, Egypt
3 Department of Poultry Diseases, Veterinary Research Division, National Research Centre, Dokki, Giza, Egypt

which are widely used in domestic animals and human for treatment of certain types of illness or in the improvement of growth rate. Improper administration for disease therapy (higher or sub-therapeutic doses) and as growth promoting agents (low doses for long period) can result in antibiotic residues in milk and dairy products and can contribute to the development of microbial drug resistance and the spread of resistant bacteria, including those with serious health consequences in animals (IFT, 2006; Stolker *et al.*, 2007) and possess a potential risk to the consumer due to the development of allergic reactions and interference with growth of intestinal micro-flora (Dewdney *et al.*, 1991).

1. **Aminoglycosides** (e.g. Streptomycin, kanamycin, amikacin, neomycin, apramycin).

The differences in substitutions in the basic ring structures between the various aminoglycosides are the reason for the relatively minor variations in antimicrobial scales, duration of action, resistance and toxicity forms. Aminoglycosides given in therapeutic dosages mainly cause ototoxicosis, but may also cause nephrotoxicosis, allergy and neuromuscular disturbances. With respect to the solubility of aminoglycosides, it is high (10-500 g L^{-1}). They are basic strongly polar polycationic compounds (Thiele-Bruhn, 2003). The amino groups of aminoglycosides can be positively charged by protonation under acidic conditions. The positive charge may facilitate adsorption to soil clay minerals that typically possess a negative charge (Huang *et al.*, 2001). Despite their extensive use in livestock farming, no aminoglycosides were found in a broad study on the analysis of animal faeces (Berendsen, *et al.*, 2013).

2. **Amphenicols** (Chloramphenicol, thiamphenicol, florfenicol):

One of the commonly used antibiotics for several years for the treatment or as a prophylactive in the farms of poultry, calves, pigs, sheep and fish is the chloramphenicol. Bone marrow depression is the greatest serious toxic side effect of chloramphenicol. These toxic symptoms was recorded in newborn infants giving large doses of chloramphenicol, these symptoms appeared in the form of vomiting, hypothermia, cyanosis and circulatory collapse followed by death. Moreover, other symptoms may be appearing such as neuritis, encephalopathy with dementia and ototoxicity, while its metabolites could be genotoxic. Therefore, chloramphenicol is restricted in many countries, while it is totally prohibited for use in food-producing animals within the European Union and the USA (Lozano and Arias, 2008).

3. **Beta-lactams** (Penicillins, cephalosporins).

Penicillin and its derivatives caused allergic reactions in some peoples. The adverse effects associated with cephalosporins are similar to those described for penicillins.

4. **Macrolides** (Lincomycine-macrolide Erythromycin, spiramycin, kitasamycin, josamycin, desmycosin, mirosamycin, tilmicosin, leucomycin, tylosin).

Macrolides is usually used for the treatment of staphylococcal infections in sheep, goats, calves and pigs; moreover, it is used as a feed additives for increasing the growth rate in growing animals. The long term administration of lincomycine is established to cause gastrointestinal disorders represented in vomiting, nausea and diarrhoea which that may consider fatal. Also, macrolides may cause adverse side effects such as polyarthritis, urticaria, skin rashes, hepatic damage and haematological disorders (WHO, 1989). With respect to the solubility of macrolides, it greatly varies, it ranged between 0.15 and 45 mg L^{-1} (Thiele-Bruhn, 2003). Tylosin is unstable in either acidic or alkaline media and relatively stable under neutral pH media. The degradation of tylosin in the nature is affected by many factors such as organic matter in soil, clay particles, and organic components in manure (Rabølle and Spliid, 2000; Kolz *et al.*, 2005). During a study carried out in USA at 1999 and 2000 on surface waters, it was reported that tylosin is the most frequently detected antibiotic (Kolpin *et al.*, 2002).

5. **Nitrofurans** (Furazolidone, nitrofurazone, furaltadone, nitrofurantoin).

Different types of nitofurans are used as therapeutic treatment or as prophylactive of bacterial and protozoal infectious diseases in different species of farm animals (cattle, poultry, rabbits, pigs and fish). The routine usage of nitrofurans in food-producing animals has been debatable as residues of such drugs may be carcinogenic and mutagenic. Some studies reported that nitrofurazone is a carcinogenic but not genotoxic agent, while furazolidone has possessed both carcinogenic and genotoxic action (WHO, 1993). In addition nitrofurans metabolites can be found in animal proteins (meat and eggs) for several weeks or months specially in farmyard birds receiving nitrofurans as anticoccidial agents. Due to the serious side effects of nitrofurans and its metabolites, its systemic use is prohibited in food producing animals in many countries as in Europe and USA (EMA, 2008).

6. **Quinolones** (Ciprofloxacin, danofloxacin, difloxacin, enrofloxacin, flumequine, marbofloxacin, norfloxacin, ofloxacin).

Administration of quinolone antibiotics can cause adverse side effects in the GIT such as gastrointestinal disorders as vomiting, diarrhoea, nausea, headache, visual disturbances and insomnia. In addition, some toxic symptoms may be occur such as pruritus, rashes and epidermal necrolysis (Pérez-Jiménez *et al.*, 2011). With regard to solubility of fluoroquinolones, it possess poor water solubility at pH 6-8 (amphoteric property) and insensitive to hydrolysis, resistant to microbial degradation and increased temperatures, but they can be degraded by UV light (Thiele-Bruhn, 2003) and were found to be very persistent in manure and soil matrixes (Boxall *et al.*, 2004, 2012).

7. **Sulphonamides** (Sulfadiazine, sulfadimethoxine, sulfamethazine, sulfadoxine, sulfaethoxypyridazine, sulfaguanidine, sulfamerazine, sulfamethoxazole, sulfapyridine, sulfamethoxydiazine, sulfamethoxypyridazine, sulfamonomethoxine, sulfathiazole, sulfaquinoxaline):

Sulphonamides residues in animal products may cause hypersensitivity reactions, mainly in the form of skin rashes. With regard to the solubility of sulfonamides, it possess high solubility (0.1 to 8 g L^{-1}), this wide variation in the solubility returned to the type of sulphonamides (Sarmah *et al.*, 2006). Also, sulfonamides are characterized by a low chelating ability and low binding constants (Sukul and Spiteller, 2006). Degradation of sulphonamides can be occurring during exposure to photo (Batchu *et al.*, 2014). Sulfonamides can potentially enter animal wastewaters, ground and surface waters, soils, sediments and in environmental samples (Thiele-Bruhn, 2003; Wei *et al.*, 2011; Zhang *et al.*, 2011).

8. **Tetracyclines** (Chlortetracycline, oxytetracycline, demeclocycline, doxycycline, methacycline, minocycline).

Oxytetracycline can induces bacterial resistance in coliform microorganisms in GIT of human beings, which result from improper dosage and consequently require higher doses to give efficient antibacterial activity. With respect to the presence of tetracyclines in the environment, tetracyclines are stable in acid media, but not in alkaline conditions, and constitute salts in both conditions (Doi and Stoskopf, 2000; Halling-Sørensen *et al.*, 2002). They are susceptible to photo-degradation (Doi and Stoskopf, 2000). Chelating agents reduces bioavailability and thus reduces the antibacterial activity of tetracyclines. There is minimal degradation of tetracycline in manure (Bansal, 2012). The estimation rate of tetracyclines in manure ranged from 84.9 to 96.8% with a maximum concentration of residual chlortetracycline recovery reaching 764.4 mg kg^{-1} (Pan *et al.*, 2011). Tetracyclines (particularly tetracycline and chlortetracycline) were found to be more persistent in soils than in manure (Bansal, 2012).

METHODS FOR DETERMINATION OF ANTIBIOTIC RESIDUES

One or more of the different antibiotic drug classes (aminoglycosides, amphenicols, beta-lactams, macrolides, nitrofurans, quinolones, sulphonamides and tetracyclines) could contaminate animal products (meat, milk and egg) or their by products. Therefore, it is of great importance to determine the concentrations of antibiotics or their metabolites in the serum, tissues or by products of animals which considered essential for both farmers or breeders and consumers (Mitchell *et al.*, 2003).

Recently different methods for detection of drug residues in animal product and by products samples were developed for rapid estimation of antibacterial drug residues.

One of the assays routinely applied in many countries for detection of beta-lactam antibiotics is the microbial inhibition assays, in which *Bacillus stearothermophilus* was used as the test microorganism due to its sensitivity to some antibiotics particularly β-lactam antibiotics.

Different methods were applied for detection of antibiotics residues at or low the permissible limit such as the tube test and (multi-) plate test systems and many of immunological methods such as ELISA, RIA or biosensor methods (Ferguson *et al.*, 2002; Pikkemaat *et al.*, 2009). All the dependence methods used for detection of antibiotics are validated in accordance with the Council Directive 2002/657/EC (EC, 2002).

With regard to poultry samples, many methods are applied now for detection of drug residues in poultry tissues, comprises microbiological methods, chromatography methods, ELISA and immunochemical methods (Kaya and Filazi, 2010). The microbiological assays are preferred method as they are cheap, easy to perform and able to measure a large number of samples at the same time (Karraouan *et al.*, 2009; Javadi *et al.*, 2011). Four plate test (FPT) which are characterized by high sensitivity and specificity are used for determination of levels of drug residues in poultry tissues and are approved by European Union as a standard assay.

ADVERSE EFFECTS OF ANTIBIOTICS DRUGS RESIDUES

The challenging cause of resistance to antibacterial drugs are the widespread uses of sub-therapeutic doses of antibiotics for long time as growth promoter and lack of perfect control of administration, the risk of drug accumulation and their residuals in animal tissues and their product will increase (Meredith *et al.*, 1965; Lemus *et al.*, 2008). In addition it was recognized to favor the selection, spread, and the establishment of permanent resistant strains in the environment (Andremont, 2003; Kumar, *et al.*, 2005). Owing to the widespread non-therapeutic use of antibacterial drugs and is, therefore, no longer accepted within the EU (EC, 2003).

Many researches focused on the main uses of antibiotics in livestock animals, they found that 87% of antibiotics have been broadly used in farm animals for treatment, control or prevention of infectious diseases and 13% as food supplement to increase growth and productivity (Dipeolu and Alonge, 2002; Donoghue, 2003; Mahgoub *et al.*, 2006).

Antibiotic residues and their metabolites in poultry meat may cause several adverse effects on consumers such as direct toxicity, developing resistant bacteria, and allergies (Kirbis *et al.*, 2007) and leads to adaptation of normal micro flora in the GIT, and exposure to low doses of antibiotics for long term via contaminated foods can gain resistance (Myllyniemi *et al.*, 2004; Javadi *et al.*, 2011). Therefore, due to the high risk of antibiotic residues they established the maximum limits of drug residues (MRLs), which are the maximum concentration of drug residues that could legally allowed to be in the food product without causing adverse effects to the consumers (Myllyniemi *et al.*, 2004; Reyes Herrera *et al.*, 2005).

ANTIBIOTIC RESISTANCE IN FOOD OF ANIMAL ORIGIN

Resistance factors were already recognized to exist in the environment earlier to the introduction of antibiotics for treatment of diseases (D'Costa *et al.*, 2011; Bhullar *et al.*, 2012), though, the variety and distribution of resistant organisms has increased intensely in the past few years (Levy, 2002). Therefore, antibiotic resistance has become a serious and growing risk to modern medicine, and began as one of the leading health distresses of the 21st century (WHO, 2014). The prospects that a continued increase in antimicrobial resistance (AMR) by 2050 will lead to 10 million people dying yearly, and a reduction of 2 to 3.5% in Gross Domestic Product (GDP) (http://amrreview.org/). Also in Europe, more attention was paid for the problem of antimicrobial resistance and gives it a high priority topic in the impending years (EC, 2015).

Antimicrobial resistance developed with the increased number, volume and variety of antimicrobial applications used in humans and animals (Levy, 2002; Kumar *et al.*, 2005). The use of antibiotics in animal production contributes significantly to the development and spread of antibiotic resistance in animals and food of animal origin (EFSA, 2015).

In equivalent with the increasing prevalence of antibiotic resistant bacteria in domestic farm animals, resistant bacteria are also more and more commonly present on food products of animal origin (Aarestrup *et al.*, 2008; Overdevest *et al.*, 2011; Tham *et al.*, 2012) and even on vegetables (Reuland *et al.*, 2014; Hoek *et al.*, 2015). Some studies which carried out in the Netherlands found that the use of fluoroquinolones caused an amazing increase in the prevalence of ciprofloxacin resistant Salmonella isolates from retail poultry meat; between 2000 and 2007 the prevalence rose from 0 to 60% (MARAN, 2015). Also, another study in the Netherlands concerning presence of ESBL producing micro-organisms in retail poultry with a danger values which reached 100% on conventional and 84% on organic muscle samples (Cohen Stuart *et al.*, 2012). Moreover, ESBL producing bacteria are found in low level in meat of other animal species (MARAN, 2015).

There are relationship between the appearance of fluoroquinolone resistance in poultry and human Campylobacter isolates, the risk of resistant bacteria being transmitted to human being via food is believed to be low (Food Safety authority of Ireland, 2015). Raw food products obviously hold a more substantial risk for transfer of bacteria and thus also antimicrobial resistance. Besides the direct transfer of resistant bacteria, intact DNA coding for resistant might be transmitted through foods, and the potential for uptake by bacteria in the human gut is uncertain (EFSA, 2008).

ANTIBIOTIC RESISTANCE IN LIVESTOCK

At any time an animal given a dose of antibiotics, there is an opportunity for bacteria to induce resistance to this antibiotic or which similar in structure. Bacteria may exhibit intrinsic (natural) and acquired resistance. Intrinsic one it's a self-defensive mechanism of microorganism in which induced immune action against action of antibiotic drugs. This is a natural (intrinsic) property to all members of a species and is unrelated to the over/misuse of antibiotics. Acquired resistance occurs when the bacteria was previously susceptible to the same drug and become resistant to this drug after second exposure, and have the ability to multiply and spread in the presence of the same antibiotic. Bacteria can acquire resistance in two ways: vertically, through gene transfer i.e. by mutations or horizontally, via gene transfer gained from either new genetic material from resistant bacterium or from the environment. The different types of horizontal gene transfer occurred in the bacteria are included: conjugation, transformation or transduction (Aminov, 2011).

The mechanisms by which the bacteria resist the action of antibiotics through: (1) increased expression of efflux pumps, (2) permeability changes in the bacterial cell membrane which limit the amount of antibiotic penetrating the bacterial cell membrane, (3) physical modification/ inactivation of the antimicrobial agent, (4) enzymatic inactivation of the antibiotic, and (5) modification of the molecular binding sites (McDermott *et al.*, 2003; Alekshun and Levy, 2007).

The prevalence of antibiotic resistant bacteria in farm animals is depending on many factors such as the quantities of antibiotics used, type of antibiotics, administration route, and species of animals (Levy, 2001; Catry *et al.*, 2003). There is clear evidence on the relationship between the use of antibiotics and increased resistance development in farm animal production (Dunlop *et al.*, 1998; Aarestrup, 1999; Kruse *et al.*, 1999). A clear example is the rapid development of fluoroquinolone resistant bacteria from poultry in the 1990's, shortly after the introduction of these antibiotics for treatment of poultry (Jacobs-Reitsma *et al.*, 1994). In the Unites States the increasing prevalence of fluoroquinolone resistant Campylobacter in humans provoked the US Food and Drug Administration in 2005 to ban the use of enrofloxacin in poultry. Fluoroquinolones are considered "critically" or "very" important to human medicine (Category I) by the World Health Organization (WHO, 2007). Nevertheless, they are still allowed for veterinary use in Europe. Antibiotic resistance occurs in zoonotic pathogens such as *Salmonella* and *Campylobacter* spp., as well as commensal bacteria. Commensal flora plays an important role in physiological and metabolic processes as well as in the development of the animal's immune system (Ivanov and Honda, 2012). In particular the intestine contains incredible numbers of bacteria that are exposed to resistance provoking antibiotic concentrations during the treatment of an infection or the application of growth promotors. Subsequently, forms an effective and important reservoir for antibiotic resistance (Acar and Moulin, 2006). Not surprisingly, resistance prevalence and profiles of commensal organisms are very similar to their zoonotic counterparts (MARAN, 2015). A particular worrying trend is the increasing occurrence of multidrug resistance. For example, in 2012 more than 60% of the commensal *E. coli* strains from broiler chickens in the Netherlands were found to show resistance to two or more classes of antibiotics (MARAN, 2015). Antimicrobial resistance formed in livestock may be transmitted to humans. Livestock associated MRSA is widely found in farmers and veterinarians (Voss *et al.*, 2005; Wulf *et al.*, 2008). Also the significance of livestock as a reservoir for ESBL (Extended Spectrum Beta-Lactamase) -producing bacteria is increasingly being recognized as a threat to human health care (Dohmen *et al.*, 2015).

REFERENCES

Aarestrup, F.M. (1999): Association between the Consumption of Antimicrobial Agents in Animal Husbandry and the Occurrence of Resistant Bacteria among Food Animals. J. Antimicrob. Agents, 12: 279-285.

Aarestrup, F.M.; Wegener, H.C. and Collignon, P. (2008): Resistance in Bacteria of the Food Chain: Epidemiology and Control Strategies. Expert Reviews, 6(5): 733-750.

Acar, J.F. and Moulin, G. (2006): Antimicrobial Resistance at farm Level. Rev. Sci. Tech. Off. Int. Epiz, 25(2): 775-792.

Alekshun, M.N. and Levy, S.B. (2007): Molecular Mechanisms of Antibacterial Multidrug Resistance. Cell, 128(6): 1037-1050.

Aminov, R.I. (2011): Horizontal Gene Exchange in Environmental Microbiota. Front. Microbiol., 2: 158.

Andremont, A. (2003): Commensal Flora may Play Key Role in Spreading Antibiotic Resistance. ASM News, 69: 601-607.

Bansal, O.P. (2012): A Laboratory Study on Degradation of Tetracycline and Chlortetracycline in Soils of Aligarh District as Influenced by Temperature, Water Content, Concentration of Farm yield Manure, Nitrogen and Tetracyclines. Proc. Nat. Acad. Sci. India, Section B: Bio. Sc., 82(4): 503-509.

Batchu, S.R.; Panditi, V.R. and Gardinali, P.R. (2014): Photodegradation of Sulfonamide Antibiotics in Simulated and Natural Sunlight: Implications for their Environmental Fate. J. Environm. Sci. Health, 49(3): 200-211.

Berendsen, B.J.A.; Pikkemaat, M.G.; Romkens, P.F.A.M.; Wegh, R.; van Sisseren, M.; Stolker, A.A.M. and Nielen, W.M.F. (2013): Occurrence of Chloramphenicol in Crops through Natural Production by Bacteria in Soil. J. Agric. Food Chem., 61: 4004-4010.

Bhullar, K.; Waglechner, N.; Pawlowski, A.; Koteva, K.; Banks, E.D.; Johnston, M.D.; Barton, H.A. and Wright, G.D. (2012): Antibiotic Resistance is Prevalent in an Isolated Cave microbiome. PLoS ONE, 7(4): e34953, 11 p.

Boxall, A.B.; Rudd, M.A.; Brooks, B.W.; Caldwell, D.J.; Choi, K.; *et al.* (2012): Pharmaceuticals and Personal Care Products in the Environment: What are the big Questions? Environ. Health Perspect., 120(9): 1221-1229.

Boxall, A.B.A.; Fogg, L.A.; Blackwell, P.A.; Kay, P.; Pemberton, E.J. and Croxford, A. (2004): Veterinary Medicines in the Environment. Rev. Environ. Contam. Toxicol., 180: 1-91.

Catry, B.; Laevens, H.; Devriese, L.A.; Opsomer, G. and de Kruif, A. (2003): Antimicrobial Resistance in Livestock. J. Vet. Pharmacol. Ther., 26: 81-93.

Cohen Stuart, J.; van den Munckhof, T.; Voets, G.; Scharringa, J.; Fluit, A. and Hall, M.L. (2012): Comparison of ESBL Contamination in Organic and Conventional Retail Chicken Meat. Int. J. Food Microbiol., 154(3): 212-214.

D'Costa, V.M.; King, C.E.; Morar, L.K.M.; Sung, W.W.L.; Schwarz, C.; Froese, D.; Zazula, G.; Calmels, F.; Debruyne, R.; Golding, G.B.; Poinar, H.N. and Wright, G.D. (2011): Antibiotic Resistance is Ancient. Nature, 477: 457-461.

Dewdney, J.M.; Maes, L.; Raynaud, J.P.; Blanc, F.; Scheid, J.P.; Jackson, T.; Lens, S. and Verschueren, C. (1991): Risk Assessment of Antibiotic Residues of beta-lactams and Macrolides in Food-products with regard to their Immunoallergic Potential. Food and Chemical Toxicology, 29: 477-483.

Dipeolu, M.A. and Alonge, D.O. (2002): Residues of Streptomycin Antibiotic in Meat Sold for Human Consumption in some States of SW Nigeria. Archivos de Zootecnica, 51: 477-480.

Dohmen, W.; Bonten, M.J.; Bos, M.E.; van Marm, S.; Scharringa, J.; Wagenaar, J.A. and Heederik, D.J. (2015): Carriage of Extended-spectrum β-lactamases in pig farmers is associated with occurrence in pigs. Clin. Microbiol. Infect., 21(10): 917–923.

Doi, A.M. and Stoskopf, M.K. (2000): The Kinetics of Oxytetracycline Degradation in Deionized Water under Varying Temperature, pH, Light, Substrate, and Organic Matter. J. Aquat. Anim. Health, 12: 246-253.

Donoghue, D.J. (2003): Antibiotic Residues in Poultry Tissues and Eggs: Human Health Concerns? Poultry Science, 82: 618-621.

Dunlop, R.H.; McEwen, S.A.; Meek, A.H.; Clarke, R.C.; Black, W.D. and Friendship, R.M. (1998): Associations among Antimicrobial Drug Treatments and Antimicrobial Resistance of Fecal *Escherichia coli* of swine of 34 farrow to Finish Farms in Ontario, Canada. Prev. Vet. Med., 34: 283-305.

EC (2002): Commission Decision 2002/657/EC of 14 August 2002 on Implementing Council Directive 96/23/EC Concerning the Performance of Analytical Methods and the Interpretation of Results 2002/657/EC. Official Journal of European Union L221, 8-36.

EC (2003): Commission Decision 2003/181/EC of 13 March 2003 on Amending Decision 2002/657/EC as Regard the Setting of Minimum required Performance Limits (MRPLs) for Certain Residues in Food of Animal Origin. Official Journal of European Union, L71, 17.

EC (2015): Commission Staff Working Document Progress Report on the Action Plan against the Rising Threats from Antimicrobial Resistance. SANTE/10251/2015.

EFSA (2008): Foodborne Antimicrobial Resistance as a Biological Hazard, Scientific Opinion of the Panel on Biological Hazards. The EFSA Journal, 765: 1-87.

EFSA (2015): EU Summary Report on Antimicrobial Resistance in Zoonotic and Indicator Bacteria from Humans, Animals and Food in 2013. The EFSA Journal, 13(2): 4036, 178 pp.

EMA (2008): Maximum Residue Limit Assessment Reports, Penicillins: Summary Report - Committee for Veterinary Medicinal Products. Retrieved from http://www.ema.europa.eu/ema/.

Ferguson, J.P.; Baxter, G.A.; McEvoy, J.D.G.; Stead, S.; Rawlings, E. and Sharman, M. (2002): Detection of Streptomycin and Dihydrostreptomycin Residues in Milk, Honey and Meat Samples using an Optical Biosensor. Analyst, 127: 951-956.

Food Safety Authority or Ireland (2015): Report of the Scientific Committee of the Food Safety Authority of Ireland. Potential for Transmission of Antimicrobial Resistance in the Food Chain. ISBN 978-1-910348-01-7.

Halling-Sørensen, B.; Sengeløv, G. and Tjørnelund, J. (2002): Toxicity of Tetracyclines and Tetracycline Degradation Products to Environmentally Relevant Bacteria, including selected Tetracycline-resistant Bacteria. Arch. Environ. Contam. Toxicol., 42: 263-271.

Hoek, van A.H.; Veenman, C.; van Overbeek, W.M.; Lynch, G.; de Roda Husman, A.M. and Blaak, H. (2015): Prevalence and Characterization of ESBL- and AmpC-producing Enterobacteriaceae on Retail Vegetables. Int. J. Food Microbiol., 204: 1-8.

Huang, C.-H.; Renew, J.E.; Smeby, K.L.; Pinkston, K. and Sedlak, D.L. (2001): Assessment of Potential Antibiotic Contaminants in Water and Preliminary Occurrence Analysis. J. Contemp. Water Res. Educ., 120: 30-40.

IFT (The Institute of Food Technologists) (2006): Comprehensive Reviews Food Science and Food Safety, Institute of Food Technologist, 5(3): 71-137, ISNN 1541-4337.

Ivanov, I.I. and Honda, K. (2012): Intestinal Commensal Microbes as Immune Modulators. Cell Host Microbe, 12(4): 496-508.

Jacobs-Reitsma, W.F.; Koenraad, P.M.; Bolder, N.M. and Mulder, R.W. (1994): In vitro Susceptibility of Campylobacter and Salmonella Isolates from Broilers to Quinolones, Ampicillin, Tetracycline, and Erythromycin. Vet. Q., 16(4): 206-208.

Javadi, A.; Mirzaie, H. and Khatibi, S.A. (2011): Effect of Roasting, Boiling and Microwaving Cooking methods on Enrofloxacin Residues in Edible Tissues of Broiler. African Journal of Pharmacy and Pharmacology, 5(2): 214-218.

Karraouan, B.; Bouchrif, B.; Ziyate, N.; Talmi, A.; Yahia, Kh.I.S.; Cohen, N. and Fassouane, A. (2009): Evaluation of Multi-plate Microbial Assay for the Screening of Antibacterial Residues in Poultry Muscle. European Journal of Scientific Research, 35(2): 311-317.

Kaya, S.E. and Filazi, A. (2010): Determination of Antibiotic Residues in Milk Samples. Kafkas Univ. Vet. Fak. Derg., 16: 31-35.

Kirbis, A. (2007): Microbiological Screening method for Detection of Aminoglycosides, β-lactames, macrolides, tetracyclines and quinolones in meat samples. Slov. Vet. Res., 44(1/2): 11–18.

Kolpin, D.W.; Furlong, E.T.; Meyer, M.T.; Thurman, E.M.; Zaugg, S.D.; Barber, L.B. and Buxton, H.T. (2002): Phamaceuticals, Hormones, and other Organic Wastewater Contaminants in US Streams, 1999-2000: A National Reconnaissance. Environ. Sci. Technol., 36: 1202-1211.

Kolz, A.C.; Moorman, T.B.; Ong, S.K.; Scoggin, K.D. and Douglass, E.A. (2005): Degradation and Metabolite Production of Tylosin in Anaerobic and Aerobic Swine-manure Lagoons. Water Environ. Res., 77: 49-56.

Kruse, H.; Johansen, B.K.; Rorvik, L.M. and Schaller, G. (1999): The use of Avoparcin as a Growth Promoter and the Occurrence of Vancomycin-resistant Enterococcus species in Norwegian Poultry and Swine Production. Microb. Drug Resist., 5: 135-139.

Kumar, K.; Gupta, S.C.; Baidoo, S.K.; Chander, Y. and Rosen, C.J. (2005): Antibiotic uptake by Plants from Soil Fertilized with Animal Manure. J. Environ. Qual., 34: 2082-2085.

Lemus, J.A.; Blanco, G.; Grande, J.;Arroyo, B.; Garcia-Montijano, M. and Martinez, F. (2008): Antibiotics Threaten Wildlife: Circulating Quinolone Residues and Disease in Avian Scavengers. PLoS ONE, 3(1): 1-6.

Levy, S.B. (2001): Antibiotic Resistance: Consequences of Inaction. Clin. Infect. Dis., 3: S124-S129.

Levy, S.B. (2002): The Antibiotic Paradox. How the Misuse of Antibiotics Destroys their Curative Powers, Book Review 2nd edn. Int. Microbiol., 5: 155-156.

Lozano, M.C. and Arias, D.C. (2008): Residuos de farmacos en alimentosde origen Animal: panorama actual en Colombia. Rev. ColombCienc Pecu., 21: 121-135.

Mahgoub, O.; Kadim, I.T.; Mothershaw, A.; Al Zadjali, S.A. and Annamalai, K. (2006): Use of Enzyme Linked immunosorbent assay (ELISA) for Detection of Antbiotic and Anabolic Residues in Goat and Sheep Meat. World Journal of Agricultural Sciences, 2(3): 298-302.

MARAN (2015): Monitoring of Antimicrobial Resistance and Antibiotic Usage in Animals in the Netherlands in 2014. Retrieved from http://www.wageningenur.nl/nl/Expertises- Dienstverlening/ Onderzoeksinstituten/ Central-Veterinary-Institute/Publicaties-CVI/MARAN Rapporten.

McDermott, P.F.; Walker, R.D. and White, D.G. (2003): Antimicrobials: Modes of Action and Mechanisms of Resistance. Int. J. Toxicol., 22(2): 135-143.

Meredith, W.E.; Weiser, H.H. and Winter, A.R. (1965): Chlortetracycline and Oxytetracycline Residues in Poultry Tissues and Eggs. Applied Microbiology, 13(1): 86-88.

Mitchell, P.; Petfalski, E.; Houalla, R.; Podtelejnikov, A.; Mann, M. and Tollervey, D. (2003): Rrp47p is an exosome-associated Protein required for the 3′ Processing of Stable RNAs. Mol. Cell Biol., 23(19): 6982-69892.

Myllyniemi, A. L. (2004): Development of Microbiological methods for the Detection and Identification of Antimicrobial Residues in Meat. National Veterinary and Food Research Institue, Helsinki, Finland.

Overdevest, I.; Willemsen, I.; Rijnsburger, M.; Eustace, A.; Xu, L.; Hawkey, P.; Heck, M.; Savelkoul, P.; Vandenbroucke-Grauls, C.; van der Zwaluw, K.; Huijsdens, X. and Kluytmans, J. (2011): Extended spectrum β-lactamase genes of Escherichia coli in chicken meat and humans, The Netherlands. Emerg. Infect. Dis., 17(7): 1216–1222.

Pan, X.; Qiang, Z.; Ben, W. and Chen, M. (2011): Residual Veterinary Antibiotics in Swine Manure from Concentrated Animal Feeding Operations in Shandong Province, China. Chemosphere, 84(5): 695-700.

Pérez-Jiménez, J.; Fezeu. L.; Touvier, M.; Arnault, N.; Manach, C.; Hercberg, S.; Galan, P. and Scalbert, A. (2011): Dietary intake of 337 Polyphenols in French Adults. Am. J. Clin. Nutr., 93(6): 1220-1228.

Pikkemaat, M.G.; Rapallini, M.L.B.A.; Oostra-van Dijk, S. and Elferink, J.W.A. (2009): Comparison of Three Microbial Screening methods for Antibiotics using Routine Monitoring Samples. Analytica Chimica Acta, 637: 298-304.

Rabølle, M. and Spliid, N.H. (2000): Sorption and Mobility of Metronidazole, olaquindox, oxytetracycline and tylosin in Soil. Chemosphere, 40(7): 715-722.

Reuland, E.A.; Al Naiemi, N.; Raadsen, S.A.; Savelkoul, P.H.; Kluytmans, J.A. and Vandenbroucke-Graul, C.M. (2014): Prevalence of ESBL-producing Enterobacteriaceae in raw vegetables. Eur. J. Clin. Microbiol. Infect. Dis., 33(10): 1843–1846.

Reyes-Herrera, I.; Schneider, M.J.; Cole, K.; Farnell, M.B.; Blore, P.J. and Donoghue, D.J. (2005): Concentration of Antibiotic Residues vary between different Edible Muscle Tissues in Poultry. Journal of Food Protection, 68(10): 2217-2219.

Sarmah, A.K.; Meyer, M.T. and Boxall, A.B.A. (2006): A Global Perspective on the use, Sales, Exposure Pathways, Occurrence, Fate and Effects of Veterinary Antibiotics (VAs) in the Environment. Chemosphere, 65(5): 725-759.

Stolker, A.A.M.; Zuidema, T. and Nielen, M.W.F. (2007): Residue Analysis of Veterinary Drugs and Growth-promoting Agents. Trends in Analytical Chemistry, 26: 967-979.

Sukul, P. and Spiteller, M. (2006): Sulfonamides in the Environment as Veterinary Drugs. Rev. Environ. Contam. Toxicol., 187: 67-101.

Tham, J.; Walder, M.; Melander, E. and Odenholt, I. (2012): Prevalence of Extended-spectrum betalactamase- producing Bacteria in Food. Infect. Drug Resist., 5: 143-147.

Thiele-Bruhn, S. (2003): Pharmaceutical Antibiotic Compounds in Soils—A Review. J. Plant Nutr. Soil Sci., 166: 145-167.

Voss, A.; Loeffen, F.; Bakker, J.; Klaassen, C. and Wulf, M. (2005): Methicillin-resistant Staphylococcus aureus in Pig Farming. Emerg. Infect. Dis., 11(12): 1965-1966.

Wei, R.C.; Ge, F.; Huang, S.Y.; Chen, M. and Wang, R. (2011): Occurrence of Veterinary Antibiotics in Animal Wastewater and Surface Water Around Farms in Jiangsu Province, China. Chemosphere, 82: 1408-1414.

WHO (World Health Organization) (1989): In Evaluation of Certain Veterinary Drug Residues in Food, Thirty-fourth Report of the Joint FAO/WHO Expert Committee on Food Additives, Technical Report Series 788.

WHO (World Health Organization) (1993): In Evaluation of Certain Veterinary Drug Residues in Food, Fortieth Report of the Joint FAO/WHO Expert Committee on Food Additives, Technical Report Series 832.

WHO (World Health Organization) (2007): Report of the FAO/WHO/OIE, Expert Meeting on Critically Important Antimicrobials. Rome, Italy, 26-30 November 2007. Retrieved from http://www.who.int/foodsafety/publications/antimicrobials/en/

WHO (World Health Organization) (2014): Antimicrobial Resistance: Global Report on Surveillance. World Health Organization. Retrieved from http://www.who.int/drugresistance on 19-05-2014.

Wulf, M.W.; Sørum, M.; van Nes, A.; Skov, R.; Melchers, W.J.; Klaassen, C.H. and Voss, A. (2008): Prevalence of methicillin-resistant Staphylococcus aureus among Veterinarians: An International Study. Clin. Microbiol. Infect., 14(1): 29-34.

Zhang, D.D.; Lin, L.F.; Luo, Z.X.; Yan, C.Z. and Zhang, X. (2011): Occurrence of Selected Antibiotics in Jiulongjiang River in Various Seasons, South China. J. Environ. Monit., 13: 1953–1960.

Pages: 56-83

Animal Biodiversity and Fisheries
Edited by: **Dr. Rashmi Tripathi; Dr. Vijay Sharma & Dr. Pawan Kumar 'Bharti'**
ISBN: 978-93-88854-06-1
Edition: **2019**
Published by: **Discovery Publishing House Pvt. Ltd., New Delhi (India)**

4

Comparative Analysis of Milk Production and Reproductive Performances of Dairy Cattle Breeds and Crosses in Three up Country Farms in Sri Lanka

Jayantha T.M.[1]; Silva G.L.L.P[2]
Esakkimuthu M[3*] and Ranathunga L.N.[4]

ABSTRACT

This study was conducted to determine the effect of five factors, namely genotype, parity, calving month, bull breed and farm, on selected production and reproduction traits, i.e. birth weight, lactation length, total milk yield, days to peak, 305-day milk yield, number of services and mature equivalent yield of dairy cattle in three Up Country farms belong to National Livestock Development Board. A total of 1500 dairy cow records were collected covering the period from January, 2013 to August, 2016, using herd register and *Alpro* windows software maintained at Bopaththalawa, Manikpalama and Dayagama farms. Records were obtained from five different genotypic groups (Friesian (F), Jersey (J), 75% F × 25% J, 50% F × 50% J, and 25% F × 75% J) using available pedigree records and visual observations. Analysis of variance was performed using SAS software package and means of genotypes were compared using Duncan's Multiple Range Test. Production and reproduction traits were significantly ($P<0.05$) affected by the five genotypes tested in the study. The highest performance in production was shown by the 50% F × 50% J cattle group. The highest production and reproduction performance levels were recorded by September to February calvings. It was also revealed that the highest production was obtained at the fourth parity of cows regardless of the

[1,2] Department of Animal Science, Faculty of Agriculture, University of Peradeniya Sri Lanka
[3] Kerala Agricultural University, India
[4] Aquinas College of Higher Studies, Colombo 08, Sri Lanka

genotype. Use of semen from pure Friesian bulls resulted in the lowest number of services per calf. Among the three farms, Dayagama farm showed the highest milk production and Manikpalama farm showed the highest reproduction performance. Further, the results revealed that the 50% F x 50% J was the best performing genotype in Dayagama farm while pure Friesian performed the best in Manikpalama farm.

Keywords: Cattle breeds, Genotype, Milk Production, Up country

INTRODUCTION

Dairy industry of Sri Lanka has a significant contribution to the economic development of the country. It is also a traditional industry that has been practiced for thousands of years. While being a source of employment it plays an important role in alleviating poverty. Although the dairy industry has occupied an important place in Sri Lankan economy, its contribution towards uplifting the nutritional status of the people is still low. In the year 2014 total number of milking cows in Sri Lanka were 540,100 and other cows were 174,440 (National Livestock Statistics, 2014). Local milk production of Sri Lanka is not sufficient to meet the demand. The rest has to be fulfilled by importing of milk at a high cost. Per capita consumption of milk by Sri Lankans is lower than the other South Asian nations. It is about 32kg, compared to 72kg and 180kg per capita consumption, in India and Pakistan, respectively (Ranawana., 2008). In order to meet the required amount of dairy products, the performance of dairy animals should be increased; particularly dairy cattle in relation to milk production. Even though good management practices facilitate performance of animals; breeding and selection are the best approaches to permanently improve genetic potential. Genetic improvement is an important overall strategy to increase profitability of dairy cattle operations. Especially for economic purposes and to sustain important traits such as high milk production. Identification and evaluation of factors that affect the genetic improvement and mating strategies in a population are essential to evaluate genetic improvement (Sarakul *et al.*, 2010). Dairy animals generate a continuous flow of income and act as a cushion against income shocks arising due to crop failure for people with poor resources.

Milk is a 'cash crop' for smallholders, converting low value agricultural byproducts, crop residues and cheap family labour into a value added market commodity. Small-scale dairying is predominant in Sri Lanka. Its efficiency as an integrated farming system provides financial health and social securities to thousands of rural dwellers in the country. Sri Lanka imports 70,000-75,000 Mt. of milk powder annually by spending a colossal sum of Rs. 30 billion. For self-sufficiency, 482 million liters of milk should be produced annually in Sri Lanka. Therefore to meet this objective, in 2013 phase 01 of the National Dairy Development project was implemented in Bopaththalawa, Manicpalama and Dayagama farms which are under the National Livestock Development Board (NLDB). There are different genotypes in these three farms. This study intends to identify the most suitable genotype which has the maximum production and reproduction performance in the local environment. The objectives of this study is to compare the milk production and reproduction performances of different cattle breeds and crosses reared in three farms; to compare the milk production and reproduction performances of different cattle breeds and crosses kept in a farm; to evaluate the factors contributing to the variation of production and reproduction performance of cattle reared in three farms.

REVIEW OF LITERATURE

Cattle Population in Sri Lanka

According to the Department of census and statistics, the cattle population in Sri Lanka is about 1,088,110 heads in 2015. The highest cattle population which is 106,470 heads is reported in Kurunagala district, and Kegalle becomes the district with the lowest number of animals where the value is less than 13,000 herds in 2015 (Table 4.1). The highest cattle population was recorded in 2012 (Fig 4.1)

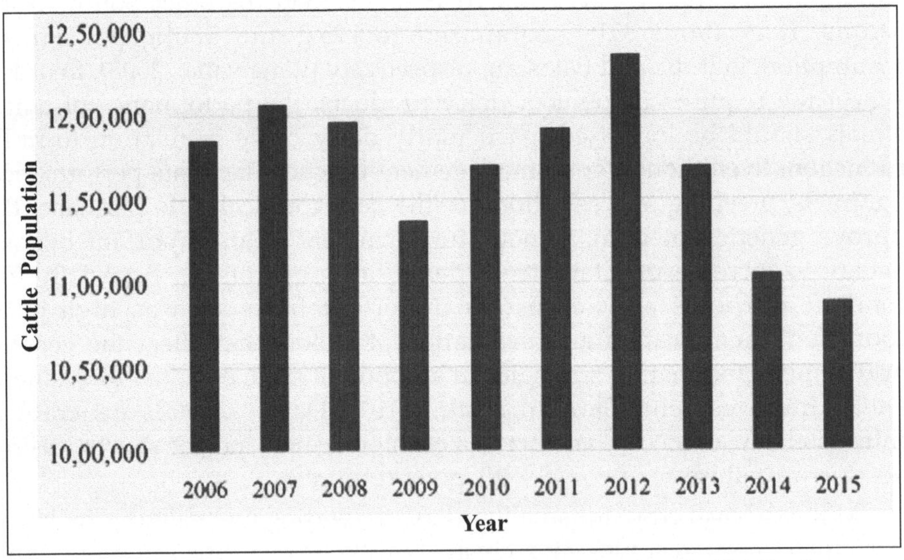

Fig. 4.1: Cattle population in Sri Lanka, 2006-2015 in Sri Lanka

Source: National Livestock Statistics., 2015

Table 4.1: Cattle population in Sri Lanka during 2006-15

District	2006	2007	2008	2009	2010	2011	2012	2013	2014	2015
National Total	1,184,710	1,206,490	1,195,610	1,136,860	1,169,670	1,191,850	1,235,535	1,169,040	1,104,780	1,088,110
Colombo	11,430	11,780	10,540	12,130	10,850	11,330	11,670	12,450	11,690	10,940
Gampaha	34,520	32,490	33,260	30,830	31,890	31,530	31,930	32,460	32,090	30,680
Kalutara	16,900	18,000	18,180	18,800	19,360	18,910	19,920	18,630	18,190	20,600
Kandy	30,430	29,330	27,870	26,590	26,480	26,410	26,250	23,890	23,990	22,530
Matale	25,640	24,500	20,450	20,850	21,830	21,880	20,135	20,050	20,780	22,600
Nuwaraeliya	27,200	28,710	29,820	29,560	29,820	28,750	29,560	30,010	30,940	36,590
Galle	17,540	16,880	17,450	16,900	16,450	14,350	16,330	14,560	13,990	14,730
Matara	15,780	14,980	13,750	13,940	12,710	12,400	12,620	13,360	13,390	13,340
Hambantota	53,000	54,400	46,260	43,160	43,120	40,930	39,600	33,340	32,380	30,350
Jaffna	51,760	53,000	53,000	66,150	61,700	63,430	61,050	59,770	58,570	62,800
Kilinochchi	33,000	33,000	33,000	-	-	32,250	31,580	31,790	38,720	40,950
Mannar	24,700	24,900	24,050	24,530	36,190	39,590	42,270	42,740	39,770	46,130
Vavuniya	35,530	38,630	42,775	42,970	61,320	87,720	94,540	64,950	36,630	43,600
Mullativu	32,100	36,680	36,680	-	21,180	30,560	53,560	47,960	34,670	44,400
Batticaloa	64,360	67,540	63,810	65,740	69,610	63,140	72,470	75,570	72,410	75,700
Ampara	69,600	70,600	100,965	97,830	79,590	73,450	78,970	91,750	94,920	95,140
Trincomalee	48,270	48,770	50,035	56,070	61,890	57,570	57,690	60,710	51,160	50,310
Kurunegala	145,890	146,520	141,720	138,340	136,530	132,640	118,680	111,760	136,900	106,470
Puttalam	78,300	79,900	72,540	69,640	73,170	69,220	70,380	65,970	60,930	60,720
Anuradhapura	155,240	151,980	158,855	146,500	140,850	133,320	134,870	121,740	97,940	97,580
Polonnaruwa	39,600	42,070	32,600	45,940	45,860	35,290	38,220	38,290	40,100	37,690
Badulla	69,610	71,610	64,480	66,880	64,840	65,820	74,480	63,260	62,900	49,230
Moneragala	74,790	78,850	74,810	75,140	75,340	71,700	68,240	61,750	52,750	47,160
Ratnapura	16,800	19,870	17,450	17,430	18,620	18,800	19,370	20,590	18,950	17,570
Kegalle	12,720	11,500	11,260	10,940	10,470	10,860	11,150	11,690	10,020	10,300

Source: National Livestock Statistics 2015

Although the importance of the consumption of milk has been emphasized in many ways, the milk production in Sri Lanka is not adequate enough to meet the demand of the country. This low production is associated with a diverse set of factors, such as lack of knowledge, non-descript genotypes in animals resulting low yield, poor management practices, inadequate nutrition and other essential resources and veterinary services. These factors lead to impaired fertility, delayed conception, increased age at first calving and extended calving interval exerting adverse effect on milk yield causing low profit.

Dairy Cattle Production in Sri Lanka

The dairy sector forms an integral part of agriculture in Sri Lanka by providing draught power, milk, meat, transport and manure apart from its direct contribution to the gross domestic production (GDP) of the country (Silva *et al.*, 2008). Livestock accounts for only about 1.2% of the GDP (Ranaweera, 2007) while the country depends largely on imports to fulfill its demand for milk and milk products.

Dairy Cattle Productionzone in Sri Lanka

The cattle are reared in five major agro climatic zones belong to Up Country, Mid Country, The Coconut Triangles, Low Country Wet Zone, and the Dry Zone. It is estimated that in Mid and Up country areas 60% of the cattle population is dairy cows. In the coconut triangle and wet zone the proportion of dairy cows is around 40% whereas in the dry zone it is around 35%. At present dairy industry in Sri Lanka primarily depends on natural pasture and fodder. The total land area utilized for livestock production in combination with crops is estimated to be about 670,000 ha with an estimated 50,000 ha under improved pastures (Rajaguru, 1986). Cattle type found in different zone are given in table 4.2.

Up-country

This zone lies above 1200 meters a.m.s.l. and is characterised by tea plantations and dairy production from cattle kept in two systems, the estate- and village-based systems. In the estate-based system many of the employees in the tea estates rear dairy cattle, generally the European breeds, Ayrshire, Friesian and Jersey, and their crosses. Average milk yields are reported as up to 8 litters/cow/day or about 2,500 litters/cow/lactation. Manure is often sold. In the village-based system majority of the smallholders are crop-livestock farmers, growing vegetables and paddy. Manure is a major product from their cattle, milk is only a secondary source of income (Ibrahim *et al.*, 1999).

Mid-country

Crosses of European dairy breeds are an increasing proportion of the smallholder cattle herd. There are many crosses of Indian breeds two and milk yields are correspondingly low. They are reported to be about 6 litters/

cow/day or around 1,500 litters/cow/lactation. Land sizes are small encouraging the adoption of zero grazing, with generally two cows and their progeny. There is an increasing dependence on fodder from off-farm and on concentrate purchases, which are influenced by the level of household income.

Table 4.2: Population type and husbandry practices of cattle in different zone in Sri Lanka

Zone	Population	Animal type	Husbandry Practices
Up and Mid Country	121,000	Pure exotic, crosses and Zebu crosses	Zero grazing small herds, some tethering
Wet Low Country	142,000	Pure exotic, crosses and Zebu crosses Indigenous cattle	Limited grazing, Medium size grazing
Dry Low Country	1,104,000	Indigenous cattle, Zebu cattle and their crosses	Free grazing, Large herds, small herds in irrigated schemes
Coconut Triangle	177,000	Crosses of exotic breeds, Zebu types, Indigenous cattle	Limited grazing, Tethered under coconut palms, Medium size herds

Source: Ibrahim *et al.*, 2000

Coconut Triangle and Wet Lowlands

In this zonecattle forms an integral part of the farming systems. This farming system helps in weed control and provides manure to the coconut lands. Cattle is kept in almost all the rice growing areas. Pure Indian breeds or their crosses are managed under intensive or semi intensive system in this area. The cattle milk is generally converted to curd which has a high demand locally. In both zones cattle graze on the fallow paddy fields, as well as on the natural pastures under the coconut plantations and in non-cultivated areas, including common grazing areas (Ibrahim *et al.*, 1999).

Dry Lowland Zone

Predominantly indigenous Zebu are kept in this zone. Although Sahiwal and crossbred cattle in the dry zone are becoming more common, especially in the Mahaweli irrigated areas. These cattle form an important capital asset for the peasant farmers and there is the possibility to sell milk which is becoming an important source of income. Herd sizes average between 10 - 25 with some having more than 100 animals. The average production of milk extracted for human consumption from the indigenous breeds is about 1 liter/cow/day, with 2-3 times more from Sahiwal (Ibrahim *et al.*, 1999).

Dairy Cattle Farming System in Sri Lanka

Agriculture can be simply defined as cultivation of crops and rearing of animals. Despite the fact that crop cultivation is dominant in Sri Lanka's agriculture system a large number of livestock production systems could be seen within the country. Most production systems are crop based farming systems and livestock based farming system. These production systems are mainly depend on the agro-ecological and socio-economic conditions. Cattle production systems can be categorized into several subsystems on the basis of the climatic factors and resource distributions (Ibrahim *et al*, 1999).

Plantation Crop Based Cattle Farming System

This system could be seen in the Hill and Mid country of the wet Zone and humid part of the Intermediate Zone. Main cattle breeds such as Ayrshire, Friesian and Jersey and their crossbreds are reared in this system. Stall feeding is very common under this system. Fodder from roadsides and farm boundaries are used for feeding under this system. Cost of production is high and annual milk yield vary within between 800-1200 litters/cow/lactation. There is extensive use of AI in the area. Sometimes there is pasture cultivation. Hence grazing is very limited. Animal loan system is not common and extension services are at very poor level (Chandrasiri, 2002).

Kandyan Home Garden System in the Mid Country

This system is very common in the wet and intermediate zones of the hill and Mid-country. Especially to rear temperate crossbreds such as Jersey, Ayrshire and Friesian and their crosses. Annual milk yield between 900 - 1200 litters/cow. Although the system is very complicated and cost of production is high, this is a very sustainable system. Other than the animal component, tall forest trees, plantation crops, fruit crops, spices and various flower plants are included in the integrated system. Manure is mainly used for paddy cultivation and other crops or sometimes manure is sold (Ibrahim *et al.*, 1999).

Coconut Based Cattle Farming System

Kurunagala and Puttalam districts are mainly included in this farming system. Animals are allowed to graze natural pastures in the coconut lands, fallow paddy fields and non-cultivated areas. Mainly local crosses with improved breeds such as Jersey, Sahiwal and Sindi are reared under this system. Their milk yield is around 300-400 litters/annually. Animals are allowed to graze in natural pastures in the coconut lands, fallow paddy fields and non-cultivated areas. Cut grasses like *Bracharia Spp.* are often fed with locally available coconut Ponca or rice bran. Thus, cost of production is generally low (Chandrasiri, 2002).

Dry Zone Extensive System

Indigenous and Indian crossbreds of cattle form an important source of income for farmers at these zones. There is no use of concentrates at all. When villus are not available for grazing during rainy season due to flood condition, animals are moved to high lands and grazed on "Savana". They graze on large irrigated paddy lands, bunds, scrub jungles, tank beds and villus. Hence cost of production is very low. Although the land size is large their annual milk yield is about 200-400 litters/cow, which is very low. Although many herds in the area are managed extensively; semi intensively and intensively managed herds could be seen (Chandrasiri, 2002).

Off-farm Income Based Peri-Urban Dairy Farming System

High producing purebred temperate breeds and temperate crossbred dairy cattle are kept indoor and fed with purchased forages and 4-5 Kg of concentrates daily. This system could be seen in and around the major cities such as Colombo and Homagama. Although the cost of production is very high due to animal feed, labor, housing etc. These animals are high producers. Their annual milk yield is around 1500 -2000 litters/ cow (Chandrasiry, 2002).

Dairy Cattle Breeds in Sri Lanka

Indian and European are two types of major dairy breeds in Sri Lanka. They are adapted to different climatic zones. Milk production of different cattle breeds are given in Table 4.2.

Characteristics of European Dairy Breeds

Bos Taurus (Friesian, Jersey and Ayrshire) are main European cattle breeds in Sri Lanka. Pure and crossbred animals of mentioned breeds are raised mainly in up country farms. They lack the prominent hump (Ibrahim, 2000) and the dewlap in contrast to Indian breeds and their level of production is significantly greater than that of Indian breeds. In addition to that their body size is relatively larger than Indian breeds.

Friesian Breed

The origin of the breed is Netherlands. They possess a black and white coloured coat with sharp margins in between. They have relatively larger body size where a male and a female animal weighs about 1000kg and 675kg respectively. A healthy calf weighs 40 to 45 kg or more at birth and mature cow typically stands 147 cm tall at the shoulder. Heifer should be bred by 13 to 15 months of age, when they weigh over 360 kg. Head is long with flat forehead with narrow and slightly rounding withers. They have a well formed capacious udder producing up to 6150 liters of milk with 3.7% fat content in 305 day lactation (Briggs, 1969; Bogart 1977; Ibrahim, 2000).

Jerseybreed

The breed is originated in the island of Jersey in England. They have comparatively smaller body size weighing males and females, 675 kg and 450 kg respectively. Their body is brown in colour with or without white patches. The specific characteristics of their body includes marble eyes, double dish head, straight top lines, and level rumps, sharp withers. The udder is small but strong and produces up to 4000 liter of milk per lactation (Briggs, 1969; Bogart 1977; Ibrahim, 2000). Jersey cattle are mainly found in the Hill and Mid Country. Considerable numbers of Jersey cattle could be seen in coconut plantations and the Wet Zone (Ibrahim *et al.*, 1999).

Table 4.3: Average milk production of different cattle breeds

Type of Cattle	Breed of Cattle	Milk Production (1/305 days)
Bos indicus	Sahiwal Red Sindhi Indigenous	2000-2500 1500-2000 500-600
Bos Taurus	Friesian Jersey Ayrshire	3000-3500 2500-2800 2500-2800
Crosses	Friesian× Indigenous Jersey × Indigenous	1200-1500 1060-1250

Source: Silva, 1996

Ayrshirebreed

Scotland is the land of origin of this breed. Ayrshires are red and white, and purebred Ayrshires only produce red and white offspring. There are multifocal white colour patches in the mahogany colour coat giving a characteristic picture. Straight rumps, long horns that are turned upwards are considered as some of the significant features of this breed. Ayrshires are medium-sized cattle, male up to 850 kg and a female animal up to 550 kg at maturity. The udder is large and strong producing 4840 liters of milk per lactation with 4.2 percentage of fat (Briggs, 1969; Bogart 1977; Ibrahim, 2000). Ayrshire is found in Hill and Mid Country but not as purebreds.

Characteristics of Indian Dairy Breeds

Bos indicus (Sahiwal, Red sindhi, Indigenous) are main Indian cattle reeds in Sri Lanka. Typically Indian breeds are low productive, draft animals. They are adapted to heat stress, and have a high amount of milk fat.

Indigenous Cattle

At present, the native cattle in Sri Lanka *(Bos indicus varceylonicus)* called "Lankan Cattle"or "Batu Haraka" are the locally-adapted cattlein the country, descending from the ancient cattle introductions (Silva *et al.*, 2008). They are the locally adapted cattle in the country that are being used for milk and meat production and for draught purposes as well. These animals are small in body size. Although they are poor producers, they are highly adapted to the local harsh environment. The coat color of local cattle may be black or tan with white spots and barrel shape body. Thus, they appear to be a meat type. The body measurements of local cattle are as follows. The indigenous Cattle are mainly found in Dry Zone of the country and island wide distribution could be seen.

Sahiwal Breed

Their colour can range from reddish brown through to the more predominant red, with white on the neck, and the underline. In males the colour darkens towards the extremities, their head, legs and tail area. The males have big humps. Their height at withers are 136 and 120 cm for males and females, respectively. Cows average a 2270 kg of milk during a lactation while suckling a calf and much higher milk yields have been recorded too. Other characteristics are high milk yields, ease of calving, drought resistant, bloat tolerant, good temperament, lean meat with even fat cover and heat tolerance (Upazila *et al.*, 2016).

Red Sindhi Breed

The Red Sindhis are originated in Pakistan. They are normally a deep, rich red color, but this can vary from a yellowish brown to dark brown and characteristics are hardiness, heat resistance and high milk yields. The average over 1700 kg of milk is possible after suckling their calves, but under optimum conditions there have been milk yields of over 3400 kg per lactation.The average height of a Red Sindhi cow is 116 cm with a body weight of 340 kg. Bulls average a height of 134 cm and average a body weight of 420 kg (Dowell, 2016).

Production Parameters of Dairy Cattle

Milk composition is economically important to milk producers and processors, and nutritionally important to consumers. There are factors which affect milk composition and production performance. Such as breed, genetic variation within breed, health, environment, management practices, and diet. The production parameters are total milk yield, milk fat, milk protein, carbohydrates and minerals.

Milkyield

Milk yield is the basic economic advantage of dairy cattle. Major factors which determine milk yield are breed characters and the environment. Milk yield has a correlation with genotype, and environment, and their (G × E). Climatic factors such as temperature, humidity, atmospheric pressure, light and rainfall significantly affect the lactating cow. Dairy cattle in many subtropical, tropical and semi-arid regions are highly impacted by the above climatic factors.

Milk Fat

Milk fat in the mammary gland is synthesized via the malonyl coenzyme A pathway. Milk fat content varies in different breeds. (Woodford *et al.*, 1986). For example, milk fat in indigenous dairy cattle are less than the European Dairy cattle breeds. The milk fat varies during the stages of lactation. In addition, the environment highly affects on the milk fat composition. (Milam *et al.*, 1986). Milking process also directly affected by the milk fat percentage. Incomplete milking leads to decrease of milk fat percentage. Mastitis is a main cause of decline in milk fat and milk composition (Kitchen., 1981). The diets that increase propionate production have the greatest effect on milk fat percentage.

Protein in Milk

Non Protein Nitrogen (NPN) and true proteins are two types of total protein (crude protein) which are found in milk. The total protein percentage of milk is generally considered to be about 3.5, of which 94 to 95% is in the form of true protein. Casein and Whey are the two types of true proteins found in milk of which casein represent 80% and whey represent 20%. (Davies *et al.*, 1983; Jenness, 1985). The protein contain varies with the cattle breeds. The highest amount of casein is present in Jersey breed and low amount of casein is present in Frisian breed (Gaunt, 1980). The age significantly influenceson the protein percentage and composition in milk (Jenness, 1985). Milk protein percentage decreases in cows older than 3 years, with a 0.4% unit drop being reported over five lactations. The stage of lactation is influenced by the milk protein content. During early lactation stage the highest amount of milk protein is present and decreases during the later lactation stages (Kroeker *et al.*, 1985). Mastitis and udder inflammation causes the increase in protein content.

Carbohydrate in Milk

Lactose is a predominant carbohydrate in milk. Other carbohydrates found in milk are monosaccharaides, sugar phosphates, nucleotide sugars, free neutral and acid oligosaccharides, and glycosyl groups of peptides and proteins (Jenness, 1985). The principal biological function of lactose is to regulate water and osmatic levels in milk. In generated, there is an average of 4.6 percentage lactose content in milk.

Minerals in Milk

The mineral content of milk is derived from minerals found in circulating body fluids. The major minerals found in milk are ash, calcium, phosphorus, and magnesium and their percentage differs according to the breeds. The average ash content varied from 0.74% for Frisian to 0.83% for Jerseys. The highest amount of calcium and phosphorus are present in milk from Jerseys (Cerbulis and Farrel, 1976). Due to the presence of colostrum, the highest amount of mineral are found in early lactation stage. Due to udder inflammation and mastitis, sodium and chloride percentage increases whereas potassium, calcium and phosphorus percentages decrease (Kitchen, 1981).

Different Reproduction Parameters of Cattle

Reproduction is an important consideration in the economics of cattle production. Nevertheless, economics of cattle production depends largely on the feeding and management of cattle. In order to obtain the maximum milk production from cow, maximum numbers of lactations have to be obtained with her economic life (Kollalpitiya *et al.*, 2012).To improve the reproductive performance of herds, dairy producers must understand the complex interactions of milk production, reproduction, nutrition, genetics, and management. Recommended improvements in management, such as detection of oestrus, insemination technique, herd health programs, and nutrition, are key factors to improve reproductive performance to ensure high production (Foster *et al.*, 1988).

Birth Weight

Birth weight depends on the breed, dam and sire body weight, and varies other factors such as herd-year-season of birth, sex of the calf and parity number of the dam. Reduction of the birth weight means low weaning weight. It effects the reduction of income. Hence, delayed puberty, takes the time for calving etc. Since breeding animal selection is very important, effective to consider appropriate selection index. Birth weight and many other productive traits are directly correlated. The birth weight directly affects maternal weight (Guti, *et al.*, 2007).

Conception Availability and Conception Rate

Conception availability study is economically important. It causes the increase of progeny to farmer. Factors affecting conception availability can be classified, as bull, AI, cow, environment factors, health, Body Condition Score and Negative Energy Balance. Conception availability depends on the stud bull. Stud bull activity and performance is very important to the holding conception rate. Bull performance are semen quality, semen concentration, fertility availability, age of the bull, healthy of the bull. Fertile bull selection is very important in natural breeding centers. Conception availability depends on the cow too. Some factors depend only on the cow, such as estrus cycle, accept the semen, quality oocyte, activity of the ovary, accept the embryo in uterine, delayed ovulation, abnormal uterine environment, age of the heifer and heifer performance (Dhaliwal *et al.*, 1996).

Uniform production can be obtained using the Artificial Insemination. Conception availability depends on the AI. Successful AI depends on performance and skills of the AI technician, detection the heat time, time of the AI, storage of the semen, time of the ovulation, site of insemination, concentration of the semen, quality of the semen etc. Low conception rate could be observed due to decrease of Body Condition Score (Roche *et al.*, 2007). Negative Energy Balance affects to the conception rate. Negative energy balance is common for high producing cows in early lactation and their mobilized body fat is used to produce milk (Inchaisri *et al.*, 2010). Conception rate depends on the environmental factors. Heat stress is the main environment factors that affect conception rate and signified by increasing the body temperature by two degrees for 48 straight hours. Consumption of alkaloids from fungus redirects the ability of an animal dissipate heat. Animals in confused condition and sound stress are also affecting the conception rate (Raheja *et al.*, 1989). Heavy metals and some minerals cause the conception. Heavy metals such as Hg, Cd, and high level of S, Fe, Mo, and low level of Cu, Se, Mn, Zn, P, are containing in the feed. Like that protein level affects the conception rate. High legume in pasture that increases the CP more than 22-23% reduces the conception rate and some hormones affect the conception during the stress conditions (Gates, 2013).

Successfulness of AI

Successfulness of Artificial Insemination (AI) depends on difference factors, such as semen collection, semen storage, heat detection, site of the AI, time of the AI, performance of the insminer. It has many advantages such as reduction of the cost of bull, prevent inbreeding, prevent disease spread, prevent damage to the cow, uniformity in production, easy to control and handling. AI started for dairy cows many years ago. Efficiency of AI has not been fully understood. Some factors are needed to assess the present situation of AI and to find out the factors affecting it. Estimated factors are 80% of environmental, 50% of that is explained by nutrition variances (Inchaisri *et al.*, 2010).

Calving Interval

Heifers come to puberty at 18months of age. Animals at this stage are suitable for servicing. Carving interval depends on the different factors such as affect to fitness trait, fertility, longevity and heat stress. Calving interval is the most important parameters in dairy farm. Calving interval should be hold for 365 day. It can be held by manipulation technique and management techniques. At present success of fertility in the dairy cow decreases, with long calving interval from 13.6-16.5 months (Evans *et al.*, 2006). Heifers or cows with lower weight also affect because they are less likely to be pregnant. First calving at older age affect increasing of culling. Heifer's body weight directly affect puberty, but not by her age. Body weight can be increased by proper feeding and growth management. Breeding heifers should be 2/3 of their matured body weight. Calving and maturity depend on significant genotype by environment interaction (Penasa *et al.*, 2010).

Heat stress is more interacting with fertility, lactation peak, oestrus cycle, pregnancy wastage on the lactation dairy cow. Pregnancy availability, conception availability decrease with heat stress. Ovarian cyst is more affected during the warm period and during the cold period. Pregnancy rate is decreasing up to 6% and inactive ovaries percentage increase up to 8% in the warm period and increases the milk yield about per 1000kg. But some dairy breeds are resistant to the heat, such as Brown Swiss. They are heat resistant to the production and reproduction performance compared to Holsteins cattle breed. Dam milk production is very important to increase the calf performance. Calving interval is the time between one calving to another calving. Calving interval of a good cow is around 12 months. It is

Causley maximizing the production. Some challenges affect the calving interval, such as insemination taking place and risk of fertility. Some problem in fertility, such as silent heat, ovarian cyst, increase with milk production, early conception and some environmental factors also affect it (Evans *et al.*, 2006).

Dairy Developmentprogram in Sri Lanka

The following programs have been developed for implementation in the dairy sector during the period of 2010 to 2015. NLDB was the most recent program implementation agency identified in "Mahinda Chinthana".

Large Scale Dairy Development Program

Under the major Dairy Development Project Phase I in 2012/2013, 2,000 European type high yielding cattle were imported to Sri Lanka, and accommodated in the three upcountry farms namely Bopaththalawa, Dayagama and Manikpalama. Later, with the agreement between NLDB and Wellard Company, Australia another consignment of 2,500 herds of European crossbred type cattle were imported and housed hold in Ridiyagama farm at Ambalanthota in March/April 2015. Parallel to the above importation the NLDB has decided to develop all infrastructure facilities at Ridiyagama farm such as pasture/fodder developments, construction of cattle sheds, storage facilities, introduction of modern machinery and Equipment etc (Anuranga, 2014).

Target Milk Production of Large Scale Dairy Development Program

After importation of 2,500 cattle, Ridiyagama farm has become the largest dairy farm in Sri Lanka which could produce approximately 15 million L of milk annually from the year 2016. In addition, around 600-700 heifer calves could be issued to the public annually by this project. After completion of the Sri Lanka Dairy Development Project, it predicted that the total annual milk production of NLDB would be 33 million L by end of year 2017. Then the total contribution of NLDB to the National Milk Grid would be 51 million L of milk with inclusion of milk produced by the follower stocks issued to the public. The overall percentage of contribution of NLDB would increase up to 7-10% against the self-sufficient requirement of the country (Anuranga., 2014).

Medium Scale Dairy Development Program

Absence of reasonable number of medium scale investors is an inherent weaknesses of the dairy industry in this country. Medium scale dairy development program is introduced to construct the correct structure for the dairy industry. It has been suggested to provide assistance to 1000 investors to establish vertically integrated partially mechanized medium-scale dairy farms having a minimum initial stock of twenty upgraded breeding animals in WZ, and elite native breeding animals or upgraded animals in DZ and IMZ. They are strongly encouraged to go for processing activities and find their own market for direct sales of their branded farm products at urban, peri-urban and rural markets. These farms will also be developed as private cattle breeder farms (Anuranga, 2014).

Target Milk Production of Medium Scale Dairy Development Program

According to the targets of the project there will be thirty thousand initial stock in these farms to contribute twenty five and half million liters of milk annually to national grid. At the end of the year 2015 onward it was expected to have 265,000 upgraded heifers, and 200,000 replacement stock contributing to the national herd keeping the total herd a constant. The replacement stock will give additional one liter of milk than their mothers. Therefore, finally 166.9 Millionliters of milk will be added to national grid. There will be 15000 out grower farmers as beginners keeping two native cows giving at least 2 liters of milk contributing 10.95 million liters of milk annually to the national grid (Anuranga, 2014).

Smallholder Dairy Farms Development Program

Smallholder dairy farmers are the only group of people who have safeguard the domestic dairy industry under enormous amount of hardships and difficulties in the past. However, they have to be adequately rewarded financially, socially or by any other meaningful way. Ensuring of a minimum amount of daily income enough to cover monthly family expenses is one way of satisfying these farmers and is the best way of producing milk for the country. Hence the Sri Lanka Dairy Development Project targeted to work with 120, 000 farmers having 690,000 breedable cows to produce 530 million liters of milk annually (Anuranga, 2014).

MATERIALS AND METHODS

Data collection from Bopaththalawa, Dayagama and Manikpalama belong to the NLDB, located in Nuwara Eliya district of central province of Sri Lanka. These farms belong to agro-ecological zone of up country wet zone. Since 2013 these farms keep different cattle genotypes imported from Australia.This farm is located 1676m above sea level. In this area South Western monsoon is the main rainfall which occurs during May to September. The average rainfall varies from 2500mm and 3800mm annually and over 200 to 250 average rainy days. The monthly average temperature varies from 18°C to 28°C, and minimum temperature has been recorded between 8°C to 15°C. Humidity is around 75% to 85%. The main cattle type of Bopaththalawa farm is 50% cross bred from Holstein Frisian and jersey breeds. The Dayagama and Manikpalama farms rear pure Holstein Frisian, pure Jersey and their cross breeds. Dayagama farm has more Jersey cattle where as Manikpalama farm has more Holstein Friesian cattle.

The data need in the study covered period from 2013 January to 2016 September byeach farm. The book of records and Alpro Windows system maintained at each farm were need to extract data. Data included farm type, cow ID, genotype, cow birth day (birth year, birth month, birth date), sire ID, sire genotype, dame ID, dame genotype and number of lactation. In addition, details such as bull breed, bull ID, no of services, calf sex, calf ID, calf birth weight, lactation length, 305day projection yield, mature equivalent, total milk yield, days to peak, peak yield and calving date (calving year, calving month, calving date) have been recorded.

Cattle genotypes were identified and coded as follows; Pure Frisian (F),Pure jersey (J), 75% Frisian 25% Jersey (75%F X 25%), 50% Frisian 50% Jersey (50%F X 50%J), and 25% Frisian 75% Jersey (25%F X 75%J). Bull genotypes recorded were pure Frisian(1), pure Jersey (2) and 25% Frisian 75% Jersey (5) and the dame genotypes found were pure Frisian (1), pure Jersey (2) and their crosses.

The statistical analysis were consider out using Analysis of Variance and Chi Squire method. Mean comparisons were done by method was Duncan's multiple range test. The data analysis by SAS computer package (Version University edition 21016). The model made for the analysis of each farm is model 1.

Model 1:

$Y_{ijkl} = \mu + Breed_i + Parity_j + CM_k + error_{ijkl}$

Where,

Y_{ijkl} = traits of the lth cow i th cow breed in j^{th} parity of kth calving month (traits= calf birth weight, lactation length, total milk yield, mature equivalent,

days to peak, peak milk yield,305 day projected yield)

μ = Grand mean

$Breed_i$ =effect of ith breed (1,2,3,4,5)

$Parity_j$= effect of jth parity (1,2,3,4)

CM_k= effect of kth calving month (1, 2, 3, 4....12)

$error_{ijkl}$= residual effect

The individual performance was analyzed with the model 2

Model 2

$Y_{ijkl} = \mu + Breed_i + Parity_j + BB_k + error_{ijkl}$

Where,

μ = Grand mean

Y_{ijkl}= no of services of the lth cow i^{th}bull breedin j^{th}parity of kth bullbreed

$Breed_i$=effect of ith breed (1,2,3,4,5)

$Parity_j$ = effect of jth parity (1,2,3,4)

BB_k = effect of kth (1,2,5)

$error_{ijkl}$ = residual effect

RESULTS AND DISCUSSION

Bopaththalawa, Manikpalama and Dayagama farms have the animal management practices under semi-intensive system. Veterinary care practices, feeding management and the farm environment were animals in all three farms. Table 4.4 show the overall assessment of parameters measured in all farms.

Table 4.4: Description on the variables measured in all farms

Variable	Total Number	Mean	Std Dev.	Minimum	Maximum
Calf birth weight (Kg)	2634	25.53	4.43	12.00	45.00
305day projected yield (L)	2936	4638.63	1233.10	956.00	8877.00
Total milk yield (L)	2937	5299.17	1844.18	1024.40	15075.40
Days to peak (Day)	2937	73.52	37.99	30.00	199.00
Peak milk yield (L)	2937	24.65	5.69	6.33	58.99
Age (Day)	2937	1159.48	355.36	570.00	2090.00
Mature equivalent factor	2936	0.93	0.04	0.74	0.99
Lactation length (Day)	2937	386.74	131.92	251.00	1497.00
Mature equivalent (L)	2937	4958.07	1303.90	972.00	9191.00

Since Bopaththalawa farm had 50%F X 50%Jcattle, the performance of different cattle genotypes were compared between Manikpalama and Dayagama farms where F, J, 75%F X 25%J, 50% FX 50%J and 25%F X 75%J genotypes were present.

Calf Birth Weight

Calf birth weight (CBW) was significantly different among genotypes ($P<0.05$) in Manikpalama farm. The mean CWT was highest in pure Friesian and the lowest in pure Jerseyin Manikpalama farm. Dayagama farm showed no significant difference ($P>0.05$) in CBW among genotypes ($P>0.05$). (Table 4.5). The CWT significantly differed ($P<0.05$) according to the parity (Table 4.6). Parity four recorded the highest mean CBW in both Manikpalama and Dayagama farms. However, Bopaththalawa farm recorded the highest mean CBW in parity one (Table 4.6). CBW significantly varied according to calving months ($P<0.05$). The highest mean CBW was recorded in November and the lowest mean CBW was recorded in July. (Table 4.7)

Lactation Length

Lactation length (LL) did not significantly ($P>0.05$) differ according to the genotypes and the parity. The highest mean LL was recorded in pure Friesian and the lowest was 25%F X 75%J in Manikpalama farm. However in Dayagama farm the highest LL was recordedin 25%F X 75%J and the lowest in 50%F X 50%J (Table 4.5). LL significantly differ according to calving month ($P<0.05$). The highest mean LL was recorded in February and the lowest was recorded in November in all the farms. But, Dayagama farm did not show a significant difference between calving month and LL (Table 4.7).

Table 4.5: Comparison of Calf birth weight, Total milk yield, Lactation length and Days to peak in different genotypes between Dayagama and Manikpalama farms

Trait	Genotypes	Manikpalama	Dayagama	Overall Farm
Calf birth weight (Kg)	Pure Friesian	29.6^{a}	-	29.6^{a}
	Pure Jersey	25.0^{c}	23.2^{a}	23.8^{c}
	75%F X 25%J	26.3^{c}	23.8^{a}	25.6^{b}
	50%F X 50%J	25.6^{bc}	24.1^{a}	25.4^{b}
	25%F X 75%J	26.2^{b}	23.3^{a}	26.0^{b}
Lactation length (Day)	Pure Friesian	408^{a}	-	408^{a}
	Pure Jersey	367^{b}	391^{a}	394^{ab}
	75%F X 25%J	371^{b}	392^{a}	379^{b}
	50%F X 50%J	371^{b}	386^{a}	397^{ab}
	25%F X 75%J	350^{b}	426^{a}	356^{c}
Total yield (L)	Pure Friesian	5778^{a}	-	5778^{a}
	Pure Jersey	4405^{c}	5243^{b}	4941^{c}
	75%F X 25%J	4957^{b}	6557^{a}	5402^{c}
	50%F X 50%	5000^{b}	6580^{a}	5438^{b}
	25%F X 75%J	4656^{c}	5629^{b}	4729^{b}
Days to peak (Day)	Pure Friesian	75.6^{a}	-	75^{ab}
	Pure Jersey	74.5^{a}	69.7^{a}	71^{b}
	75%F X 25%J	79.7^{a}	72.3^{a}	77^{a}
	50%F X 50%J	80.7^{a}	68.5^{a}	71^{b}
	25%F X 75%J	79.0^{a}	70.2^{a}	78^{a}

Means not followed by the same superscript in a column within trait are significantly different ($P<0.05$).

Table 4.6: Comparison of Calf birth weight, Lactation length, Total milk yield, Days to peak, peak milk yield in different parity among three farms

Traits	Parity	Bopaththalawa	Manicpalama	Dayagama	Overall Farm
(1)	(2)	(3)	(4)	(5)	(6)
Calf birth weight (Kg)	1	26.3^{a}	24^{d}	22.4^{a}	23.9^{a}
	2	24.9^{ab}	25.6^{c}	24.0^{b}	25.0^{c}
	3	25.0^{ab}	30.2^{b}	25.3^{b}	28.2^{d}
	4	22.0^{b}	31.9^{a}	28.0^{a}	31.7^{a}
Lactation length (Day)	1	417^{a}	404^{a}	406^{a}	414^{a}
	2	414^{a}	373^{b}	399a	396^{a}
	3	369^{a}	348^{bc}	325^{a}	350^{b}
	4	266^{a}	328^{c}	365^{a}	328^{b}
Total milk yield (L)	1	4695^{a}	5366^{a}	5722^{a}	5319^{b}
	2	6467^{a}	4986^{b}	5784^{a}	5546^{a}
	3	5748^{a}	4334^{b}	5271^{a}	5061^{b}
	4	5259^{a}	3701^{c}	7056^{a}	3763^{c}

(Table Contd...)

(1)	(2)	(3)	(4)	(5)	(6)
Days to peak (Day)	1	75.6^{a}	89.2^{a}	80.4^{a}	83^{a}
	2	58.3^{a}	72.1^{b}	59.4^{a}	65^{b}
	3	62.7^{a}	69.6^{b}	62.4^{a}	66^{b}
	4	92.0^{a}	81.7^{a}	31.0^{a}	81^{a}
Peak milk yield (L)	1	22.8^{a}	22.9^{c}	20.9^{b}	22^{d}
	2	25.6^{a}	25.5^{b}	23.3^{b}	25^{c}
	3	26.5^{a}	29.6^{a}	25.5^{b}	28^{b}
	4	25.5^{a}	29.3^{a}	35.5^{a}	29^{a}

Means not followed by the same superscript in a column within trait are significantly different (P<0.05).

Total Milk yield

Total milk yield (TMY) significantly differs according to the genotype (P<0.05). The highest mean TMY was recorded in pure Friesian and pure Jersey in Manikpalama farm. The highest mean TMY was reported from 50%F X 50%J crosses and the lowest was recorded from pure Jersey in Dayagama farm (Table 4.5). TMY significantly differ according to the parity (P<0.05) Table (4.6). Bopaththalawa and Dayagama farms did not show a significant difference in TMY according to parity (P>0.05). But, Manikpalam farm showed a significant difference in TMY according to parity (P<0.05). The highest mean TMY in Manikpalama farm was reported in parity one and the lowest in parity four (Table 4.6). TMY significantly differs according to the calving month (P0<05). The maximum mean TMY was reported from September to February (Table 4.8) in the all the farms. This period provided the optimum climatic condition for European cattle; hence animal are in the most comfortable environment study those period.

Table 4.7: Comparison of Calf birth weight and Lactation length in different Calving months among three farms

Traits	Calving month	Bopaththalawa	Manicpalama	Dayagama	Overall Farm
(1)	(2)	(3)	(4)	(5)	(6)
Calf birth weight (kg)	January	23.7^{cd}	25.9^{defg}	24.5^{abc}	24.9^{e}
	February	23.1^{d}	26.0^{defg}	24.5^{abc}	24.8^{ef}
	March	25.2^{ab}	27.4^{bcdef}	24.7^{ab}	26.5^{bc}
	April	26.2^{a}	28.1^{abc}	25.5^{a}	26.9^{bc}
	May	25.9^{ab}	26.5^{cdef}	23.4^{cd}	25.5^{de}
	June	25.5^{ab}	25.5^{fg}	23.4^{d}	24.8^{ef}
	July	26.1^{a}	24.4^{g}	22.0^{e}	23.9^{f}
	August	25.1^{ab}	25.7^{efg}	23.0^{d}	25.0^{de}
	September	25.3^{ab}	27.5^{bcd}	24.1^{ab}	26.8^{bc}
	October	24.6^{bc}	29.3^{a}	25.2^{a}	27.3^{ab}
	November	25.5^{ab}	29.7^{a}	24.0^{bcd}	28.0^{a}
	December	24.6^{bc}	28.5^{ab}	24.0^{bcd}	26.0^{cd}

(Table Contd...)

(1)	(2)	(3)	(4)	(5)	(6)
Lactation length (Day)	January	361^{c}	381^{ab}	411^{a}	390^{abc}
	February	466^{a}	356^{abc}	430^{a}	412^{a}
	March	421^{abc}	387^{ab}	374^{a}	399^{ab}
	April	435^{ab}	383^{ab}	407^{a}	411^{a}
	May	399^{bc}	373^{ab}	379^{a}	387^{abc}
	June	403^{bc}	368^{abc}	399^{a}	389^{abc}
	July	411^{abc}	388^{ab}	398^{a}	402^{a}
	August	413^{abc}	389^{ab}	392^{a}	402^{a}
	September	389^{bc}	392^{a}	349^{a}	387^{abc}
	October	384^{bc}	338^{bc}	371^{a}	360^{cd}
	November	365^{c}	341^{bc}	367^{a}	352^{d}
	December	367^{c}	320^{c}	423a	365^{bcd}

Means not followed by the same superscript in a column within trait are significantly different (P<0.05).

Days to Peak Milk yield

Days to peak milk yield (DPMY) significantly differ according to the genotypein overall comparison (P<0.05). But, Manikpalama and Dayagama farms did not show a significant difference in according to the DPMY according to genotypes (P>0.05). The highest mean DPMY was reread in recorded in 50%F X 50%J performed from 50%Friesian 50%Jersey crosses in Manikpalama and 75%F X 25% J crosses in Dayagama farms (Table 4.5). The DPMY significant differs according to the parity (P<0.05). But, Bopaththalawa is do not show a significant difference according to DPMY and parity (P>0.05) (Table 4.6).The highest mean DPMY was shown in parity four in Bopaththalawa farm and the lowest DPMY was reported in parity four in Dayagama farm (Table 4.6). DPMY significantly differs according to the Calving month (P<0.05). The highest mean DPMY was recorded from Manikpalama in June and the lowest milk yield was recorded from Manikpalam farm in April (Table 4.8).

Table 4.8: Comparison of Total milk yield and Days to peak in different calving months among three farms

Traits	Calving month	Bopaththalawa	Manikpalama	Dayagama	Overall Farm
(1)	(2)	(3)	(4)	(5)	(6)
Total milk yield (L)	January	5213^{de}	5310^{abcd}	5930^{ab}	5446^{ab}
	February	6702^{a}	5587	5196^{b}	5877^{a}
	March	5171^{e}	5491^{ab}	5602^{ab}	5885^{cb}
	April	5575^{bcde}	5013^{abcde}	5625^{ab}	5330^{cb}
	May	4964^{e}	4732^{de}	5358^{b}	4960^{c}
	June	5226^{de}	4601^{e}	5763^{ab}	5146^{bc}
	July	5502^{cde}	4996^{bcde}	5711^{ab}	5339^{bc}
	August	6184^{abcd}	5117^{bcde}	5708ab	5386^{bc}
	September	6224^{abc}	5406^{abc}	5513^{ab}	5546^{ab}

(Table Contd...)

(1)	(2)	(3)	(4)	(5)	(6)
	October	5701bcde	4796de	5982ab	5276bc
	November	6501ab	4825de	5479ab	5295bc
	December	6184abcd	4872cde	6519a	5620ab
Days to peak (Day)	January	77.3abc	68.5efd	60.0a	68cde
	February	78.9ab	68.9efd	77.6a	72bcd
	March	82.7a	58.5ef	64.5ab	68cde
	April	68.3bcd	54.9f	67.8ab	61e
	May	59.2de	64.4efd	59.9ab	62e
	June	63.3cde	101a	80.3a	84a
	July	65.8bcde	86.4b	75.3ab	78ab
	August	66.3bcde	83.1bc	65.8ab	78abc
	September	52.6e	70.3cde	55.0b	65de
	October	56.7de	88.3b	68.7ab	76abc
	November	75.4abc	83.4bc	66.7ab	79ab
	December	78.4ab	74.1bcd	80.3a	76abc

Means not followed by the same superscript in a column within trait are significantly different (P<0.05).

Peak Milk yield

Peak milk yield (PMY) significantly differs genotypes (P<0.05) according to the (Table 4.10) The highest PMY was reported in pure Friesian and the lowest by 25%F X 25%J crossbred in Manikpalama farm. The highest mean PMY was reported by 50%F X 50%J and the lowest reported by pure Jersey in Dayagama farm (Table 4.6). PMY significantly differs according to the parity (P<0.05). But, Bopaththalawa did not show a significant difference in PMY as the parity change.

Table 4.9: Comparison of Peak yield and mature equivalent in different Calving months among three farms

Traits	Calving month	Bopaththalawa	Manicpalama	Dayagama	Overall Farm
(1)	(2)	(3)	(4)	(5)	(6)
Peak yield (L)	January	25.7abc	27.5c	22.6bc	25d
	February	26.8a	30.5a	22.6bc	27ab
	March	24abcd	29.5ab	22.4bc	26abc
	April	26.3ab	27.5c	22.5bc	26cd
	May	24.0cd	25.1d	21.5bc	23e
	June	238cd	22.1e	21.5c	22f
	July	23.3d	23.0e	21.9bc	22f
	August	24.3bcd	25.2d	22.2bc	24e
	September	26.7a	27.5c	25.4a	27abc
	October	24.1cd	28.7abc	25.3a	26abcd
	November	25.7abc	29.7ab	24.1ab	28a
	December	25.2abcd	28.1bc	25.3a	26bcd

(Table Contd...)

(1)	(2)	(3)	(4)	(5)	(6)
Mature equivalent (L)	January	5149^{bcd}	4957^{abc}	5053^{bc}	5127^{bcd}
	February	5565^{ab}	5254^{a}	4788^{c}	5316^{ab}
	March	4185^{f}	5078^{ab}	5108^{abc}	4759^{ef}
	April	4490^{ef}	4886^{abc}	5164^{abc}	4864^{def}
	May	4303^{ef}	4581^{cd}	5139^{abc}	4687^{f}
	June	4654^{def}	4485^{d}	5314^{abc}	4811^{def}
	July	4866^{cde}	4745^{bcd}	5365^{abc}	4979^{cdef}
	August	5223^{abc}	4949^{abc}	5230^{abc}	5081^{bcde}
	September	5467^{ab}	5247^{a}	5351^{abc}	5307^{ab}
	October	5721^{ab}	4689^{bcd}	5823^{a}	5204^{abc}
	November	5720^{ab}	4738^{bcd}	5133^{abc}	5025^{bcde}
	December	5830^{a}	5009^{ab}	5753^{ab}	5477^{a}

Means not followed by the same superscript in a column within trait are significantly different ($P<0.05$).

The highest mean PMY was reported in parity four in Manikpalama farm and the lowest in parity one in Dayagama farm. (Table 4.6). PMY significantly differs according to the calving month ($P<0.05$) (Table 4.9). All the farms showed a high mean PMY during September to March. The mean PMY was reported highest in March and the lowest in September in Bopaththalawa farm. The PMY was reported the highest in November and the lowest in June in Manikpalma farm. In Dayagama farm PMY was reported in highest in December and the lowest in June (Table 4.9).

Table 4.10: Comparison of Peak yield, Mature equivalent, 305day projected yield and Number of services in different cattle genotypes between Dayagama and Manikpalama farms

Trait	Genotypes	Manicpalama	Dayagama	Overall Farm
Peak yield (L)	Pure Friesian	28.3^{a}	-	28^{a}
	Pure Jersey	23.8^{c}	21.0^{b}	22^{d}
	75%Fries25%Jers	25.7^{b}	25.1^{a}	25^{b}
	50%Fries50%Jers	25.7^{b}	25.9^{a}	25^{b}
	25%Fries75%Jers	24.1^{c}	21.8^{b}	23^{c}
Mature equivalent (L)	Pure Friesian	5418^{a}	-	5418^{a}
	Pure Jersey	4354^{c}	4933^{b}	4764^{b}
	75%Fries25%Jers	4764^{b}	6037^{a}	5128^{b}
	50%Fries50%Jers	4857^{b}	6112^{a}	4965^{b}
	25%Fries75%Jers	4665^{b}	4977^{b}	4689^{c}
305d projected yield (L)	Pure Friesian	5111^{a}	-	5111^{a}
	Pure Jersey	4111^{c}	4568^{a}	4043^{c}
	75%Fries25%Jers	4463^{b}	5584^{a}	4775^{c}
	50%Fries50%Jers	4550^{b}	5689^{a}	4637^{b}
	25%Fries75%Jers	4361^{b}	4511^{b}	4372^{c}
No of services	Pure Friesian	4.7^{a}	-	4.78^{b}
	Pure Jersey	3.6^{a}	7.4^{a}	6.2^{a}
	75%Fries25%Jers	4.7^{a}	7.2^{a}	5.5^{ab}
	50%Fries50%Jers	4.1^{a}	6.0^{a}	5.4^{ab}
	25%Fries75%Jers	4.6^{a}	6.0^{a}	4.6^{b}

Means not followed by the same superscript in a column within trait are significantly different ($P<0.05$).

Mature Equivalent

Mature equivalent (ME) significantly differs according to the genotypes (P<0.05) (Table 4.10). The highest ME was reported by pure Friesian and the lowest by pure Jersey in Manikpalama farm. The ME was 50%F X 50%J and the lowest was reported by the 25%F X 75%J in Dayagama farm (Table 4.6). ME does not show a significant difference as the parity (P<0.05). However, Bopaththalawa farm did not show a significant difference in ME according to the parity (P>0.05). The highest ME reported in parity four in Dayagama farm and lowest reported parity four in Manikpalama farm (Table 4.11). The ME did not show a significant difference (P<0.05) according to the calving month. The highest ME was reported in December and the lowest was reported in March in Bopaththalawa farm. The highest mean ME was reported in September and the lowest was reported in June in Manikpalama farm. The highest mean ME was reported in October and the lowest was reported in February in Dayagama farm. The highest ME was reported from September to February in all the farms (Table 4.11).

Table 4.11: Comparison of Mature equivalent 305d projected yield and Number of services in Parity and among three farms

Traits	Parity	Bopaththalawa	Manicpalama	Dayagama	Overall Farm
Mature equivalent (L)	1	3991[a]	5238[a]	5345[b]	4987[a]
	2	5660[a]	4674[b]	5262[b]	5099[a]
	3	5273[a]	4636[b]	5232[b]	4894[a]
	4	5660[a]	3812[c]	7154[a]	3877[b]
305d Projected yield (L)	1	3534[b]	4660[a]	4740[b]	4421[b]
	2	5422[a]	4484[a]	5044[b]	4853[a]
	3	5186[a]	4561[a]	5232[b]	4805[a]
	4	5514[a]	3780[b]	7015[a]	4843[c]
No of Services	1	3.5[a]	6.8[a]	9.0[a]	6.7[a]
	2	7.7[a]	5.9[a]	7.7[a]	7.3[a]
	3	5.4[a]	4.1[b]	6.5[a]	5.0[b]
	4	3.0[a]	3.5[b]	4.0[a]	3.5[c]

Means not followed by the same superscript in a column within trait are significantly different (P<0.05).

The 305 day Projected yield

The 305 day projected yield significantly according to the genotypes (P<0.05) (Table 4.10). The highest mean 305 day projected yield was reported from pure Friesian and the lowest was reported from pure Jersey in Manikpalama farm. In Dayagama farm it was crosses and the lowest 305 day projected yield significantly differ according to genotypes (P<0.05) (Table 4.8). But Manikpalama farm did not show a significant difference of 305 day projected yield according to parity. The highest mean 305dayprojected yield was reported from parity four and the lowest reported from parity one in Bopaththalawa farm. The highest mean 305 day projected yield was reported from parity four and the lowest reported from parity one in Dayagama farm (Table 4.8).

Table 4.12: Comparison of 305 day projected yield in different Calving months among three farms

Traits	Calving months	Bopaththalawa	Manicpalama	Dayagama	Overall Farm
305 day projected yield (L)	January	4965^{bc}	4837^{ab}	4882^{bc}	4889^{bc}
	February	5245^{ab}	5232^{a}	4592^{c}	5057^{ab}
	March	3834^{e}	4899^{ab}	4837^{c}	4492^{de}
	April	4150^{de}	4617^{bc}	4706^{c}	4491^{de}
	May	3963^{e}	4298^{cd}	4704^{c}	4335^{e}
	June	4327^{de}	4158^{d}	4838^{c}	4427^{e}
	July	4516^{cd}	4362^{cd}	4893^{bc}	4569^{d}
	August	5121^{ab}	4606^{bc}	4893^{bc}	4776^{cd}
	September	5295^{ab}	4875^{ab}	5186^{abc}	4988^{bc}
	October	5494^{ab}	4533^{bc}	5620^{a}	4997^{abc}
	November	5579^{a}	4610^{bc}	4933^{bc}	4875^{bc}
	December	5606^{a}	4899^{ab}	5506^{ab}	5241^{a}

Means not followed by the same superscript in a column within trait are significantly different ($P<0.05$).

The 305 day milk yield has been estimated from individual test day records that are usually taken at monthly intervals. Additionally, genetic evaluation of dairy system including sires and cows are generally based on 305 day lactation yield (Ulutas *et al.*, 2010). 305 day projected yield significantly differs according to the calving months ($P<0.05$). The highest mean 305day projected yield was reported from November to February (Table 4.12) in all the farms.

Number of Services

Manikpalama and Dayagama farms did not show a significant difference number of services (NS) according to genotypes ($P>0.05$) (Table 4.10). Only Manickpalama farm showed a significant difference NS according to the parity ($P<0.05$). The highest mean NS was recorded in parity one and the lowest in parity four (Table 4.11). Dayagama farm did not show a significant difference in NS and according to bull semen ($P>0.05$) But, Manikpalama farm showed a significant difference in NS according to bull semen ($P<0.05$). The highest NS was recorded from Friesian Jersey cross bull semen and the lowest was recorded from pure Friesian bull semen in Manikpalama farm (Table 4.13).

Table 4.13: Comparison of No of services in different bull breeds (semen types) among three farms

Traits	Bull Breed (Semen Type)	Bopaththalawa	Manikpalama	Dayagama	Overall Farm
No of service	Pure Frisian	-	4.2^{b}	7.6^{a}	5.2^{a}
	Pure Jersey	-	4.7^{ab}	6.9^{a}	6.8^{a}
	Frisian Jersey cross	-	6.7^{ab}	-	6.7^{a}

Means not followed by the same superscript in a column within trait are significantly different (P<0.05).

Table 4.14: Comparison of types of calving in different farm by affected genotypes

Farm	Genotypes	Abort	Male	Female	Still birth	Total
Manikplama	Pure Friesian	6	113	148	16	283
	Pure Jersey	2	118	136	23	279
	75%F X 25%J	1	206	215	27	449
	50%F X 50%J	7	158	174	23	362
	25%F X 75%J	1	54	61	8	124
Dayagama	Pure Jersey	1	257	210	29	497
	75%F X 25%J	0	76	90	10	176
	50%F X 50%J	0	30	31	10	71
	25%F X 75%J	0	5	4	1	10
Overall farm	Pure Friesian	6	113	148	16	283
	Pure Jersey	3	375	346	52	776
	75%F X 25%J	1	282	305	37	625
	50%F X 50%J	7	487	453	104	1051
	25%F X 75%J	1	59	65	9	134

Different Types of Calving

The highest numbers of still births and abortions were recorded in Manikpalama farm. The overall highest number of still births were recorded by the pure Jersey. The male:female ratio of newborns remained almost 1:1, and were approximately similar in all the farms (Table 4.14)

CONCLUSION

Milk production and reproduction performance depend on the Calving month, genotypes, bull breed, farm and parity. Dayagama farm showed the highest production peformence than the Manickpalama farm. Both Dayagama and Bopaththalawa farms shaved the highest production and reproduction performance in the 50%F X 50%J crosses genotypes. The highest production and reproduction performance were shown from September to February calving months.

REFERENCES

Anuranga, B.K.H.D. (2014): DCP, a Potential Shield to uplift Local Milk. Scientific Research Journal, 2(3): 20-25.

Bandara, D.M.D.S., Premaratne, S. and Dematawewa, C.M.B. (2011): Production and Economic Characteristics of Intensive and Semi-Intensive Dairy Cattle Management Systems in Vegetable Based Farming System in Welimada, Sri Lanka. Trop. Agric. Res.22(3), 314-323.

Bogart, R. (1977): Scientific Farm Animal Production. Burgess Publishing Company Co. Inc., New York, USA.

Briggs, M.H. (1969): Modern Breeders of Livestock. Macmillan Publishing Company, Minneapolis, USA.

Cerbulis, J., and H.M. Farrell, Jr. (1976): Composition of the Milk of Dairy Cattle. II. Ash, Calcium, Magnesium and Phosphorus J. Dairy Sci. 59:589.

Chandrasiri, A.D.N. (2002): Country Report on The State of Animal Genatic Resources (Sri Lanka).

DAPH, (2015): Department of Animal Production and Health, State Organization which is Responsible for Providing Technical Leadership to Livestock, Gannoruwa, 47 Peradeniya, Sri Lanka. http://WWW.daph.gov.lk/web/index., (Accessed on 10/10/ 2016).

Davies, D.T., C. Holt, and W.W. Christie. (1983): The Composition of Milk. Ch. 5 in Biochemistry of Lactation, T. B. Mepham, editor., ed. Amsterdam: Elsevier.

DCS, (2011): Department of Census and Statistics, Central Statistical Agency in Sri Lanka, which is Responsible for Collection, Analysis and Dissemination, Sri Jayawardhanapura Kotte, Sri Lanka. http://WWW.statistics.gov.lk., (Accessed on 23/ 10/2016).

Dematawewa, C.M.B. and Beger, P.J. (1998): Genetic and Phenotypic Parameters for 305-day Yield, Fertility, and Survival in Holsteins. J. Dairy Sci. 81, 2700-2709.

Dhaliwal, G.S., Murray, R.D. and Dobson, H., (1996): Effects of Milk yield, and Calving to First Service Interval, in Determining Herd Fertility in Dairy Cows.

Dowell, l., Dash, A.K. and Alam, R., (2016): Production Performance of Different Cross Breeds of Milch Cow in., 3(6), pp. 29-33.

Evans, R.D. and Garcia-Peniche, T.B. (2006): Effects of Calving Age, Breed Fraction and Month of Calving on Calving Interval and Survival Across Parities in Irish Spring-calving Dairy Cows. Livestock Science, 100(2-3), pp. 216-230.

Foster, W.W, McGilliard, M.L. and James R.E. (1988): Association of Herd Average Genetic and Environmental Milk yield with Dairy Herd Improvement Variables. J Dairy Sci 71, 3415-3424.

Gates, M.C.(2013): Evaluating the Reproductive Performance of British Beef and Dairy Herds using National Cattle Movement Records. The Veterinary Record, 173(20), p. 499.

Gaunt, S.N. (1980): Genetic Variation in the yields and Contents of Milk Constituents. Int. Dairy Fed. Bull. Doc.125:73.

Guti, J.P., Haque, M.R. and Haque, A.P. (2007): Genetic Relationships among Calving Ease, Calving Interval, Birth Weight and Weaning Weight in the Asturiana de los Valles Beef Cattle Breed. Journal of Animal Science, 85(1), pp. 69-75.

Ibrahim, M.N.M., Staal, S.J., Daniel, S.L.A. and Thorpe, W. (1999): Appraisal of the Sri Lanka Dairy Sector, Volume 1. Synthesis Report. Department of Animal Science, University of Peradeniya; International Livestock Research Institute, Nairobi, Kenya and Ministry of Livestock Development and Estate Infrastructure, Colombo, Sri Lanka. pp 7.

Ibrahim, M.N.M. and Zemmelink, G. (2000): A Comparative Evaluation of Integrated Farmmodels with the Village Situation in the Forest-Garden Area of Kandy, Sri Lanka. Asian-Aus.J. Anim. Sci. 13(1), 53-59.

Inchaisri, C., Coffey, M.P. and Brotherstone, S.(2010): Effect of Milk yield Characteristics, Breed, and Parity on Success of the First Insemination in Dutch Dairy Cows. Journal of Dairy Science, 93(11), pp. 5179-87.

Jalatge, E.F.A. (1986): Crossbreeding of Cattle in Sri Lanka.

Jenness, R. (1985): Biochemical and Nutritional Aspects of Milk and Colostrum. Ch. 5 in Lactation, B.L. Larson, Editor., ed. Ames: Iowa State University Press.

Jeyamalar, J., Packthynathan, M. and Mahusoon, M.M., (2003): Comparison of Characteristics of Cattle Production Under Up Country Wet Zone and Low Country Dry Zone Condition in Sri Lanka., p. 79.

Kitchen, B.J. (1981): Bovine Mastitis: Milk Compositional Changes and related Diagnostic Tests. J. Dairy Res.48: 167.

Kollapitiya, K.M.P.M.B., Premarathna, S, and Peiris, B.L. (2012): Reproductive and Productive Performance of Up-Country Exotic Dairy Cattle Breeds of Sri Lanka.Trop. Agric. Res. 23 (4): 319-326.

Kothalawala, K.A.C.H.A. (2014): Livestock Statistical Bulletin

Kroeker, E.M., K.F., Ng-Kwai-Hang, J.F., Hayes, and J.E. Moxley. (1985): Effect of beta-lactoglobulin Variant and Environmental Factors on Variation in the Detailed Composition of Bovine Milk Serum Proteins. J. Dairy Sci.68: 1637.

Lee, D.H., Han, K.J. & Park, B.H., (1999): Genetic Relationship between Milk Yields, Calving Ease and Days Open at First Lactation of Holstein Cows in Korea.

Milam, K.Z., Coppock, C.E., West, J.W., Lanham, J.K., Nave, D.H., Labore, J.M., Stermer, R.A. and Brasington, C.F.(1986): Effects of Drinking Water Temperature on Production Responses m lactating Holstein Cows in Summer. J. Dairy Sci. 69:1013.

Raheja, K.L., Burnside, E.B. and Schaeffer, L.R.(1989): Heifer Fertility and its Relationship with Cow Fertility and Production Traits in Holstein Dairy Cattle. Journal of Dairy Science, 72(10), pp. 2665-2669.

Rajaguru, A.S.B. (1986): Livestock Development Policy Plan for Sri Lanka. Report of the Society for Researchers on Native Livestock 11: 37-64.

Ranawana, S. (2008): Dairy Industry in Sri Lanka: Problems and Prospects. Economic Review, 34(5): 47.

Ranaweera, N.F.C. (2007): Improved Market Access and Smallholder Dairy Farmer Participation for Sustainable Dairy Development. Lessons Learned Sri Lanka. FAO Report. pp. 5-21.

Roche, J.R., Rekik, B. and Gengler, N. (2007): Associations Among Body Condition Score, Body Weight, and Reproductive Performance in Seasonal-calving Dairy Cattle. Journal of Dairy Science, 90(1), pp. 376-91.

Rogers, G.L., and J.A. Stewart. (1982): The Effects of some Nutritional and no Nutritional Factors on Milk Protein Concentration and yield. Aust. J. Dairy Technol. 37:26.

Penasa, M., Hafez, E.S.E. and Hafez, B. (2010): Crossbreeding Effects on Milk yield Traits and Calving Interval in Spring-calving Dairy Cows. Journal of Animal Breeding and Genetics, 127(4), pp. 300-307.

Sarakul, J.E., Coffey, M.P. and Brotherstone, S.(2010): The Genetic Relationship between Calving Interval, Body Condition Score and Linear Type and Management Traits in Registered Holsteins. Journal of Dairy Science, 83(11), pp. 2664-2671.

Silva, G.L.L.P., Herath, H.M.S.P. and Chandrasiri, A.D.N.(2008): Indigenous Cattle Types and Production Systems in Sri Lanka.

Upazila, M., Dash, A.K. and Alam, R. (2016): Production Performance of Different Cross Breeds of Milch Cow in., 3(6), pp. 29-33.

Woodford, J.A., Jorgensen, N.A. and Barrington, G.P. (1986): Impact of Dietary Fiber and Physical form on Performance of Lactating Dairy Cows. J. Dairy Sci. 69:1035.

Pages: 84-105

Animal Biodiversity and Fisheries
Edited by: **Dr. Rashmi Tripathi; Dr. Vijay Sharma & Dr. Pawan Kumar 'Bharti'**
ISBN: 978-93-88854-06-1
Edition: **2019**
Published by: **Discovery Publishing House Pvt. Ltd., New Delhi (India)**

5 Effect of *mangiferin* on Pharmacokinetic, Antidiabetic and Hepatotoxicity of Pioglitazone in Albino Rats

R.M. Singh[1]; A.R. Kulkarni[1]; S.T. Shukla[2*]
K. Ganguly[1]; K. Chaturvedi[1]; V.H. Kulkarnil[1]
R.K. Mishra[3*]; Ankita Gupta[2]

ABSTRACT

Relevance of mangiferin: Herbal Antidiabetic preparations are often used as an add-on therapy in diabetics. Mangiferin indica (Anacardiaceae) stem bark contains a rich content of Mangiferin and is used traditionally in Indian Ayurvedic system to treat diabetes. Mangiferin has been reported to be potent Alpha-Glucosidase inhibitor that also shows modulation of CYP450 enzyme that inhibits CYP3A4 enzyme.

Aim of the study: the present investigation aims to examine effect of mangiferin on pharmacokinetic, antidiabetic and hepatotoxicity of pioglitazone in albino rats or induced diabetic rats.

Materials and methods: Streptozotocin (STZ) was purchased from Enzo Life Sciences, Switzerland. Insulin was purchased from Biocon, India. DTNB was obtained from Sigma. Tris-HCL buffer form Renkem. DPPH, Deoxy-D-Ribose, Mannitol, Trichloroacetic acid (TCA) were purchased from Himedia. Total Cholesterol Kit & Total Triglyceride Kit form ERBA diagnostics Mannheim GMBH, Germany. *Mangifera indica* stem barks were collected from the Kyarkop region of Dharwad, Karnataka, India.

Result: Mangiferin may influence the kinetic, diabetic and hepatotoxicity effect of pioglitazone which is particularly crucial, as any

1 Department of Pharmacology, S E T's College of Pharmacy, Dharwad, Karnataka (India)
2 Department of Pharmacology & Toxicology, Patanjali Research Institute. Haridwar, Uttarakhand (India)
3 Patanjali Bhartiya Ayurvigyan Evum Anusandhan Sansthan, Haridwar, Uttarakhand (India)

increment in its plasma level may raise safety concerns. Pharmacokinetic study was carried out by administrating Pioglitazone orally (10mg/kg) alone and in combination with Mangiferin (200mg/kg) pretreated in alloxan induced diabetic rats and its plasma levels were determined at various time points (0h, 1h, 2h, 4h, 8h, 12h, 18h, 24h) after oral administration by HPLC. Mangiferin pretreatment increased AUC0-" of pioglitazone. Pharmacodynamic effects of Pioglitazone with Mangiferin were evaluated in alloxan induced diabetic rats. The blood samples were collected from diabetic rats at different time intervals up to 24hrs and blood glucose was estimated. Mangiferin (200mg/kg, p.o) pretreatment has significantly altered the onset of Antidiabetic effect of Pioglitazone from 26.67% to 31.5% and significantly enhanced the peak Antidiabetic effect from 69.25% to 73.99%. Duration of Antidiabetic effect was raised from more than 24hrs. Hepatotoxicity activity was estimated and Mangiferin significantly reduces the level of AST and ALT enzymes alone and in combination with pioglitazone.

Conclusion: The study indicates that Therapeutic drug monitoring has to be required to readjust the therapeutic dose of Mangiferin and pioglitazone when they used concomitantly.

Keywords: Mangiferin, Pioglitazone, Pharmacokinetic, Pharmacodynamic, Antidiabetic, Hepatotoxicity.

GRAPHICAL ABSTRACT

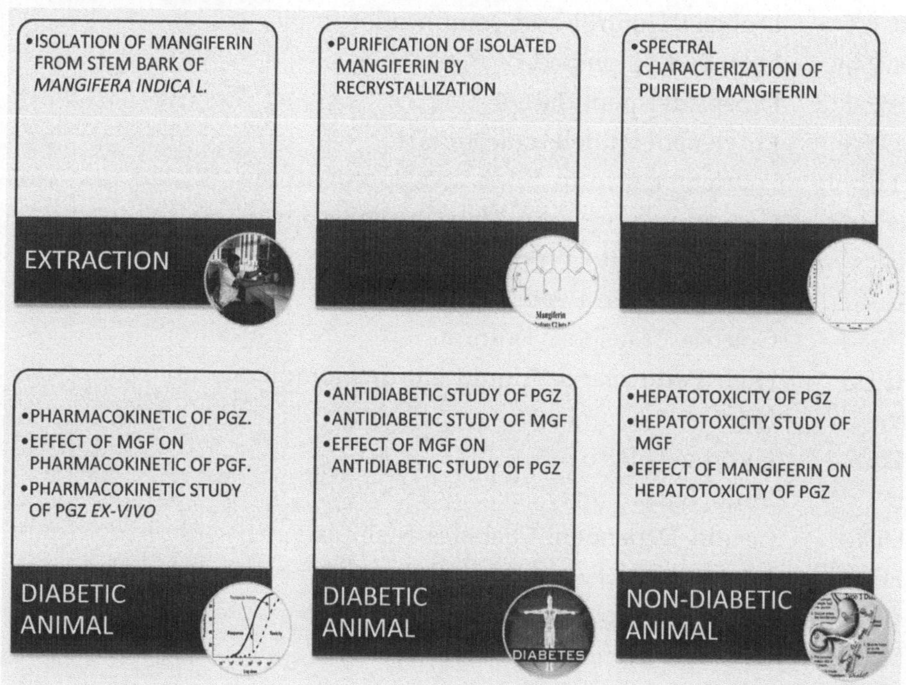

LIST OF ABBREVIATIONS

ACCORD	Action to Control Cardiovascular Risk in Diabetes
ALT	Alanine Transaminase
AST	Aspartate Transaminase
ATP	Adenosine Triphosphate
AUC	Area Under Curve
AUC0-∞	Area Under Curve
BGL	Blood Glucose Level
C AMP	Cyclic Adenosine Monophosphate
CCK	Cholecystokinin
CGMP	Cyclic Guoanosine Monophosphate
Cmax	Maximum Concentration
Conc.	Concentration
CPCSEA	Control and Supervision of experiments on experimental animals
CYP-450	Cytochrome -P450
CYP-3A4	Cytochrome-3A4
CYP-2C8	Cytochrome-2C8
CYP-2C9	Cytochrome-2C9
DB	Dried Bark
DCCT	Diabetes Control and complication trails
DMSO	Dimethyl Sulphoxide
DPP-4	Dipeptidyl peptidase-4
EDTA	Ethylenediaminetetraacetic acid
FTIR	Fouriers Trasform Infra Red Spectroscopy
GC-MS	Gas chromatography Mass Spectroscopy
GIP	Gastric inhibitory polypeptide
GLP-1	Glucagon Like Peptide -1
Glut-4	Glucose Transport Isoform
HPLC	High Performance Liquid Chromatoraphy
hr.	Hour
H2O2	Hydrogen Peroxide
IB	Inner Bark
IDDM	Insulin Dependent Diabetes Mellitus.
IFCC	International Federation of clinical Chemistry
i.p	Intra peritoneal
IP3	Ionositol triphosphate

IU	International Unit
K.el	Constant Elimination Rate
Kg.	Kilogram
Kir.62	Potassium inward rectifier
LDH	Lactate Dehydrogenase
LPL	Lipoprotein Lipase
LDH	Lactate Dehydrogenase
Max.	Maximum
MDH	Malate Dehydrogenase
MGF	Mangiferin
Mg.	Miligram
Min.	Minimum
Mm	Mili Molar
M.w.	Molecular Weight
N	Number of group
NAD	Nicotinamide adenine dinucleotide
NIDDM	Non Insulin Dependent Diabetes Mellitus
NSAID	Non Steroidal Anti-inflammatory Drug
NYHA	New York Heart Association
OFR	Oxidative Free Radicals
PDE	Phosphodiesterase
PEPCK	Phosphenol pyruvate Carboxy Kinase
PGZ	Pioglitazone
Pio	Pioglitazone
PKA	Protein Kinase A
PKC	Protein Kinase C
PLC	Phospholipase C
p.o.	Per Oral
PPAR-α	Peroxisome Proliferator Activating Receptor-Alpha
PPAR-γ	Peroxisome Proliferator Activating Receptor-Gamma
S.E.M	Standard Error Mean
SGOT	Serum Glutamate Oxaloacetate Transaminase
SGPT	Serum Glutamate Pyruvate Transaminase
SOD	Superoxide Dismutase
STZ	Streptozotocin
SUR	Sulphonylurea Receptor
TG	Triglyceride

Tmax	Maximum Time
TZD's	Thiazolidinediones
U.V/	Viseable Ultra violet/viseable spectroscopy
UKPDS	UK prospective diabetes studies
%	Percentage
°C	Degree Celsius
µg.	Microgram

INTRODUCTION

Drug interaction is the modification of the effect of one drug (object drug) by the prior or concomitant administration of another drug (precipitant drug). Drug interaction may either enhance or diminish the intended effect of one or both drugs. It may modify the diagnostic, preventive or therapeutic activity of either drug (Kohler *et al.*, 2004) In poly pharmacy, it is important to determine the incidence and frequency of occurrence of drug interactions, which serious implications, in hospitalized patients. In addition, it is also important to find out agents that are most likely to produce hazardous interactions (Sunilkumar *et al.*, 1998).As per survey, the incidence of drug interaction ranges from 3 to 5% in patients taking a few drugs to 20% in patients receiving many drugs. According to a report that, the drug interaction may be fourth to sixth leading cause for death in United States (Alan *et al.*, 2001). Pioglitazone hydrochloride ([(±)-5-[[4-[2-(5-ethyl-2-pyridinyl)ethoxy] phenyl]methyl]-2,4-] thiazolidinedione) hydrochloride is an oral antidiabetic agent used in the treatment of type 2 diabetes mellitus (also known as non-insulindependent diabetes mellitus (NIDDM) or adult-onset diabetes). Pioglitazone decreases insulin resistance in the periphery and liver, resulting in increased insulin dependent glucose disposal and decreased hepatic glucose output. It acts primarily by increasing insulin sensitivity in target tissues. Pioglitazone is a potent and highly selective agonist for peroxisome proliferator-activated receptor-gamma (PPARγ). PPARγ receptors are found in tissues important for insulin action such as adipose tissue, skeletal muscle, and liver. Activation of PPARγ nuclear receptors modulates the transcription of a number of insulin responsive genes involved in the control of glucose and lipid metabolism, and in the maturation of preadipocytes, predominantly of subcutaneous origin. It is used both as monotherapy and in combination with sulfonylurea or insulin in the management of type 2 diabetes mellitus, NIDDM). Currently, it is marked under the trade name Actos® (http://www.actos.com/pi.pdf, 2004; Chilcott *et al.*, 1792). Pharmacological studies indicate that Pioglitazone improves sensitivity to insulin in muscle and adipose tissues and inhibits hepatic gluconeogenesis (Smith, 2001). Pioglitazone orally well absorbed within two hrs, metabolized by hepatic cytochrome CYP2C isozyme and CYP3A4 to active metabolites. The metabolites of pioglitazone mainly eliminated in bile (Rang & Dale, 2005). Mangiferin, a xanthone glucoside, is an active phytochemical present in various plants including *Mangifera indica Linn.* Family: Anacardiacae, Genus: Mangifera). Mangiferin is present in leaves, fruits, stem and roots of *Mangifera indica.* The natural C-glucoside xanthone Mangiferin [2-C-β-D-gluco-pyranosyl-1,3,6,7- tetrahydroxyxanthone; C19H18O11 ; Mw., 422.35; melting point, anhydrous 271°C (Miura *et al.*, 2001; Nunez *et al.*, 2002; Muruganand *et al.*, 2002). Mangiferin has been reported to posse's antioxidant, antitumor, antiviral, immunomodulatory activities (Sanchez *et al.*, 2000; Ghua *et al.* 1996, Zheng and Lu YU, 1990; Leiro *et al.*, 2004). Mangiferin rich plants are widely used medical plants in India for the treatment of immune-deficiency diseases such as arthritis, diabetes, hepatitis, cardiac and mental disorders (Ichiki *et al.*, 1998). Being a polyphenolic antioxidant, Mangiferin has strong antioxidant, antilipid peroxidative, immunomodulatory, cardiotonic, hypotensive, wound healing, antidegenerative and Antidiabetic activities (Andreu *et al.*, 2005). Mangiferin, has recently been shown to have antidiabetic activity in KK/Ay mice, a genetic model of non-insulin-dependent diabetes mellitus (NIDDM) with hyperinsulinemia (Miura *et al.*, 2001). Mangiferin have been reported to be potent alpha-glucosidase inhibitors that have been shown to inhibit increases in serum glucose levels (Yoshikawa *et al.*, 2001). Mangiferin also shows modulation of certain P450 enzymes (Rodeiro *et al.*, 2008). Since pioglitazone has the possibility of interacting with enzyme inducers or inhibitors of CYP3A4 and CYP2C8 and Mangiferin being a CYP450 enzyme modulator. This study is carried out to evaluate the effect of Mangiferin on the pharmacokinetics, hypoglycemic and hepatotoxicity activity of Pioglitazone in experimental animals. As pioglitazone in known to cause hepatotoxicity they are contraindicated in patients with pre-existing liver disease. The toxic effects of these drugs in combination may be enhanced or protected. Hence in the present study we undertake the hepatotoxicity activity along with the pharmacokinetic and pharmacodynamic aspect. Pharmacokinetic parameters will be assessed by measuring the AUC (area under curve) in rats using HPLC (high performance liquid chromatography) whereas the pharmacodynamic parameters will be assessed by measuring the blood glucose level by Trinder's method and hepatotoxicity studies will be carried out by measuring the AST, ALT levels along with histopathology to assess the extent of liver damage. All the six parameters will be done using the drugs individually and in combination. Both pharmacodynamic as well as hepatotoxicity studies will be carried out in rats.

MATERIAL AND METHODS

Chemicals

Alloxan, DMSO, Acetone, Tween 80, Glucose was purchased from S d Fine-chem. ltd. Pioglitazone was purchased from Micro Labs ltd., HP.

Chloroform and Formaldehyde from RFCL, New Delhi. Sodium Chloride was obtained from Himedia lab. Pvt. Ltd. Heparin buffer form Neon pharma. Petroleum Ether and Glucose kit form Transassia Bio medicals LTD, Daman.

Instruments

HPLC has purchased from Shimadzu LC-20AT Japan. Autoanalyser has been purchased MayGun technology Co. Ltd.- MS-500E. U.V/ Vis Spectrophotometer has brought from Labindia: UV 3000+, India. FTIR from NICOLET (USA) Model 5700, GC-MS from Shimadzu Japan.

Plant Material

Mangifera indica stem barks were collected from the Kyarkop region of Dharwad (Karnataka, India) in the month of September 2010. The stem barks were inspected to be healthy, collected and were washed with water thrice in the bucket and dried overnight over a cotton cloth. After that the materials were grounded to fine powder using a domestic electric grinder.

Animal

Male Wister albino rats weighing between 200-250gms were used for the experiments. Animals were housed for a week in the laboratory before the start of the experiment. Rats were fed with standard rodent diet (Lipton India Ltd) and water ad libitum. Ethical committee clearance was obtained prior from college ethical committee for the present study.

Methods

Extraction of Mangiferin

Powdered stem barks were passes through the sieve no.20 and around 100 gram of powder was successively extracted with petroleum ether (2×300ml; 4 hr each time) and acetone (400 ml 4 hr each time) soaked for 24hrs to remove tannins. Finally bark extracted with 70% ethanolic solvent (2×400 ml; 4hr each time). The ethanolic fraction was concentrated using distillation unit and evaporated on water bath. Then mangiferin was separated as a yellow colour powder. Confirmative tests for isolated mangiferin were performed by dissolving isolated mangiferin in aqueous ethanol showed deep yellow colour solution due to presence of mangiferin. In addition, alcoholic solution of isolated mangiferin when treated with ferric chloride gave deep green colour while with ferric chloride and hydrochloric acid it produced greenish yellow precipitate immediately due to presence of mangiferin (Dineshkumar *et al.*, 2010).

Isolation, Purification and Characterization of Mangiferin from Mangifera indica L. stem barks

Mangifera indica stem barks were collected from the Kyarkop region of Dharwad (Karnataka, India) in the month of September 2010. A herbarium specimen was kept in Department of Pharmacognosy (SETCPD/

Ph.cog/herb/29/09/2010), SET's College of Pharmacy, Dharwad.The stem barks were inspected to be healthy, collected and were washed with water thrice in the bucket and dried overnight over a cotton cloth. After that the materials were grounded to fine powder using a domestic electric grinder. Powdered stem barks were passes through the sieve no.20 and around 100 gram of powder was successively extracted with petroleum ether (2×300ml; 4 hr each time) and acetone (400 ml 4hr each time) soaked for 24hrs to remove tannins. Finally bark extracted with 70% ethanolic solvent (2×400 ml; 4hr each time). The ethanolic fraction was concentrated using distillation unit and evaporated on water bath. Then mangiferin was separated as a yellow color powder. Confirmative tests for isolated mangiferin were performed by dissolving isolated mangiferin in aqueous ethanol showed deep yellow color solution due to presence of mangiferin. In addition, alcoholic solution of isolated mangiferin when treated with ferric chloride gave deep green color while with ferric chloride and hydrochloric acid it produced greenish yellow precipitate immediately due to presence of mangiferin (Singh *et al.*, 2005).

Purification of Mangiferin by Crystallization

The Mangiferin obtained is dissolved in 70% of ethanol and heated in the water bath for 30 minutes and filtered, the filtrate obtained is again reheated for a suitable period for super saturation and then cooled at room temperature. The yellow powder of Mangiferin was obtained after the complete evaporation of the solvent (Singh *et al.*, 2005).

Determination of Melting Point

Small amount of Mangiferin was taken in a melting point capillary tube and placed in the melting point apparatus (make) and then it was switched on and the temperature was gradually increased. At certain temperature range the Mangiferin was melted and this temperature was notes as melting point of Mangiferin (Singh *et al.*, 2005).

Spectral characterization of Mangiferin

FTIR

The IR spectra of isolated impurity and mangiferin were recorded by FTIR spectrophotometer using KBr method at 25°C. The technical specification it includes IR source: Aiun Standard ETC Ever-Glo TM, Detector: DTGS with KBr window, Laser: Helium-Neon Laser head, Interferometer: Vectra aluminum Interferometer, Range: 350-7800cm^{-1}, Resolution: 0.5 cm-1 to 4 cm^{-1}.

GC-MS

The isolated Mangiferin is dissolved in the DMSO and subjected to GC-MS (Muruganand *et al.*, 2002).

UVspectra

A pinch of isolated Mangiferin was dissolved in the alcohol and U.V spectra were observed in the range of 200 nm to 500 nm (Chaudhari *et al.*, 1971).

Liquid Chromatography

The HPLC Analysis of isolated Mangiferin was performed with Shimadzu LC-20AT equipment including a diode- array UV detector. A phenomex C18(2) 100A Analytical column (250 4.60 mm, 5 micron was used and operated at 25°C. The mobile phase used consisted of methanol-2% glacial acetic acid (40:60,v:v) and was delivered by a pump at a flow rate of 1.0 ml/min. The diode array detector was set at 318 nm and the measurement was performed by injecting 20µl of isolated Mangiferin dissolved in methanol in the injector port (Hou *et al.*, 2010).

Pharmacokinetic Studies

Pharmacokinetic studies were done in rats. The animals were divided into two groups containing six animals each. One group received pioglitazone in 1% Tween 80 (10 mg/kg) alone while the other group received pioglitazone in 1% Tween 80 (10 mg/kg) along with Mangiferin (200mg/kg). The drugs were administered by oral route using a gastric gavage tube. The blood samples were drawn from the retro orbital plexus at time intervals of 0, 1, 2, 4, 8, 12, 18 and 24 hrs respectively and collected in heparinised glass tubes which was then centrifuged at 6000 rpm for 15 min, from this plasma were taken and the plasma volume were measured and added to 10 ml glass tubes and extracted with triplicate volume of chloroform in separating funnel by vigorous shaking, the lower chloroform layer were collected and same procedure repeated thrice for each sample. The collected organic phase was evaporated to dryness and the residue was reconstituted with 2ml methanol from this 25 µl was injected into the HPLC system the column used was C18 the mobile phase was methanol with a flow rate of 0.5 ml/min the eluent was monitored by ultra-voilet detection at 230nm. The area under curve was obtained. Actual concentration was calculated from the standard graphs of the drugs administered from which the slope and the correlation co-efficient (R2) values were estimated and these values were further used to calculate the plasma concentration in µg/ml. The formula for this was: Plasma concentration (µg/ml)={(AUC) of test*1*100}/(slope*0.5*2),Where: 20µl = is the amount of sample injected into the HPLC system, 0.5ml = amount of the plasma taken, 100µl = the amount of methanol used to reconstitute the sample.

Anti-diabetic Activity

Anti-diabetic activity was done in rats. Rats received an intraperitoneal injection of Alloxan 150mg/kg of single dose, after 48hrs they were confirmed diabetic by estimating the blood glucose level (Sikarwar *et al.*,

2009). Animals showing fasting blood glucose level 250 were considered diabetic. Animals were divided into four groups containing six animals each. The first group received citrate buffer alone and served as control whereas, the second group received pioglitazone (10mg/kg), third group Mangiferin (200mg/kg) and fourth group received combination of Mangiferin (200mg) and pioglitazone (10mg). Blood samples were obtained by retro orbital flexes in order to measure the blood glucose level. The blood glucose level was estimated by trinder's method using autoanalyser. The instrument was calibrated by using the standard solution (Glucose 100mg/dl) from the kit.

Principle

Glucose in sample is oxidized to yield gluconic acid and hydrogen peroxide in the presence of Glucose oxidase. The enzyme peroxidase catalyses the oxidative coupling of 4- aminoantipyrin with phenol to yield a coloured quinoneimine complex with absorbance proportional to the concentration of glucose in the sample.

$$\text{Glucose} + O_2 + H_2O \xrightarrow{\text{Glucose oxidase}} \text{Gluconic acid} + H_2O_2$$

$$H_2O_2 + \text{phenol} + 4\text{AAP} \xrightarrow{\text{Peroxidase}} \text{Quinoneimine Dye} + 2H_2O$$

Hepatotoxicity Studies

Hepatotoxicity studies were done in rats. Animals were divided into four groups containing six animals each. The first group served as the control whereas the second and third group received pioglitazone (10mg/kg) And Mangiferin (200mg/kg) individually. The fourth group received a combination of pioglitazone (10mg/kg) and mangiferin (200mg/kg). After a week's treatment with the drugs, the animals blood were removed by retero orbital plexus upto 2ml in the effendroff tube, the blood were allowed to clot at room temperature for 15 min. after that the serum is obtained by centrifugation at 3500 RPM for 15 min. soon after AST and ALT level in serum were measured by kinetic method using kit from ERBA diagnostics in Autoanalyser. After the completion of AST and ALT analysis, the rats were sacrificed by decapitation and the liver tissues were carefully dissected out and washed with 0.9% normal saline solution and fixed in formalin (10% formaldehyde) for histopathology study.

Biochemical Parameters

Biochemical parameters, Serum was separated and analyzed spectrophotometrically for AST, ALT using diagnostic kits of ERBA diagnostics, Mannheim GMBH, Germany. Measurement of enzymatic and non-enzymatic antioxidant levels.

Histopathological Examination

Parts of isolated hepatic tissue were fixed in 10% formalin solution and then dehydrated in ascending grades of alcohol and embedded in paraffin. Four micron thickness sections were taken, stained with hematoxylin and eosin solution and examined under light microscope (Fig. 5.13).

Statistical Analysis

Results are expressed as mean S.E.M and "n" indicated the number of animals used. Differences between means were assessed by One-way analysis of variance (ANOVA) followed by Dunnet's't' test.

RESULTS

I. Isolation, Purification and Characterization of Mangiferin

Mangiferin was successfully isolated from the stem bark of *Mangifera indica* the percentage yield was found to be as 2.096% and confirmative test was carried out and it was found to be positive to all tests. Further the crude extract was purified by re-crystallization method was explained earlier Singh, *et al.*, (2005). The purified sample of mangiferin was subjected to chemical and spectral investigation, which shows pale yellow color and soluble in alcohol and DMSO and also sparingly soluble in water and acetone. Melting point of mangiferin was found 268- 275°C to range well matches with literature.

Spectral Analysis

Purified sample of mangiferin was subjected for FTIR, GC-MS, U.V, HPLC. FTIR spectra is displayed in the Fig. 5.1 and it was found that peaks at 3416.7 cm-1 are due to presence of secondary OH- bonds, peak at 2927.3 cm-1 showed presence of CH anti-symmetric stretching, 1647.8 cm-1, 1467.1 cm-1, 1198.3 cm-1 indicated presence of C-O stretching, CH-CH bending and C-O bond. Peak at 1032.8 cm-1 showed presence of C-C stretching in Mangiferin structure. In the IR spectrum, absorption characteristics of a xanthone were observed at 1647.8 cm–1 (conjugated carbonyl), as well as 1622.2, 1495.7 cm–1 (aromatic ring C=C stretching). The peaks at 3416.7 cm –1 corresponding to OH stretching suggested the presence of hydroxide bond in molecular structure. The result (Table 5.1) obtained was well matched with the standard IR spectra of Mangiferin. The Isolated Mangiferin was dissolved in DMSO and subjected to GC-MS, The mass spectrum of mangiferin (Fig. 5.2) shows a [M-H] molecular ion peak at m/z 420 ±2. (C19H17O11, calculated: 421.0776). The UV analysis was done and the λmax = 211, 241, 258,317 and 366 nm shown in (Fig. 5.3). The λmax obtained was exactly same as that of standard Mangiferin and UV absorbtion at various wave-lengths obtained in the range of 200 nm to 500 nm shown in Table 5.2. Further the HPLC analysis of the purified Mangiferin was carried out and the peak for Mangiferin was obtained at retention time 4.5 shown in (Fig. 5.4).

Table 5.1: Groups, Type of vibration and Regions of various peak observed in the spectrum of isolated Mangiferin

Groups	Type of vibration	Region in cm^{-1}
Alcohols Free O-H group	O-H str	3416.7
Cycloalkanes, CH2	C-H str	2927.3
C=C	C=C str	1647.8
Non-conjugated diene	C=C str	1622.2
-CH2-	C-H def	1495.7
-CH3	C-H def	1467.1
C-H2	C-H def	1409.8
O-H	bending	1292.8
O-H	bending	1257.3
Phenols	C-O str	1198.3
Phenols	C-O str	1093.4
C-O	C-O str	1032.8

Table 5.2: UV absorption and various wavelength obtained in the range of 200 nm to 500 nm

Sr. No.	Wavelength	Absorption
1.	366	1.402
2.	317	1.752
3.	258	3.139
4.	241	2.824
5.	211	2.037

II. Pharmacokinetic Study

In this study, we have measured the plasma concentration of animals treated with pioglitazone with and without Mangiferin. Measurement of plasma concentration was done using HPLC. Chromatogram of pioglitazone in methanol and that extracted from plasma are shown in (Figs. 5.5 and 5.6) respectively. It was observed that the retention time of pioglitazone (10mg/kg) was 5.853, 5.868, 5.851, 5.970, 5.892, 5.637, 5.949, and 5.886 minutes and that of pioglitazone (10mg/kg) and Mangiferin (200mg/kg) was 5.663, 5.673, 5.660, 5.663, 5.700, 5.673, 5.643, 5.653 minutes in plasma at time intervals of 0, 1, 2, 4, 8, 12, 18, 24 hrs respectively (Fig. 5.7 and 5.8) AUC is measured for different treatment for different intervals and is converted to plasma concentration by using standard curve plotting graph pioglitazone (10mg/kg) concentration Vs. AUC (Fig. 5.9). Results of plasma concentration of Pioglitazone alone and Pioglitazone along with Mangiferin at various intervals in plasma concentration of pioglitazone was found to be 0, 2.96, 14.46, 73.6, 2.60, 0 μg/ml at 0,1,2,4,8,12 hrs after administration respectively.

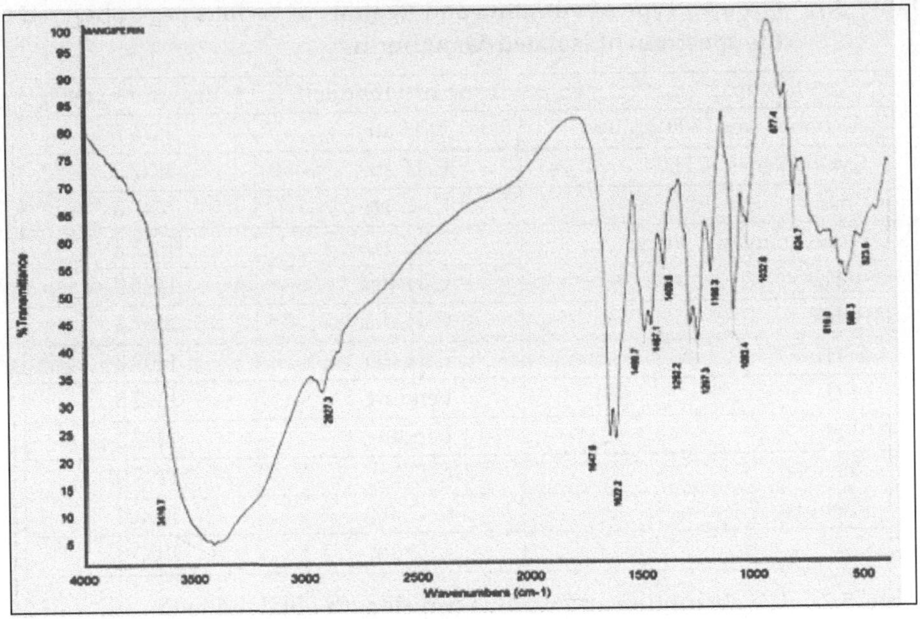

Fig. 5.1: FTIR spectral of Mangiferin

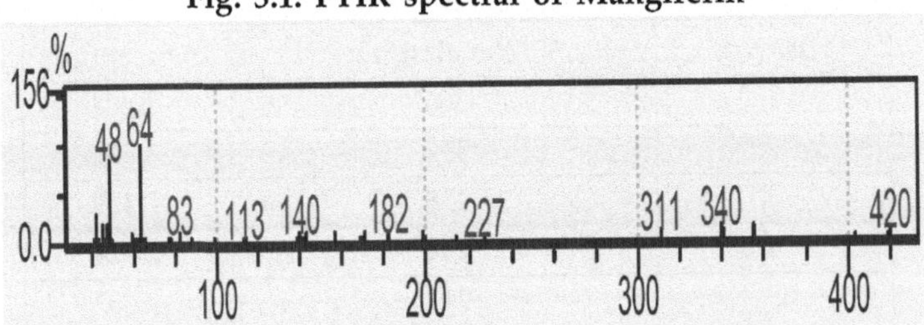

Fig. 5.2: GC-MS spectra of the mangiferin

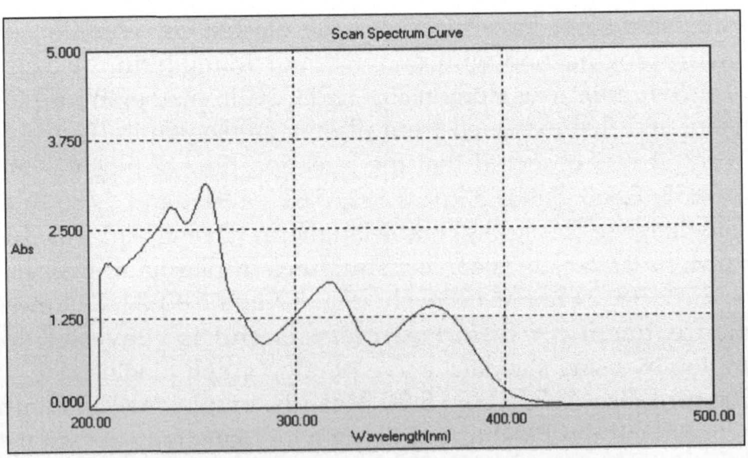

Fig. 5.3: UV absorption of Mangiferin solution in alcohol for the range of 200nm to 500nm

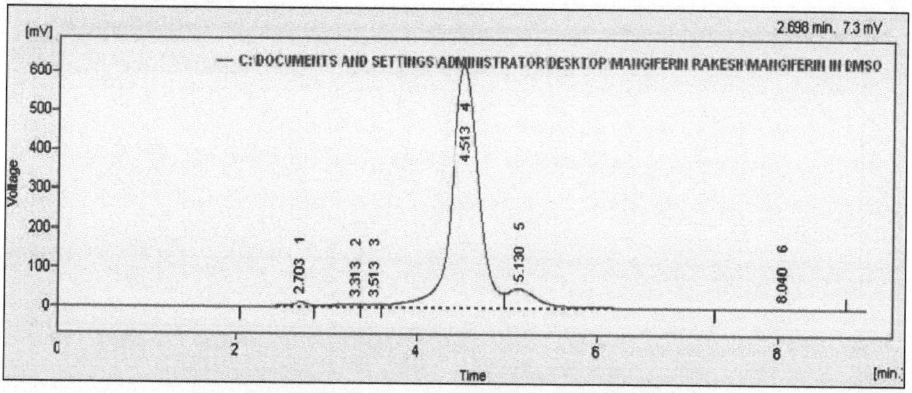

Fig. 5.4: HPLC chromatogram of Mangiferin

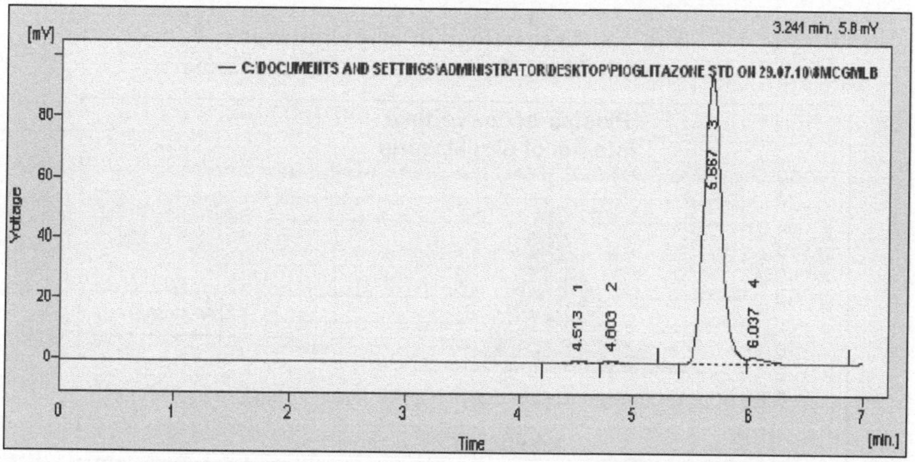

Fig. 5.5: Chromatogram of pioglitazone in methanol by HPLC

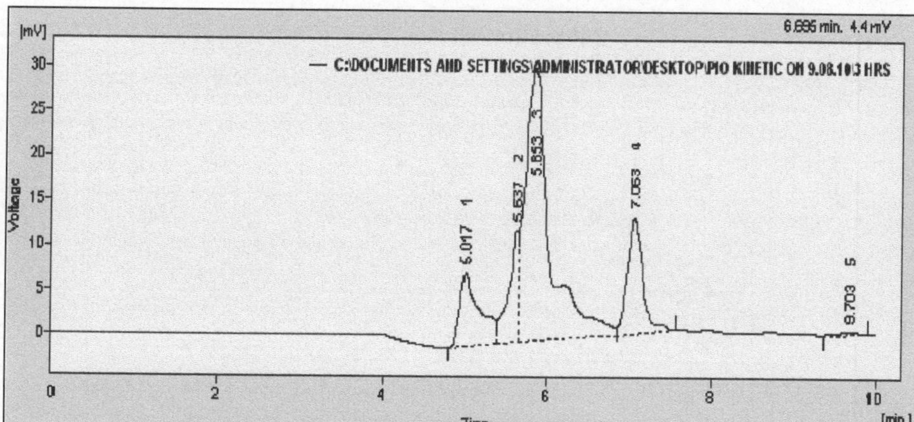

Fig. 5.6: Chromatogram of pioglitazone extracted from plasma

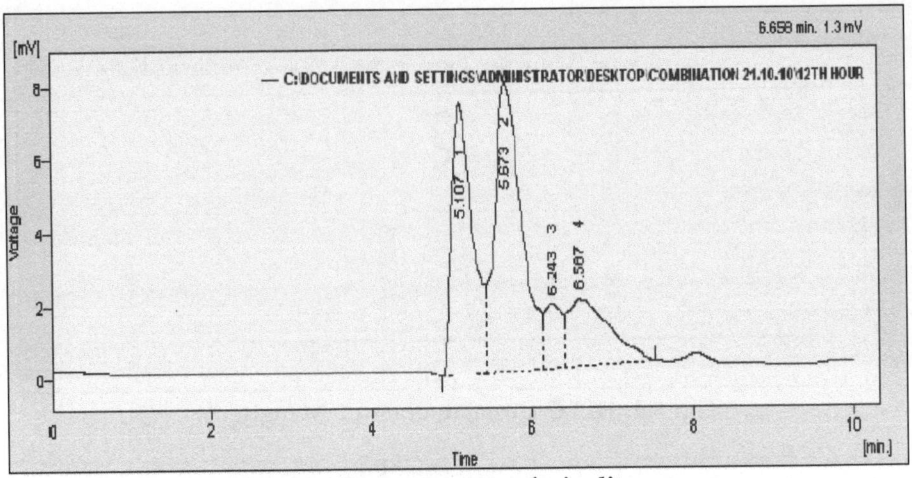

Fig. 5.7: Chromatogram of pioglitazone given with Mangiferin extracted from plasma

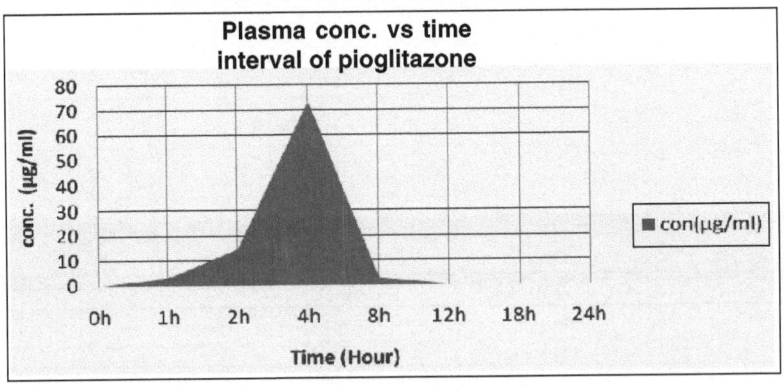

Fig. 5.8: Graph of plasma concentration Vs. Time interval of Pioglitazone

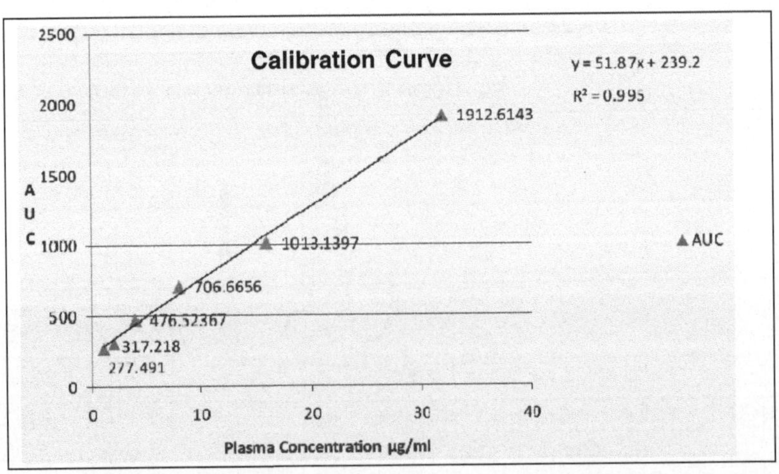

Fig. 5.9: Standard Calibration Curve of Pioglitazone

Plasma concentration of pioglitazone and Mangiferin was found to be 0, 14.018, 8.9812, 75.6, 33.8, 20.3, 8.592, 1.1432 μg/ml at 0, 1, 2, 4, 8, 12, 18, 24 hrs. after administration respectively. Dose concentration was plotted and from that various parameters such as Cmax, Tmax were calculated. Cmax, of Pioglitazone was found to be 73.6 μg/ml that of pioglitazone and Mangiferin was 75.6 μg/ml whereas the Tmax was found to be 4 hrs shown in (Fig. 5.1) for pioglitazone alone as well as combination with Mangiferin. The values Cmax as well as AUC increased when given pioglitazone and Mangiferin as compared to when given pioglitazone alone.

III. Pharmacodynamic Study

Results of blood sugar levels of animals treated with different doses of Pioglitazone and the values are compared to that of control. Mean blood sugar level of the control was found to be 439.5±9.72, 413±8.41, 439.66±8.32, 424±8.55, 422.5±9.88, 398.33±10.62, 396.33±10.97 mg/dl. The mean blood sugar level of pioglitazone (10mg/kg) treated group was found to be 437±6.40, 357.17±6.87, 320.17±7.48, 150±7.48, 134.5±7.16, 212±6.70, 330.33±6.69, 382.17±6.14. mg/dl at 0,1,2,4,8,12,18,24 hr respectively. The mean blood glucose level of Mangiferin (200mg/kg) was found to be 443.16±8.14, 433.16±4.98, 456.16±7.43, 455.16±8.66, 454.67±6.13, 449.17±5.59, 442.83±7.41, 437.17±8.32 mg/dl at 0,1,2,4,8,12,18,24 hr respectively. Effect of Mangiferin on blood sugar level, it was seen that there was no significant decrease almost comparable to control.

When pioglitazone was administered in animals in combination with Mangiferin the mean blood sugar levels of Pioglitazone (10mg/kg) and Mangiferin (200mg/kg) was found to be 429.66±7.44, 344.83±6.36, 294±6.95, 122.5±4.24, 111.17±4.85, 172.17±5.39, 286.17±4.62, 314±5.83 mg/dl at 0,1,2,4,8,12,18,24 hrs respectively. Results of Reduction in blood glucose level of control, animals treated with pioglitazone, Mangiferin and combination dose that is pioglitazone (10mg/kg) and Mangiferin (200mg/kg) are shown in Fig. 5.10. The mean percentage reduction for pioglitazone were calculated and found to be 18.22 ±1.60, 26.67±1.99, 65.71±1.46, 69.25±1.39, 51.33±2.19, 24.27±2.30, 12.42±2.13% at 1,2,4,8,12,18,24hr respectively when compared with 1st hr. Mangiferin administered alone the percentage reduction was found to be as 2.19±0.80, -2.96±0.76, -2.84±1.19, -2.68±1.45, -1.43±1.19, 0.029±1.14, 1.35±0.67 % at 1,2,4,8,12,18,24 hrs respectively. Whereas pioglitazone in combination with Mangiferin percentage reduction in glucose was found to be as 19.69±1.37, 31.5±1.80, 71.38±1.41, 73.99±1.63, 59.82±1.70, 33.28±1.68, 26.73±1.54 % at 1,2,4,8,12,18, 24h respectively. Results of % reduction blood glucose level of control, animals treated with pioglitazone, Mangiferin and combination dose that is pioglitazone (10mg/kg) and Mangiferin (200mg/kg).

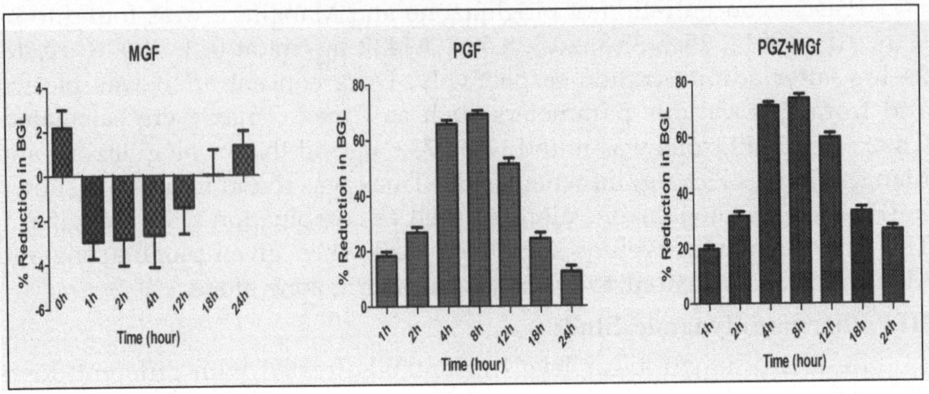

Fig. 5.10: Effect of pioglitazone, Mangiferin and pioglitazone with Mangiferin on% reduction of blood glucose level at different time intervals

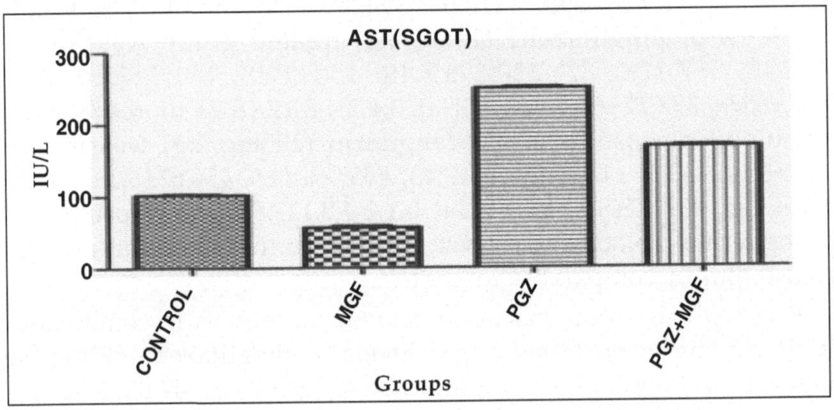

Fig. 5.11: Effect of MGF, PGZ and PGZ + MGF on AST (SGOT) levels compared with Control group

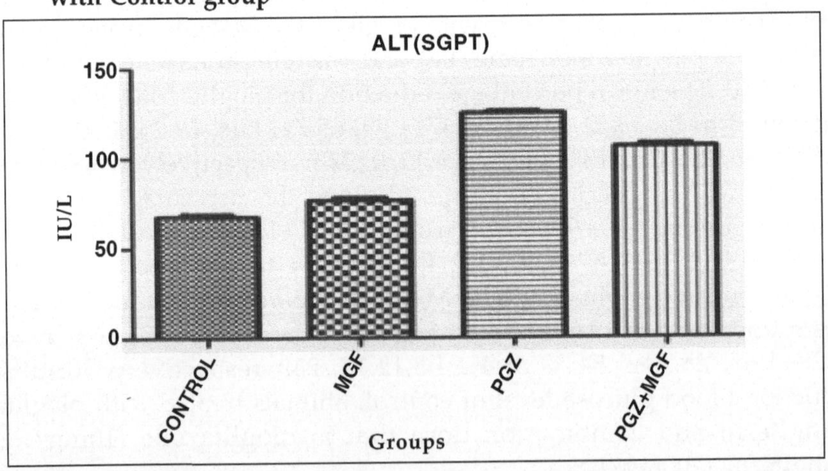

Fig. 5.12: Effect of MGF, PGZ and PGZ + MGF on ALT (SGPT) levels compared with Control group

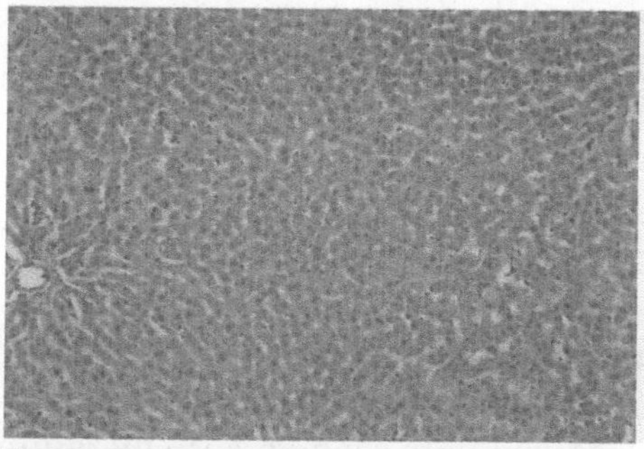

Figure A: Group I (Normal control) section of liver with normal cell structure

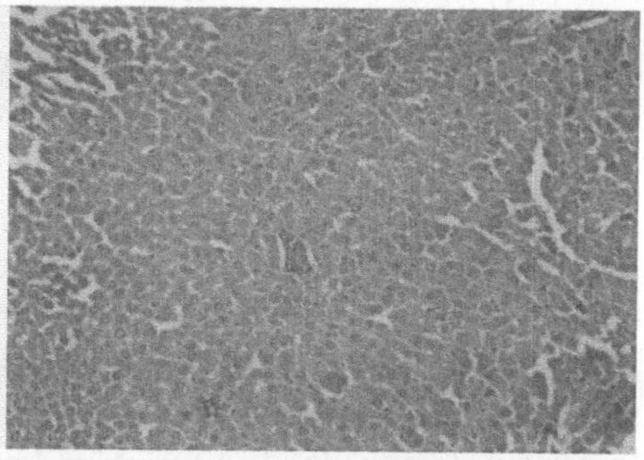

Figure B: Group (MGF treated) section of liver showing normal structure

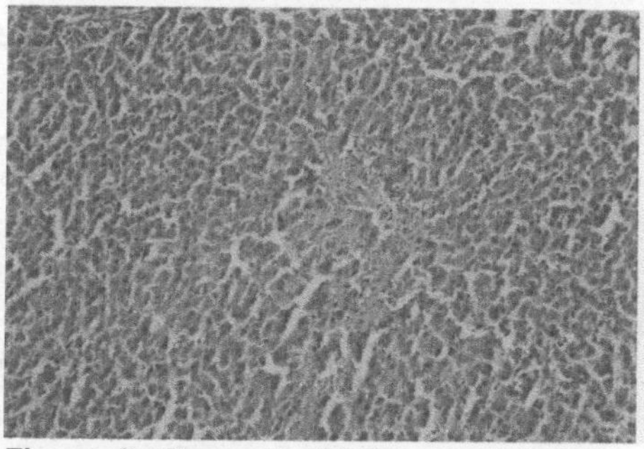

Figure C: Group III (PGZ treated) Section of liver Area of necrosis

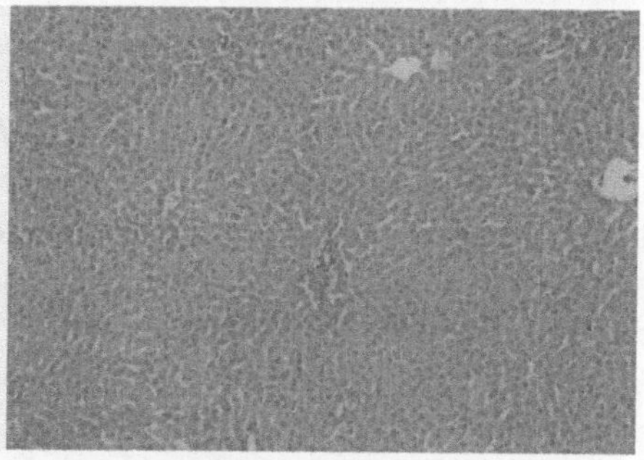

Figure D: Group IV (PGZ + MGF) Section of liver showing Reduced necrosis area

Fig. 5.13: Liver sections of animals treated with A. Control, B. MGF(200 mg/kg) treated C. PGZ (10 mg/kg) treated D. PGZ(10mg/kg) and MGF(200mg/kg)

IV. Hepatotoxicity Study

Effect of Pioglitazone, Mangiferin and Pioglitazone in combination with Mangiferin on AST(SGOT), ALT(SGPT) represented graphically in (Fig 5.11 & 5.12) respectively. Mean values of AST and ALT after treatment with pioglitazone (10mg/kg) are 249.23±1.49 and 125.06±1.01 IU/L, Mangiferin alone was found to be as 56.055±1.96 and 76.55±1.57 IU/L, whereas for pioglitazone and Mangiferin treated group together was found to be as 167.54±1.66 and 106.17±1.53 IU/L respectively.

DISCUSSION

Drug interaction occurs when effect of one drug (object drug) is modified by the prior or concomitant administration of another drug (precipitant drug). Drug interaction may either enhance or diminish the intended effect of one or both drugs. It may modify the diagnostic, preventive or therapeutic activity of either drug (Kohler *et al.*, 2004). Patients suffering from chronic disease such as diabetes often consume herbal preparations along with routinely prescribed anti-diabetic agents. In recent years, there is an increasing consumption of herbal extracts like *Mangifera indica L.* that are often administered in combination with conventional therapeutic drugs (Rodeiro *et al.*, 2008).

The present study was undertaken to investigate the effect of Mangiferin on pharmacokinetic, Antidiabetic, and Hepatotoxicity of pioglitazone. Mangiferin was successfully isolated from ethanolic extract of *Mangifera indica* L. stem bark as per the earlier method explained by Dineshkumar *et al.*, (2010) with slight modification. The isolated Mangiferin was purified by re-crystallization and subjected for various spectral analysis, the various spectra obtained was well matched with the reference literature. Mangiferin has been reported to be potent alpha glucosidase inhibitor that has shown to inhibit elevated serum glucose levels. Mangiferin also shows modulation of certain P450 enzymes where the most of the drugs are metabolized (Rodeiro *et al.*, 2008). Several studies reported that *Mangifera indica* and its polyphenol compound Mangiferin possess anti-diabetic activity. Oral administration of aqueous extract (1g/kg) of *Mangifera indica* showed hypoglycemic activity in diabetic mice (Aderibigbe *et al.*, 2001). Mangiferin showed antidiabetic activity activity in KK-Ay mice and it could be useful for treatment of Type 2 diabetes (Ichiki *et al.*, 1998). Mangiferin, 1, 3, 6, 7-tetrahydroxyxanthone-C-2-β-D-glucoside, is one such naturally occurring polyphenol that is widely found in many herbs such as *Anemarrhena asphodeloides Bung* and *Mangifera indica L.* mangiferin. The natural C-glucoside xanthone compound mangiferin has been reported in various parts of *Mangifera indica* L. leaves, fruits, stem bark heartwood and roots. This pharmacologically-active compound occurs among different angiosperm families and ferns it is widely distributed in the Anacardiaceae and Gentianaceae families, especially in the leaves and the bark (Wauthoz *et al.*, 2007). Pharmacokinetic studies were carried out by measuring the plasma concentration of pioglitazone. Prior to drug interaction studies a single dose of pioglitazone was administered in rats and plasma concentration were obtained by plotting a dose relationship curve, Cmax and Tmax were calculated. It was found to be 0, 2.95, 14.46, 73.6, 2.60, 0 µg/ml at 0, 1, 2, 4, 8, 12, 18, 24 hrs respectively the values Cmax and Tmax were found to be 73.6 µg/ml at 4 hrs. The study was repeated along with Mangiferin and peak plasma concentration were found to be 14.018, 8.98, 75.6, 33.8, 20.3, 8.592, 1.14 µg/ml at 0, 1, 2, 4, 8, 12, 18, 24 hr respectively the values Cmax and Tmax were found to be 75.6 µg/ml at 4 hr. This increase in AUC suggests the possibility of drug-drug interaction between the two. Data suggests that pioglitazone is primarily metabolized by cytochrome P450 (CYP) 2C8 isozyme and to lesser extent CPY3A4 contributing as a minor pathway (http://www.actos.com/pi.pdf, 2004). Mangiferin is a weak inhibitor of CYP3A4, because of cytrochrome P450 inhibition, pioglitazone a oral hypoglycemic agent is expected to have decreased metabolism during

Mangiferin administration. Moreover pioglitazone is contraindicated in patients with liver failure. Component of Stem bark extract of *Mangifera indica* exhibited antioxidant properties (Ichiki *et al.*, 1998). In the view of above-mentioned point we have investigated hypoglycemic activity and hepatotoxicity activity of pioglitazone with and without Mangiferin.

Effect of Mangiferin on hypoglycemic activity of pioglitazone was done by measuring the blood glucose level. Pioglitazone at a fixed dose of (10mg/kg) and Mangiferin (200mg/kg) were given to study the effect on blood glucose level and percentage of reduction in blood glucose level was observed comparatively higher than when given pioglitazone alone. Mangiferin alone was studied for Antidiabetic effect but there was no reduction in blood glucose level in acute study. Mangiferin pretreatment has significantly altered the onset of Antidiabetic effect of Pioglitazone from 26.67% to 31.5% and significantly enhanced peak Antidiabetic effect from 69.25 to 73.99%. duration of action was raised from more than 24 hrs. Literature survey shows that long-term treatment with pioglitazone could lead to hepatocellular injury. In post marketing surveillance with pioglitazone reports of hepatitis as well as elevations of hepatic enzymes to 2 or more times the upper limits of the normal have been reported. In the study undertaken pioglitazone caused 2 folds increased in the ALT and AST level while histopathological examinations show mild to moderate congestion. It was observed that co administration of these two drugs resulted in decreased ALT and AST enzyme level suggesting the hepatoprotective effect of Mangiferin which was proved in literature earlier. The major basis of drug-drug interaction of Mangiferin is due to inhibition of CYP enzymes. In this study Alpha glucosidase inhibitor mangiferin positively influence the pharmacokinetic and anti-diabetic activity of Pioglitazone in diabetic rats. Therefore, precaution should be exercised when co-administering Mangiferin with Pioglitazone. It is necessary to adopt therapeutic drug monitoring so as to readjust dose and frequency of administration of these drugs, when they are used concomitantly to avoid the patients from severe hypoglycemia.

CONCLUSION

The Mangiferin is isolated from the stem bark of *Mangifera Indica* and purified by recrystalization. The purified Mangiferin when compared with the FTIR spectra, GCMS spectrum, UV spectrum, and HPLC chromatogram of standard Mangiferin, the sample (isolated Mangiferin) showed almost similar peaks as that of standard Mangiferin. The isolated Xanthone compound Mangiferin was found to be CYP enzyme inhibitor by observing its effect on the pharmacokinetic and hypoglycemic activity of Pioglitazone in experimental animals. Mangiferin increased the AUC and Cmax, of Pioglitazone. Mangiferin and Pioglitazone when they used concomitantly the reduction in the blood glucose level is almost same at 4th hr as compare to the pioglitazone alone treated group, but the duration of antidiabetic effect was raised. Alpha Glucosidase inhibitor mangiferin positively influence the anti-diabetic activity of Pioglitazone in diabetic rats. The hepatotoxicity of Pioglitazone is also measured along with Mangiferin and it was found that Mangiferin reduces the level of liver marker enzymes AST and ALT when given alone and with Pioglitazone in non diabetic albino rats. The study indicates that Mangiferin reduces the hepatotoxicity effect produced by pioglitazone. Therefore, precaution should be exercised when co-administering Mangiferin with Pioglitazone. It is necessary to adopt therapeutic drug monitoring so as to readjust dose and frequency of administration of these drugs, when they are used concomitantly to avoid the patients from severe hypoglycemia.

REFERENCES

Alan, S., Nies, Stephan, Spielberg, P., 2001 Principles of Therapeutics: Goodman and Gilman's the Pharmacological basis of Therapeutics, Tenth ed. McGraw Hill, New York, pp. 45-65.

Andreu, G., P., Delgudo, R., Velho, J.A., Curtic, Verusi, A.E., 2005. Iron Complexing Activity of Mangiferin, a Naturally Occurring glucosylxanthone, inhibit mitochondrial Lipid Peroxidation induced by Fe (2+)-citrate. Eur J Pharmacology 47, 513.

Chaudhari, R.K., Ghosal, S., 1971. Xanthone of Canscora Decussate Schutt. Phytochemistry 10, 2425-2432.

Chilcott, J., Tappenden, P., Lloyd, M., Wight, J.,P., 2001. A Systemic Review of the Clinical Effectiveness of Pioglitazone in the Treatment of type-2 diabetes Mellitus. Clin Ther 23, 1792-1823.

Dineshkumar, B., Mitra, A., Manjunatha, M., 2010. Studies on the Anti-diabetic and Hypolipidemic Potentials of Mangiferin (Xanthone Glucoside) in Streptozotocin-induced Type 1 and Type 2 diabetic model rats. Int J adv pharma sci 1, 75-85.

Ghua, S., Ghosal, S., Chattopadhyay, U., 1996. Antitumor, Immunomodulatory and Anti-HIV Effect of Mangiferin, A Naturally Occurring Glucosylxanthone. Chemotheraphy 42, 443-451.

Hou, Y., Fan, S., Zhang, H., Gu, Y., Yu, Xuhui, Li, Baoxin, 2010. Pharmacokinetic Study of Mangiferin in Rat Plasma and Retina using High-performance Liquid Chromatography. Molecular Vision16, 1659-1668.

Ichiki, H., Miura, T., Kubo, M., Ishihara, E., Komatsu, Y., Tanigawa, K., Okada, M., 1998. New Antidiabetic Compounds, Mangiferin and its Glucoside. Biol Pharn Bull 12, 1389-1390.

Kohler G.I., Bode-Boger S.M., Busse R., Hoopmann M., Welte T., Boger R.H., 2004. Elements of Clinical Pharmacy, First ed. BS Shah Prakashan, Ahmadabad, pp. 135-48.

Leiro, J., Arranz, J.A., Yanez. M., Ubeira, F.M., Sanmartin, M.L., Orallo. F., 2004. Expression Profiles of Genes Involved in the Mouse Nuclear Factor-kappa B Signal Transduction Pathway are Modulated by Mangiferin. Int J Immunopharmacol 4, 763-778.

Miura, T., Ichiki, H., Iwamoto, N., Kato, M., Kubo, M., Sasaki, H., *et al.*, 2001. Antidiabetic Activity of Rhizome of *Anemarrhena asphodeloides* and Active Components, Mangiferin and its Glucoside. Biol Pharma Bull 24, 1009-1011.

Muruganand, S., Gupta, S., Kataria, M., Lal, J., Gupta, P.K., 2002. Mangiferin Protects the Strepozotocin induced Oxidative Damage to Cardiac and Renal Tissues in Rats. Toxicology 176, 165-173.

Nunez, A.J., Velez, H.T., Aguero, A.J., Gonzalez, G.J., Naddeo, F., Simone, D.F., Rastrelli, L., 2002 Isolation and Quanatitative Analysis of Phenolic Antioxidants, Free Sugars, and Polyols from Mango (*Mangifera indica* L) Stem Bark Aqueous Decoction used in Cuba as a Nutritional Supplement. J Agri Food Chem 50, 762.

Rang, H.P., Dale, M.M., Ritter, J.M., Moore, P.K., 2005. Pharmacology, sixth ed. Churchill Livingstone, New Delhi, pp. 407-408.

Rodeiro, I., Donoto, M.,T., Lahoz, A., Gonzalez-Lavaut, J.A., Laguma, A., Castell, J.V., *et al.*, 2008. Modulation of P450 Enzymes by Cuban Natural Products Rich in Polyphenolic Compounds in Rat Hepatocytes. Chem. Biol Interact 172, 1-10.

Sanchez, G.M., Giuliani, A., Nunez-Selles, A.J., Davison, G.P., Leon-Farnandez, O.S., 2000. Protective Effect of *Mangifera indica* L. Extracts, Mangiferin and Selected Antioxidants Against TPA-induced Biomolecules Oxidation and Peritoneal Macrophage Activation in Mice. Pharmacol Res 42, 565-573.

Singh, S.K., Kumar, Y., Sadish, K.S., Sharma, V.K., Dua, K., Samad, A., 2009. Antimicrobial Evolution of Mangiferin Analogues. Ind J Pharm 71, 328-331.

Smith, U., 2001. Pioglitazone: Mechanism of Action. Int J Clin Pract Suppl 121, 13-8.

Sripalakit, P., Neamhomb, P., Saraphanchotiwitthaya, A., 2006. High-performance Liquid Chromatographic method for the Determination of Pioglitazone in Human Plasma using Ultraviolet Detection and its Application to a Pharmacokinetic Study. J Chromatogr B 843, 164-169.

Sunilkumar, B., Lucia, P., Miglani, B.D., 1998. Possible Drug Interactions in Hospitalized Patients. The Ind J Hos Pharm 1, 91-93.

Takeda Pharmaceutical Company Limited, Actos®, 2004. Pioglitazone Hydrochloride. Full Prescribing Information. http://www.actos.com/pi.pdf/(accessed 19.12.2010).

Wauthoz, N., Balde, A., Balde, E.S., Damme, M.V., Duez, P., 2007. Ethnopharmacology of *Mangifera indica* L. Bark and Pharmacological Studies of its Main CGlucosylxanthone, Mangiferin. Int J Biomed Phamaceut Sci 1, 112-119.

Yoshikawa, M., Nishida, N., Shimoda, H., Takada, M., Kawahara, Y., Matsuda, H., 2001. Polyphenol Constituents from Salacia Spices: Quantitative Analysis of Mangiferin with Alpha-glucosidase and Aldose Reductase Inhibitor Activities. Yakugaku Zassni 121, 371-378.

Zheng, Lu YU, 1990. Antiviral Effect of Mangiferin and Isomangiferin on Herpes Simplex Virus. Chinese Med J 103, 160-165.

Sangeetha, K., Sujatha, S., Muthusamy, V., Anand, S., Nithya, N., Velmurugan, D., Balakrishnan, A., Lakshmi, B., 2010. 3beta-taraxerol of *Mangifera indica*, a PI3K Dependent dual Activator of Glucose Transport and Glycogen Synthesis in 3T3-L1 adipocytes. Biochim. Biophys. Acta. 1800, 359-366.

Pages: 106-114

Animal Biodiversity and Fisheries
Edited by: **Dr. Rashmi Tripathi; Dr. Vijay Sharma & Dr. Pawan Kumar 'Bharti'**
ISBN: 978-93-88854-06-1
Edition: **2019**
Published by: **Discovery Publishing House Pvt. Ltd., New Delhi (India)**

6

Impact of Environmental Acidic Ph on Oxygen Consumption Inan Air Breathing Murrel Fish *Channa Gachua*

Qaisur Rahman

ABSTRACT

Fishes are amongst the most diverse groups of fresh water in theworld. Among them, several groups developed air breathing mechanisms toavoid low oxygen constraints, which are common in fresh waters. These include fishes one of the most diverse groups in the world with more than 1200 species described. Such diversity is reflected also in feeding habits, fish size, swimming performance and breathing patterns, among others. The obligatory air breathing habit in the family channidae is an adaptation to low oxygen environments. Fish of this family is capable to use its stomach as a gas exchanger. Water breathing fishes, which are more active fishes in contrast are not supposed to be hypoxia tolerant fishes but are often found in hypoxic environments. The present study was aimed to investigate the total oxygen consumption of freshwater fish *Channa gachua* during exposure and acclimation to sublethal acidic pH (5.0) medium. The oxygen consumption of fish significantly depleted in all the days of exposure to sublethal acidic pH 5.0 starting from first day to fourteen days of exposure. The rate of total oxygen consumption depletion was higher on first day. From the secondday onwards a gradual decreasing trend was observed in the depletion up to 14th day of exposure. The unit of oxygen consumption of fish depends on exposure to sub lethal pH medium exhibited significant depletion when compared to control. The rate of depletion was maximumin the initial days of exposure and was reduced gradually in twelfth and fourteenth day of exposure. But at day 14th not significant decrease was observed inboth the parameters of the experimentation. This observation indicates that the fish was capable of regulatingtheir metabolic modulations

University Department of Zoology, Vinoba Bhave University, Hazaribag - 825 301 Jharkhand (India)

and physiological functions through acclimation process to be the possible reason for the successful survival of fish in acidifying water.The reduced oxygen consumption of fish on exposure to sublethal acidic medium confirms the prevalence of hypoxic condition in the surrounding medium.

Keywords: Acidic pH, oxygen consumption,*Channagachua.*

INTRODUCTION

Most of the water bodies are polluted by heavy load of industrial effluents, sewage and chemicals of industries in metropolitan cities. Water is essential for all living organisms to perform all life functions but if aquatic organisms are exposed to toxic water contents then their physiology and biochemical processes were affected badly. All these chemicals interact in various ways with cells and they can be detected by chemical analysis only. Water quality i.e. hardness, oxygen, temperature, pH etc. has a marked influence on the expression of toxicity as reported by Qaisur and Shamim (2014).The bimodal breathing system may be defined as the one in which an organ or organs of the fish at a given stage of life history utilizes both water and air in its gas exchange mechanisms. The same environmental pressure that caused the development of different air breathing mechanisms is considered to induce long and short term adaptations in fishesby Qaisurand Sadhu (2012). These adaptations are the result of adjustments in biochemical, physiological and molecular characteristics and enable the fish of the river to survive episodes of hypoxia. Environmental stress is of prime importance during the course of exposure of an animal to different acidic media by Qaisur (2011) respectively. The measure which indicates whether water is acidic or basic is known as pH. More precisely pH indicates the hydrogen ion concentration in water and is defined as the negative logarithm of the molar hydrogen ion concentration [-log H^+]. Water is considered acidic when pH is below 7 and basic when pH is above 7. Most pH values encountered fall between zero and 14. The recommended pH range for aquaculture is 6.5 to 9.0. The fish and other vertebrates have an average blood pH of 7.4 and fish blood comes into close contact with water (1 or 2 cell separation) as it passes through the blood vessels of the gills and skin. A desirable range for pond water pH would be close to that of fish blood (i.e. 7.0 to 8.0). Fish may become stressed and die if the pH drops below 5 (e.g. acidic runoff) or rises above 10 (e.g. low alkalinity combined with intense photosynthesis by dense algal blooms phytoplankton or filamentous algae by Boyd (1979). The acidic medium is known to be the highly influencing to the most organisms and therefore low pH of aquatic medium is an important aspect of environmental pollution. The oxygen consumption in fish has been considered as an index for denoting the intensity of metabolism as metabolic activity of an organism is increased by its oxygen utilization Bijay *et al.*,(2003). Respiration is an essential physiological activity of all the living organisms by which they obtain energy for carrying out all metabolic activities of the body Bhaskar and Govindappa (1985) and Krishna Murthy (1991). The rate of oxygen consumption which is the basic physiological parameterserves as an indicator of physiological stress Bhaskarand Govindappa (1985) and changes in the oxygen consumptioncould be used to evaluate any change that would occurin themetabolismdue to alterations in the environment. Such stresses like acidic mediumhave been studied by SreenivasaReddy *et al.*, (2008) pesticides by Roberts *et al.*, (1987) heavy metals by Venkata Reddy *et al.*, (2007) pulp mill effluents by Reeta *et al.* (2011) hydrocarbons by Percy (1977) and natural stresses like temperature and salinity by Bashamohideen (1984). Thus variations in respiratory activity have been used as sensitive indicators of stress in fish exposed to pollutants, in general Bashamohideen(1984) and Qaisur (2011) respectively. The above studies unequivocally suggest that the sensitive indicator of stress like oxygen consumption in fishes exposedto pollutants is considerably increased and decreased but studies involving the oxygen consumption of the whole animal with reference to sublethal effect of acidicmedia is very few in fisheswhich are of great commercial and economical value. Hence, an attempt is made in the present investigation to study the influence of acidic media on certain aspects of oxygen consumption in an air breathing fish *Channagachua* following exposure to the sublethal concentration of acidic medium atdifferent exposure periods.

MATERIALS AND METHODS

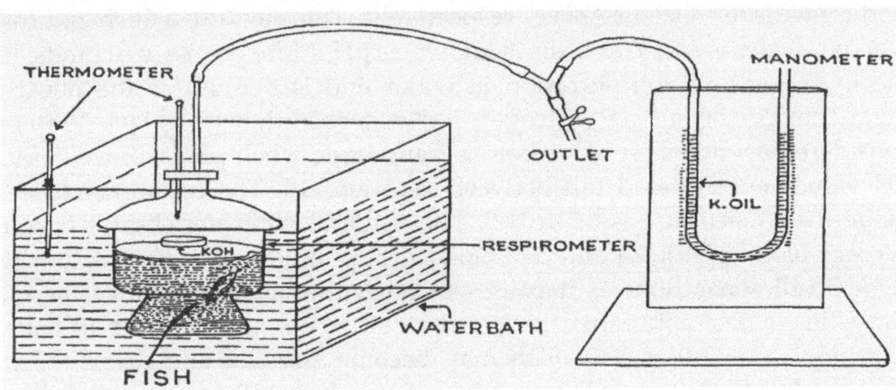

Fig. 6.1: Experimental set up for the measurements of dual mode of oxygen uptake in *Channagachua*

Live specimens of *Channagachua* were procured from local fish dealers at Hazaribag (Latitude 25° 59′N and Longitude 85° 22′E) and maintained in large glass aquaria size (90×60×60cm) with continuous flow of water. The specimens were fed on chopped goat liver daily during a minimum acclimation period of 15 days in the laboratory. Routine oxygen consumption from air and still water was measured in a closed glass respirometer containing 3 litres of water (initial O_2 content = 6.5 mg O_2/litreand pH = 7.2) and 0.51 mL of air (Fig. 6.1). The fish had free access to air through a small semicircularhole(10 cm diameter) in a disc float.Carbosorb (B.D.H) or KOH in a petridish placed on the float to absorbed CO_2. Thus the fish could exchange gases with water by way of its gills as well as with the air using the supra branchial chamber. The air phase of respirometer was connected to a differential manometer. Movement of the manometer fluid follow uptake of oxygen when the CO_2 is absorbed by Carbosorb (KOH). The fish were acclimated to the respirometers for at least 12 hours before the readings were taken. The concentration of dissolved oxygen in the water was estimated by Winkler's volumetric method Welch (1948). The oxygen uptake through gills was calculated from the difference between the oxygen levels of the ambient water in the respirometer before and after the experiment and the reading of volume of water in the respirometer. The oxygen uptake from air was measured and calculated from the reading of volume change in the manometer and by the use of the combined gas law equations and vapour pressureQaisurand Sadhu (2012). Mean values of VO_2 of a series of observations, on each fish at standard temperature pressure dry and standard errors were calculated. The experiments were conducted at 29.0 ± 1.5ºC. The pH of the ambient water was measured by an electronic pH meter systronics. The respiratory chambers were thermostated by immersion in a temperature controlled water bath. However, sexually mature *Channagachua* of almost same weight group 70-90 grams were used. The experimental individuals were divided into different groups on the basis of body weight and sex.The fish was kept in large aquaria with continuously following dechlorinated water to acclimatize them to laboratory conditions of 12 hours per day for fifteen days before they were used for experimentation. This fish is known for its adaptability to laboratory conditions and suitability to acidic media studies Bhaskar and Govindappa (1985). Hence, this fish was selected as the experimental model for the present investigation. As the smaller fish are considered to be more sensitive to toxic pollutants rather than larger one Anderson and Weber (1975) small sized fish weighing around 200 ± 50g were selected for the present investigation. After 24hours of the stipulated period, the fish were immediately used for the estimation of oxygen consumption and unit oxygen consumption in different aquatic pH media.The acidic mediawith different pH ranging between 3.0 and 7.0 with variabilityof 0.5 were prepared by adding 1 N hydrochloric acid to water. 1 N solution of hydrochloric acid was prepared separatelywith distilled water (pH=7.0) soft water chlorides (110 mg/L ± 10) carbonates (16mg/L ± 2) bicarbonates (400 mg/L ± 50) and hardness (35mg/L as $CaCO_3$± 4). The 1 N HCL was added for the purpose of obtaining different acidic media mentioned above and their pH was verified with pHmeter Elico India. As the chloride ions are least toxic hydrochloric acid was used widely for the preparation of acid media Jones (1968).

The water media having different pH range of 3.0 to 7.0 with variability of ± 0.5 pH were taken. For each pH medium in the above range 10 separate tankswere maintainedwith fisheach tank containing 10 individuals. The fishes were fed daily at 8 am with commercial fish foods and the medium in the tanks was changed at 9 a.m. The pH of the media was maintained constantly by employing special dropping system during experimentation. The number of fishdied in each of the above media was recorded at regular intervals of time up to 96 hours. The percentage ofmortality was calculated on the basis of individuals that died at each time interval. The media where the mortality of the fish was observed were taken as lethal mediaand the others where there was no mortality were taken as sublethalmedia. The oxygen consumption was determined during the temporal sequence of exposure starting from the first day till the maintenance of constant oxygen consumption by the fish on the 10th day to 14th day respectively. The sub lethal acidic media (pH=5.0) was employed as an ambient medium for acclimatization of the fish. The fish were fed daily at 8 a.m. with commercial fish food and the medium in the tanks was changed at 9 a.m. The fish were taken into the respiratory chamber containing the same pH medium at 2.00 p.m. on alternate days and the oxygen consumption was determined within a period of 1hour. After this the fishwere transferred into their respective tanks. The oxygen consumption was determined during the temporal sequence of exposure starting from the first day till the maintenance of constant oxygen consumption by the fish on the10^{th} day to 14th day. Similarly control fish in the neutral pH=7.0 were maintained and their oxygen consumption was also studied individually over the temporal sequence of time as done in the case of fish maintained under sublethal acidic media.The oxygen consumption of fish was determined by the static method describedby Qaisur (2011).The unit oxygen consumption was calculated by dividing the oxygen consumption by weight of the fish and represent asmg O_2/kg/h. All the values of-t-below 5 percent levels are considered as not significant and the value above 5 percent level is considered as significant.

RESULTS AND DISCUSSION

The pH of water plays an important role in regulation of growth and development of aquatic animals. The present study was aimed to find out the relationship between environmental acidification on the growth and development of *Channagachua*.The measurement of oxygen consumption becomes a marker to understand the overall changes that takes place in thewhole body on exposure to any stress condition. Several investigators (Sailaja *et al.*, 2009; Chavan *et al.*, 2011; Sathick *et al.*, 2011; Sindhe *et al.*,2011) reported that the level of whole oxygen consumption was an index for metabolic modulations that take place in the body on exposure to acidic stress.

The data presented in Tables 6.1 and 6.2 show changes in the total oxygen consumption and unit oxygen consumption of the freshwater fish during exposure to sublethal acidic (pH=5.0) media. The total oxygen consumption was significantlydecreased on first day of exposure to sublethal acidic (pH=5.0) medium and exhibited a non-significant change over control on 14th day of exposure. This observation indicates that the fish was capable of regulating their metabolic modulations and physiological functions through acclimation process to compensate the acidic stress imposed by the external media, which might be the possible reason for the successful survival of fish in acidified water. Decrease in total oxygen consumption might be due to hypoxic condition prevailed in external media. Another reason might be due to reduced gaseous exchange through gill surface because of excessive formation of mucous Suchismita and Gupta (2012). The other alternative could be the reduced oxygen carrying capacity of the blood due to altered blood pH on exposure to acidic media. Several investigators also reported earlier in supporting to the present study that decreased ability of fish to extract oxygen from low pH waters Packer and Dunson (1972) and Sailaja *et al.*,(2009) respectively. Investigator like Qaisur and Sadhu (2012) in *Channagachua* experimentally shown that one of the causes of thermal death is the osmoregulatory failure at temperature extremes. In a changed environmental condition organism tries to adapt and adjust to sustain its life is called acclimatization. It must try to prevent or minimise changes in its body temperature is called thermoregulation. Changes in the environment and its composition compel the fish to alter its body physiology and biochemistry in order to cope up with this novel threat.

Table 6.1: Changes of oxygen consumption during different days of exposuresin *Channagachua*

S. No.	Time in Days	Control (pH< 7.0)	Sub-lethal (pH< 5.0)	Significant value P<0.001
1.	1	0.2780±0.0510	0.1675±0.0104	-39.74
2.	2	0.2730±0.0160	0.1528±0.0115	-44.02
3.	4	0.2784±0.0144	0.1722±0.0092	-38.14
4.	6	0.2752±0.0181	0.1912±0.0128	-30.52
5.	8	0.2719±0.0161	0.2081±0.0156	-23.46
6.	10	0.2792±0.0169	0.2145±0.0144	-23.17
7.	12	0.2821±0.0150	0.2391±0.0154	-15.24 N.S*
8.	14	0.2791±0.0122	0.2391±0.0154	-44.02 N.S*

Mean ± SD, + and - indicates percentage increase and decreasep<0.001and 'NS* indicates non-significant.

Table 6.2: Changes of oxygen consumption during different day of exposure in *Channagachua*

S. No.	Time in Days	Control (pH< 7.0)	Sub-lethal (pH< 5.0)	Significant value P<0.001
1.	1	3.7252±0.0221	2.8420±0.1310	-23.70
2.	2	3.8224±0.0425	2.6051±0.1202	-31.84
3.	4	3.7235±0.0421	2.9752±0.1081	-20.09
4.	6	3.7210±0.0521	3.0244±0.0951	-18.72
5.	8	3.8314±0.0512	3.1652±0.0951	-17.38
6.	10	3.7935±0.0131	3.2826±0.0710	-13.46
7.	12	3.7624±0.0831	3.3789±0.1710	-10.19
8.	14	3.7416±0.0626	3.5914±0.1430	-4.01N.S*

Mean ± SD, + and - indicates percentage increase and decrease, p<0.001and 'NS* indicates non-significant.

Qaisur (2011) reported that the reduced oxygen consumption of fish *Channagachua* on exposure to sublethal acidic media confirms that prevalence of hypoxic condition in the surrounding media. Since the unit oxygen consumption also exhibited similar depletion trend it suggests the possibility of existence of hypoxic condition. The unit oxygen consumption of fish also exhibited non-significant change on 14th day of exposure. This observation supports and forms a basic evidence for the perfect type of acclimation by adults. Since the total oxygen consumption in animals forms a marker for the general metabolism the stabilization of total oxygen consumption on 14th days-exposed fish reflects the maintenance of normal oxygen consumption on par with the control fish. Hence, two weeks period of exposure to fish to acidic media made successful in survival through acclimation process, failure of such a regulatory mechanism, might be responsible for the mortality of fish in lethal pH media.In view of acclimation of fish to acidic media provided better metabolic adjustments at whole animal level reveal the better survival value. Thus, the changes in oxygen consumption could reflect the effect of acidic media on theaquatic fauna especially in fishes.Information on temperature tolerance and resistance is of much value in judging the eco-physiological characteristics of fishes. Qaisurand Shamim (2017) reported that in *Channagachua* the behavioural characteristics are obviously sensitive indicators of toxicant effect. It is necessary however, to select behavioural indices of monitoring that relate to the organisms behaviour in the field in order to derive a more accurate assessment of the hazards that a contaminant may pose in natural system, should be considered for species forming social organizational. If social interactions are not considered, only a certain portion of a population may be protected, and the toxicity of contaminant may be under estimated and also primarily influence modulations in the level of oxygen consumption. This also provides a platform to establish tolerable limits and safe levels of toxic agents for the biota of aquatic environment and to save the residue imbalance in aquatic bio-ecological cycles which help in involving bio detector monitoring.

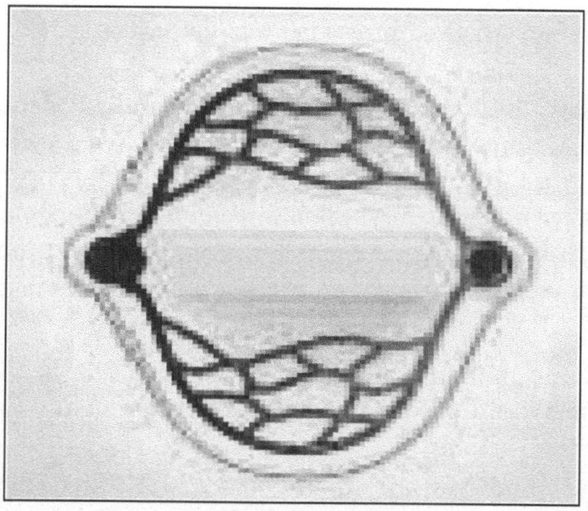

Graph 6.1: Gills of *Channagachua* showing large respiratory surface area and counter current exchange

REFERENCES

Anderson, P.D and Weber, L.J. 1975. Toxic Response as a Quantitative Function of Body size. *Toxicol. Appl. Pharmacol.*33: 471-483.

Bashamohideen, Md. 1984. Physiological Mechanisms and Behavioural Pattern during Environmental Stress and Environmental Adaptations. In: Bulletin Ethological Society of India (Vol. III) Studies in Animal Behaviour (Ed.B.S. Raoand C.S. Shetty) pp. 147-152.

Bhaskar, M. and Govindappa, S. 1985. Acclimation to Sublethal Acidic and Alkaline Media of *Tilapia mossambica* (Peters) Changes in Glycogen Metabolism of Red Muscle. *Bull. Environ. Contam.Toxicol.* 37: 113-119.

Bijay Bhushan P., Mandip and Roy, K.R. 2003. Effect of Copper Sulphate and Potassium Dichromate on Oxygen Consumption of the Air Breathing Fish *Channagachua.J.Ecotoxicol. Environ. Monit.*16(1): 71-76.

Boyd Claude E. 1979.Water Quality in Warmwater Fish pond. Auburn University, Agricultural Experiment Station.

Chavan, P.N., Afsar, S.K., Jagtap, A.R. and Mali, R.P. 2011. Effect of Temperature and Body Size on Oxygen Consumption of Freshwater Fish *Oreochromis mossambicus* from Godavari river at Nanded. *J.Ecotoxicol. Environ. Monit.*21(5): 475-480.

Jones, J.R.F. 1968. Acids and Alkaline pH Tolerance Limits. In: Fish and River Pollution. Butterworth, Co. Ltd., Canada. pp. 107-117.

Krishna Murthy, C.R. 1981. Symposium Proceedings. *Ind.J. Bio.Phys.Biochem.* 8(4): 245.

Packer, R.K. and Dunson,W.A. 1972. Anoxia and Sodium Loss Associated with Death of Brook Trout. *J.Comp. Biochem. Physiol.*, 41A: 17-26.

Percy, J.A. 1977. Fate and Effect of Petroleum Hydrocarbons in Marine Organism and Ecosystem. *J. Exp. Bio.* pp. 192-200.

Qaisur R., 2011. Studies on some Factors Affecting Aerial and Aquatic Respiration in an Air Breathing Fish *Channagachua* (Ham.) Ph.D.Thesis,Vinoba Bhave University, Hazaribag, Jharkhand, India.

Qaisur R., and Sadhu D.N. 2012. Factors Affecting Aerial and Aquatic Respiration in the Air Breathing Fish *Channagachua*. *J. Ecotoxicol. Environ. Monit.* 22(1): 17-30.

Qaisur R. and Shamim A.C. 2014. Impact of Zinc Sulphate on Biochemical Parameters in Reproductive Cycle in an Air Breathing Fish *Channagachua.J. Himalayan Ecol. Sustain. Dev.* 9: 74-80.

Qaisur R. and Shamim A.C. 2017. Impact of Sodium Cyanideon Behavior and Oxygen Consumption in an Air Breathing Fish *Channagachua.J.Res. Dev.*17: 35-45.

Reeta K., Pathak, R.N. and Rani, P. 2011. Ecological Status of River Daha in North Bihar and its Effects on Fish Diversity. *Nat. Environ.Poll. Tech.*10(2): 293-295.

Roberts, M.H.Jr., Sved, D.W., and Felston, S.P. 1987. Temporal Changes in AHHand SOD Activities in Feral Spot from the Elizabeth River a Polluted Sub Estuary. *Mar. Environ. Res.* 23: 89-101.

Sailaja, V., Madhuri, E., Ramesh Babu, Ramakrishna, K.S. and Bhaskar, M. 2009. Impact of Altered pH Media on Mortality Rate Oxygen Consumption and Excretion in Prawn. *Ecol. Environ. Conser.*15(1): 153-157.

Sathick, O., Raveendran, S. and Muthukumaravel, K. 2011. Effect of Pesticiderogar on Oxygen Consumption and Gill Histology of the Estuarine fish *Mystusgulio.J.Ecotoxicol. Environ.Monit.* 21(5): 409-414.

Sindhe, S.C.S., Butchiram, M.S., Jagadeesh Naik, M. and Indira P. 2011. Effect of Sub Lethal Concentration of Ziram on Oxygen Consumption of the Freshwater Fish *Labeorohita. J.Ecotoxicol. Environ.Monit.*21(1&2): 77-81.

Sreenivasa Reddy, A., Venkata Reddy, M. and Radhakrishnaiah, K. 2008. Impact of Copper on the Oxidative Metabolism of the Fry of Common carp *Cyprinuscarpio*(Linn.) at different PH level.*J. Environ. Biol.*29(5): 721-724.

Suchismita D., and Abhik G., 2012. Effect of Cadmium Chloride on Oxygen Consumption and Gill Morphology of Indian Flying barb *Esomusdandricus. J. Environ. Biol.*33: 1057-1061.

Venkata Reddy, M., Sreenivasa Reddy, A. and Radhakrishnaiah, K. 2007. Nickel induced Changes in Protein Metabolism of the snail *Pilaglobosa* (Swanson) *Asian J. Environ Sci.*2 (1&2): 21-27.

Welch, P.S. 1948. Limnological methods. Mcgraw Hill Book Co.Inc. New York.London. pp. 206-213.

Pages: 115-134

Animal Biodiversity and Fisheries

Edited by: **Dr. Rashmi Tripathi; Dr. Vijay Sharma & Dr. Pawan Kumar 'Bharti'**

ISBN: 978-93-88854-06-1

Edition: **2019**

Published by: **Discovery Publishing House Pvt. Ltd., New Delhi (India)**

7 Collection of Giant Prawn Seeds from Tidal Rivers and Mullet Farming – Two Established Livelihood-generating Activities in Sundarbans Region, West Bengal

Subrato Ghosh

ABSTRACT

In West Bengal (WB), the giant prawn *M. rosenbergii* seeds are available naturally in lower reaches of river Hooghly, in river Rupnarayan and in tidal rivers of Indian Sundarbans region in South 24 Parganas, which are commercially exploited by local professional giant prawn seed collectors and sold to prawn farmers. Professional *M. rosenbergii* farmers in South and North 24 Parganas and Purba Medinipur districts believe that giant prawn seeds collected from nature have much better performance in terms of growth and survivability than the hatchery-produced seeds. *Mullets (Liza sp. and Mugil sp.) or the coastal marine finfishes are excellent candidate finfish species for enhancement of aquaculture production in earthen brackishwater ponds in WB. Like sea bass, mullets too have a good market and can be produced at a low cost.* Collection of wild giant prawn seeds (post-larvae and juveniles) and pond culture of mullets have become established, sustainable and profitable livelihood-generating activities in Indian Sundarbans, which spread itself amidst North and South 24 Parganas districts in WB. Intimate conversation was made on-site with people engaged in such profession and information gathered has been lucidly described in this communication.

Macrobrachium rosenbergii Seeds

The giant prawn *Macrobrachium rosenbergii* is a suitable species for commercial pond aquaculture in WB and other states. It commands very good price in domestic market, has a fast growth rate and is noted for

Formerly Guest Lecturer, Master of Fishery Science Division, Utkal University, Bhubaneswar – 751 002, (Odisha) (India)

its compatibility to grow with major carps and lower susceptibility to diseases. It occurs in north-east coast, migrates to estuaries from Bay of Bengal for breeding. In nature, their breeding takes place in low saline waters of estuaries, thereafter larval survival and growth takes place only in brackishwater environment. After metamorphosis, post-larvae (PL; 10-15mm) migrate to freshwater habitats of rivers. Coastal tidal rivers, estuaries and Sundarban mangrove swamps are the main natural sources of giant prawn PL (Gain *et al.*, 2015). Peak breeding months of *M. rosenbergii* are March, April and May in Hooghly-Matla estuary. In WB, *M. rosenbergii* seed is available in natural sources in lower reaches of river Hooghly, in river Rupnarayan and in rivers of Indian Sundarbans region, and, as a practice, are commercially exploited by professional giant prawn seed collectors of those regions and sold to prawn farmers.

In Indian Sundarbans region, considerable information is available on the seed resources of tiger shrimp *Penaeus monodon*. Of course, in many areas, the seeds of *M. rosenbergii* are also available. Information on availability of *M. rosenbergii* seeds is not adequate. Recently culture of this species has gained importance in different brackishwater Blocks in Indian Sundarbans region. For this culture practice to take shape in a sustainable manner, the seed resources must be explored so that freshwater prawn farming can develop as a profitable enterprise. Since the culture of *M. rosenbergii* is getting momentum, for proper planning of culture of this species in freshwater impoundments, necessary information regarding the availability of seeds is required (Mahapatra *et al.*, 1995).

CREEKS AND BRACKISHWATER (TIDAL) RIVERS IN SOUTH 24 PARGANAS

In South 24 Parganas district of WB, *M. rosenbergii* seed collectors of Basanti, Kultali, Canning-I, Mathurapur-II and Diamond Harbour Blocks capture PL stage from brackishwater tidal rivers of Sundarbans region and lower stretches of river Hooghly at Diamond Harbour, where recruitment of PL is found. The Mridangabhanga river meets river Saptamukhi, and latter falls into Bay of Bengal. Nukchara nodi, Kakmara khal and Kuemuri creek are on the east of Mridangabhanga. Combination of Thikara khal, Banstara khal and Ghugudanga khal form the Saptamukhi. Major seven branches on its west are Kalnagini khal, Ghugudanga khal, Hatania-Doania creek, Patibunia creek, Edwards' creek, Chandanpiri khal and Bakkhali river. Channels and creeks on the west bank of Thakuran river are Kadrakhali khal, Moni river, Roydighi river, Sibua gang, Kali-Binmari khal, Jagadal river. Those on its east are Bainchapa khal, Guru khal, Kankalmari-Ajmalmari rivers, Dhulibasani gang, Kultoli gang, Gokultoli gang. Also in South 24 Parganas, rivers Raimangal, Bidyadhari, Jhilla, Kalindi and Jamuna, after originating from river Icchamati, spread out into wide estuaries in Sundarbans (Note: In South 24 Pgs, 'Gang' and 'Khal' are vernacular terms used for brackishwater rivulets).

Rainwater and run-off from the catchment are the only source of freshwater in Thakuran and other rivers in and around Indian Sundarbans. Decrease in salinity of the rivers occurs during monsoon; it is an effect of high monsoonal precipitation and subsequent runoff of rainwater into river basin. Salinity of Hooghly river water at Diamond Harbour is much less in comparison to that of afore-mentioned rivers/creeks.

FEATURES AND PRICE OF GIANT PRAWN PL OF RIVERS OF SOUTH 24 PGS

After the Kalboisakhi storm (occasionally accompanied by thunder), which takes place a few times every year during or slightly before the Bengali month of Boisakh (early April) in West Bengal, accompanied with north-westerly winds and wavy motion of riverine water, PL of *M. rosenbergii* 8-10mm size begins to be available in lower reaches of river Hooghly during March-April and/or April. In May, its quantity increases. During winter, river water remains calm but disquiet motion-like condition is observed in pre-monsoon time. According to Sri Buddhiswar Naskar, elderly giant prawn seed collector at Kultali Block, during March-April and April-May every year, occurrence of male PL is more (70-75%) in comparison to female PL; it fetches a very good demand and high price as males (possessing pair of giant chelate leg) attain larger size at times of harvest in grow-out monoculture prawn ponds (150gm within one year). Till May-June, these PL are sold @ Rs 1500-1600/-/1000nos, move swiftly in a circle in white porcelain dish. After the onset of monsoon, availability of PL increases further and their occurrence in other rivers is observed. In June-July, price reduces to Rs 500-600/-/1000nos., occurrence of female PL (50-55% of total quantity captured) is more. These attain 40-60gm in about eight months. During July-August and August, price of PL falls to Rs 200-250/-/1000nos. Generally, seeds obtained during June are stocked in monoculture ponds and harvested at end of 18 months to have high growth and size.

Every year, from early June (decrease in river salinity occurs after onset of monsoon), *M. rosenbergii* PL (8-10mm; white boiled rice grain size) is available in Piyali-Nabipukur and other brackishwater rivers in Indian Sundarbans region. Those are sold @ Rs 1000-1200/-/1000nos. and when stocked in grow-out ponds, 700 in every 1000nos. survive and reach adulthood stage/marketable size. The same is available in lower stretch of river Hooghly from March-April and caught at Nurpur village in Diamond Harbour-II Block and at Geonkhali; those are sold @ Rs 2400/-/1000nos. in the beginning phase to prawn farmers of Canning-I, Basanti, Kultali and other Blocks of this district. In culture ponds, 900 in every 1000nos. of these survive and reach 150-180gm in 8 months. Due to much lower salinity, availability of *M. rosenbergii* PL in Hooghly river occurs sooner (in point of time of year) in comparison to that in other afore-mentioned rivers (water of these rivers is saline as are influenced by high tides and low tides; they get more or less dry during low tide). In Sundarbans region, if onset of monsoon is delayed, availability of giant prawn PL in rivers will consequently be delayed. In June-July, prawn farmers pay Rs 2400/- for every 3100nos. PL. The same if procured during March-April and fed pellet-type supplementary feed, attain 90-140gm body weight in 8 months, excluding the weight of giant chelate legs. In auction markets, farm produced male *M. rosenbergii* large in size are weighed after the pair of chelate leg is detached from body, which is about 35-40gm.

Giant prawn PL captured from Bidyadhari, Gosaba, Raimangal, Herobhanga, Piyali-Nabipukur (tributary of river Matla) and other rivers are assembled for sale at Golabari and Nikarighata villages in Canning-I Block, Herobhanga, Delbari, Koikhali, Dongajora and Meriganj in Kultali, Amjhora and Sonakhali in Basanti, Modhukhali and Kelokhali in Gosaba Block. Some people catch 300-500nos. of PL, others capture more. These are the auction points for seeds of the economically important species *M. rosenbergii, Penaeus monodon, Mugil cephalus* (Rs 5-6/- per 1.5-2.0 inch size), *Liza parsia* (Rs 1500/-/kg; 8-10mm), *Liza macrolepis, Lates calcarifer*. Giant prawn PL is available in good quantity in Kella creek and near Kella, a small dam on Piyali river, which is near Dongajora in Kultali Block. PL 8mm size captured from Thakuran river during spring tide costs Re 1/- / piece in July-August. During monsoon, in every 24 hours, 5000-7000 PL are captured in stationary nets lengthing 50-52mts. Those are collected from nets in every 15mins. PL collected in March and March-April fetches high price, which attains 3.5-4.0 inch size by July-August. Those procured in June-July attain such a size in ponds in next five months.

During transportation of giant prawn PL to North 24 Parganas (Minakhan Block) and Howrah districts from Kultali and Basanti Blocks, seed collectors keep 8000nos. PL in 16 lits water in plastic drums; it remains alive and healthy for 18 hours, water replacement is done partially with deep tubewell water. Outside South 24 Parganas district, PL is sold at a price Rs 200/- higher of local price for every 1000nos. Giant prawn seeds (7mm) are supplied to Sri Nabin Barik at Sandeshkhali Block in empty 12lit milk containers or plastic biscuit containers; every 1000 seeds cost Rs 2000/-. These are stocked @ 30,000nos./3.5 decimal pond and in two months, these are reared to advanced juvenile stage and sold by Sri Barik @ Rs 5-6/-/piece. Mixture of soaked mustard oil cake and by-product of rice mills is fed to the growing stages daily @ 2kg/10000 seeds.

GROWTH OF RIVERINE PRAWN SEEDS IN FARM PONDS

In May 2015, Sri Ganesh Mondol, prawn farmer of Uttar Taldi village in Canning-I Block stocked 7500nos. of naturally-occurring *M. rosenbergii* seeds of 7-8mm size. It was bought (Rs. 1000/- per 1000 pieces) from prawn seed collectors in brackishwater region of Diamond Harbour, which is a low saline zone (≤2ppt). In January 2016, 120kg of marketable-size giant prawn was harvested (partial harvesting), those were found to attain 90-125gm in weight. It was sold locally @ Rs 500-550/-/kg. It attained 150gm on 14th month and in October 2016, those attained 200-250gm with giant blue claws and sold @ Rs 700-750/-/kg. In April 2017, Sri Mondol stocked 1000nos. of *M. rosenbergii* juveniles, 1.5-2.0 in size, riverine, Rs. 3.00/-/piece. It was captured at Amjhara village, located on opposite side of Canning river under Basanti Block. It attained 4 inches as on 8th July, 2017 and will be harvested at the end of six months from stocking. Additionally 2900nos. of hair-like post-larvae, lengthing 8-10mm were stocked in 1st week of June 2017, which were captured from river Roydighi in Mathurapur-II Block, bought in oxygen-packed condition @ Rs. 850/-/1000nos. It attained 1.5-2.0 inches in one month, and will grow to 75-120gm at the end of ten months. He uses less expensive 'Magic Fish Feed' brand prawn feed (2-3mm dia pellets), with 18-20% protein content, its cost is Rs 900/-/50kg sack and avoids inorganic fertilizers.

In Canning-II Block, fish farmers have experienced *M. rosenbergii* body weight of 70gm (on av.) in 6-8 months of culture in large ponds in association with major carps; early *M. rosenbergii* juveniles stocked @ 1000nos./33 dec pond. In July 2016, Sri Satyananda Maity, prawn farmer of Kultali Block procured 3700nos. of riverine *M. rosenbergii* PL (Rs 850/-) from local seed traders; those attained marketable size of 35-40gm in early January 2017 with no supplementary feed. Those were captured from tributaries of Mridangabhanga. In August, with further rainfall, salinity of paddy plots in Canning-I, Canning-II and adjacent Blocks decline. Seedlings of paddy are transplanted in such plots. Simultaneously early stages of Rohu, Catla, Mrigal, Silver carp and giant prawn when stocked in the ratio 0.6 : 0.6 : 1.2 : 1.1 : 6.5 at a total stocking rate of 23,500nos./ha, finfishes and giant prawn gave a yield of 510kg/ha in 85 days period (*Source:* Text Book on 'Perspective of Aquaculture Development in Sundarban delta' by P. Ray). Sri Narayan Maity of Satyanarayanpur village in Bali island of Gosaba Block has achieved success in producing 100-120gm *M. rosenbergii* in 7 months in 12-14 decimal rain-fed paddy plots.

RAISING PL TO JUVENILE STAGE

Some seed collectors rear the 8-10mg PL (8-12mm) to 1.0-1.5 inch size within four weeks in earthen chambers 7 feet × 4 feet × 2 feet, and sell them to prawn farmers. On 10th-12th day it attains blackish body colour. It has a high survivability rate in ponds. A black lateral band is found on the dorsal region of their body. Other collectors stock riverine PL obtained during March-April @ 50,000nos./33 dec in 10-12 dec earthen ponds and in next 50-60 days, those attain 3.0-3.5 inch size without feeding. It is sold to professional prawn farmers @ Rs 5-6/- / piece. *M. rosenbergii* PL is identified by the presence of dots in abdominal region. Presence of one/two blue dots in abdominal region are found in male PL, whereas female PL possesses brownish dots. If little amount of wheat flour is sprinkled in white porcelain dish containing different riverine prawn and shrimp PL, only *M. rosenbergii* PL will eat wheat flour and their intestinal tract near cephalic region will turn whitish, which is visible.

M. rosenbergii PL attain 2.0-3.0 inch size (6-8gm) in paddy fields or *Bheri* in 30-45 days in August-September and September, those are also sold to farmers @ Rs 5-6/- / juvenile. In Sundarbans region, during monsoon period, river water inflates during spring tide supported by monsoon downpour; it is let into agricultural tracts of 0.4-3.0 hectares *via* shallow water channels/canals (having provision of iron sluice gates) during full moon and new moon. Giant prawn PL 10-15mm in size enter and disperse in these tracts along with tidal water and water remains stagnant at 3.0-3.5 feet depth. Earth remains soft, which encourages growth of wild *M. rosenbergii* seeds upto larger juvenile stage. Those are captured in indigenous split bamboo-built traps. According to Sri Sujit Mridha, prawn farmer of Basanti Block, such juveniles attain 150-200gm at the end of one year in monoculture ponds, when stocked @ 25,000-30,000nos./ha and 40,000nos./ ha in farm ponds with paddle-wheel aerator facilities. Those are fed farm-made formulated feed comprising pulverized ground nut oil cake, powdered fish meal, shrimp meal, wheat flour and soyabean powder, or commercially available pelleted feed.

PRAWN SEEDS TRAPPED IN ENCLOSURES

In the Sundarbans, the bundhs are the most potential source of *M. rosenbergii* seeds. These bundhs or unique indigenous trapping devices are installed in the paddy fields and adjoining canals. In a bundh, different types of bamboo-made traps are fitted in the passage of giant freshwater prawn seeds. In a typical 9.15mt long bundh, 12 traps are systematically arranged. These are of two types, locally known as 'Chero' and 'Atol'. In Chero, seed collection is possible from one side only. Atols are rectangular structure and collections are taken from either side. The PL or early juveniles of this species found in the various rivers and rivulets often infiltrates into the adjoining paddy fields and canals when water is allowed in during high tide. The local prawn seed collectors and traders determine proper prices of it on the basis of gradation. According to gradations followed, grade-1 comprises *M. rosenbergii* of average length 148mm and average weight 30gm; grade-2 comprises seeds of av length 120mm and av weight 10gm and grade-3 comprises those of av length 85.5mm and av weight 9.65gm. Average collection of prawn seeds from a bundh is very high.

There is immense potentiality of *M. rosenbergii* seeds in the coastal belt of South 24 Parganas which is indicated by the innumerable number of bundhs located in this region. Seed prawns captured from the bundhs are larger in size (comprising 65.54% of total catch) and there is no need of their rearing in nurseries. Such size groups of *M. rosenbergii* are ideal for introduction in grow-out prawn monoculture ponds, composite fish culture and in paddy plots. Growing demand of giant prawn seeds in this region can be fulfilled by exploiting the potential bundhs in coastal South 24 Parganas judiciously (Mahapatra *et al.*, 1995).

Significance of *M. rosenbergi* Seed Collection

Professional *M. rosenbergii* farmers in South 24 Parganas, North 24 Parganas, Purba Medinipur and Howrah districts believe that giant prawn seeds collected from nature have much better performance in terms of growth and survivability than the hatchery-produced seeds. They prefer to stock PL or juveniles from riverine source. They purchase giant prawn seed from local fish seed/fry traders and also directly from the source. Farmers have experienced that hatchery-produced seeds cannot tolerate winter temperature. Riverine seeds have natural origin with strong vigour, greater capability to adapt new environmental condition. They are produced from large, strong and well-matured mother prawns of proper age. On 15th Jan 2018, author had a glimpse of aged adults of *M. rosenbergii* at Digha mohona fish market in Purba Medinipur, 300-350gm size, freshly captured from nearshore waters of Bay of Bengal.

Early fry of brackishwater finfishes like *Liza parsia, Mugil cephalus, Scatophagus argus, Mystus gulio, Glossogobius giuris, Rhinomugil corsula, Etroplus suratensis*; PL of *Metapenaeus monoceros, Metapeneaus brevicornis, Penaeus semisulcatus* are captured unintentionally in nets meant for collecting *M. rosenbergii* PL. Giant prawn seed collectors do not throw these away, instead they stock these stages in their small to medium-sized homestead parental ponds, old in existence, and propagate them following extensive method of farming. The rivers, numerous creeks, tidal inlets, marshes and estuaries of Sundarbans form a network and constitute its low saline brackish water body. *M. rosenbergii* has wider potentiality for culture in many brackish water areas of Indian Sundarban delta (Chand *et al.*, 2015). Low saline water culture at 4ppt and upto 7ppt has been found to be conducive for giant prawn farming, which gives better production and survival. The availability and exploitation of giant prawn post-larvae in river Hooghly and estuarine rivers of Dist. South 24 Parganas, WB has become a sustainable source of income in villages in and around Indian Sundarbans.

Prawn PL caught in Piyali-Nabipukur river

Much large sized farmed *M. rosenbergii*

Giant prawn (40-60gm size)

Giant prawn (50-100gm size)

Giant prawn (180-250gm size)

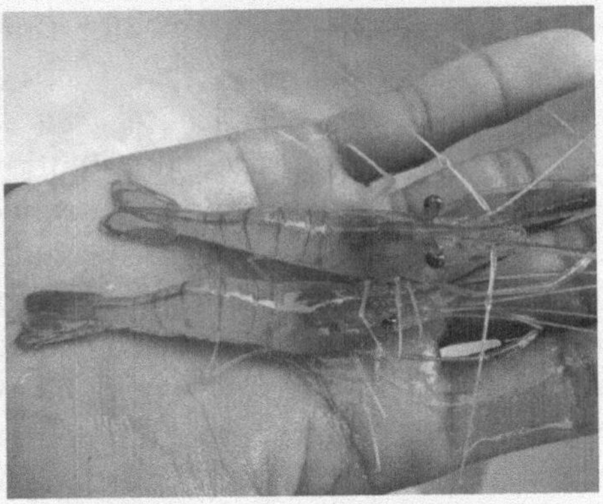

Healthy juveniles of giant prawn

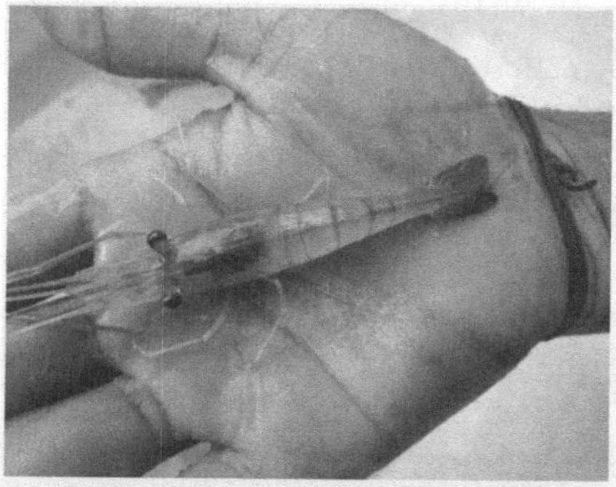

A single juvenile of *M. rosenbergii*

Porcelain dish and spoon for counting seeds

A berried female caught in Bali river, Gosaba

Polyculture of prawn and mullets practiced here

Container for transportation of prawn seeds

Trap for collecting prawn juveniles from pond

BRACKISHWATER FINFISH AQUACULTURE IN WB

Taking advantage of the strong traditional knowledge base and the unimpeding research and developmental support, land-based brackishwater aquaculture has made considerable progress in our country in terms of more area coverage, diversification of culture species and practice and improvement of farming systems (Ghosh, 2012). The traditional tide-fed auto-stocking system (trapping the natural seed, holding and fattening them in impounded tidal swamps) has slowly been improved with changes like: 1) Erection of embankments/bunds, 2) Proper pond preparation, 3) Regulation of water flow, 4) Selective stocking and 5) Feeding. The mullets *(Mugil cephalus, Liza tade, L. parsia and L. macrolepis)*, milkfish *Chanos chanos*, pearl spot *Etroplus suratensis* and sea bass *Lates calcarifer* are considered as ideal species for brackishwater finfish aquaculture in commercial terms in man-made ponds in south-eastern WB. Except pearl spot, other fishes migrate to the sea for spawning and their young ones are collected from brackishwater creeks where they are washed by the tides and are exploited for culture.

The deltaic WB is ecologically well-suited for development of commercial scale production of brackishwater fishes and prawns. The Hooghly estuary as well as other estuarine inlets and tidal streams along with their distributaries have rendered a good part of low-lying Sundarbans into saline swamps which, through embankments and other development processes, have been reclaimed into productive fish farming units. Deltaic zone of WB has an estimated 2,00,000ha swampy area, out of which 85,000ha has been considered suitable for brackishwater aquaculture and is presently practiced in 35,000ha. In WB, management practices have been evolved in early 1980s for brackishwater tiger shrimp to produce 1000kg/ha in three crops and 2000kg of finfish/ha under dugout brackishwater fish farming system; a much larger target of production can be achieved in estuarine swamps (like gher and bhery) where the natural productivity is of very high order. (*Source:* Talk delivered by Late Dr A.V. Natarajan, Former Director, ICAR-CIFRI, Barrackpore on 'Scope for scientific and commercial fish farming in West Bengal', at the National Workshop organized by the Bengal Chamber of Commerce and Industry, Kolkata on 18th Feb, 1985).

FARMING OF MULLETS

Mullets or the coastal marine finfishes can be excellent candidate finfish species for enhancement of aquaculture production in earthen brackishwater ponds. These are very much desirable from consumer point of view. In WB, even in regions where predominantly freshwater fish are preferred and sought after, mullets command high market preference. Seeds of afore-mentioned four species of mullets occur in nature along both coastlines of India; thus seed import cost is saved. These fishes are hardy, herbivorous (omnivorous and detritus-mud feeder to some extent) in feeding habit, able to tolerate high salinity fluctuations, accept supplementary feeds, high percentage of survivability is observed in farm ponds. In WB, the low-lying lands near estuaries and deltaic areas enclosed by embankments are used for traditional finfish cultivation mostly for mullets, especially during rains.

Like sea bass, mullets too have a good market and can be produced at a low cost (Pillai and Menon, 2000; *Tripathi, 2003).* Highlights of some previous studies on weight gained by mullets in culture ponds in brackishwater region in Districts North and South 24 Pgs, WB is shown in Table 7.1.

RAMPUR – THE SITE OF MULLET FARMING

In WB, district North 24 Parganas embraces the active Ganga delta slightly in the southern part (Sandeshkhali and Hingalganj) of the district; the active deltaic part is popularly known as Sundarbans which is under only in Hingalganj, Sandeshkhali-I and II Blocks of this district. In other words, the Sundarbans forest stretches only in Sandeshkhali and Hingalganj and forms a network of several tidal rivers. In six riverine Blocks of this district namely Haroa, Hasnabad, Minakhan, Hingalganj, Sandeshkhali-I and II, salinity built up due to seepage of saline water from rivers. Sandeshkhali-II is one of the six Blocks of North 24 Pgs which is included in the Indian Sundarbans area (upper Sundarbans), and is full of creeks and swamps in the deltaic region of southern Bengal.

In North 24 Pgs, professional aqua-farmers are engaged in brackishwater finfish farming throughout the year; they excavate the paddy plots to some extent to retain brackishwater even during monsoon months. Areas of brackishwater fish production, using sewage effluent mixed or normal tidal water and rain water, are found in Minakhan, Sandeshkhali and Haroa Blocks covering areas of 3373ha, 1649ha and 3965ha respectively. Area of such impounded wetlands mostly lies in the range of 20 to 40 acres (Chakrabarti, 1998). Rampur village is located in Sandeshkhali-II Block under Bermajur-II Gram Panchayat on Sorberia-Dhamakhali roadway and can be accessed *via* Sorberia on Kolkata-Basanti highway. Rampur is 4.5km from Sorberia village and 63km from eastern boundary of Kolkata city.

SRI MONORANJAN MONDAL - A PROFESSIONAL MULLET FARMER

Sri Monoranjan Mondal, aged 52, is an established and professional mullet farmer in Sandeshkhali-II Block of North 24 Pgs; his residence is at Vill. Rampur Khiristola, P.O. Rampur, PS Sandeshkhali, North 24 Pgs. He is also owner of an auction stall/point at Rampur-Bagdipara wholesale fish market. Presently Sri Mondal is having 13 perennial brackishwater ponds under his possession meant for seed rearing of mullets, total area being 1.6ha. In such dug-out 'chambers' of 0.12-0.13ha each (3 feet depth), constructed in 2002, seeds of four species of fishes are separately stocked and reared and fry/advanced fry of mullets are produced. Advanced fry are harvested and stocked in large brackishwater bodies (production units) called 'gher' in nearby region and propagated upto adulthood/table-size. Sri Mondal owns three ghers of 0.66, 1.16 and 2.64ha. Sometimes mullet fry are sold to resource-rich persons at a distance of 2-8km, who take possession of large gher on lease at Malancha village in Minakhan Block or at Sorberia village in Sandeshkhali-I.

Table 7.1: Weight gained by four species of mullets in culture ponds in brackishwater region in Districts North and South 24 Pgs, West Bengal

Sl. No.	Species cultivated	Period of culture at harvest	Weight gained	Feed used	Reference
(1)	(2)	(3)	(4)	(5)	(6)
1.	*Mugil cephalus*	7-8 months	750-1000gm	By-product of grain mills	Joseph, 2015
		upto 18 months	1500-1750gm		
2.	*Liza parsia*	1 month till February	3.4±1.3gm (6.5±0.21cm) (Initial size: 7-8mm)	No feed neither fertilizer	Mondal *et al.*, 2017
		9 months till November	58.94±2.02gm (15.2±0.19cm)		
3.	*Mugil cephalus*	1 year	872gm (426mm)	-	Rajyalakshmi, 1980
	Liza tade	6 months	211gm (267mm)	-	
	Liza parsia	3 months	27gm (120mm)	-	
4.	*Liza parsia*	6-7 months	20-25gm (Initial size: 17-20mm)	Rice polish/wheat flour and ground nut oil cake	Rajyalakshmi, 1980
		1 year	30-50gm (150-190mm)		
	Liza tade	1 year	100gm (200mm)	-	
		2 years	300-500gm (350-500mm)		
	Liza macrolepis	1 year	225mm	-	
	Mugil cephalus		800gm (400mm)	Rice bran, maize powder/wheat powder and fish meal	
5.	*Liza tade*	5 months	500gm (Initial size: 8-10cm)	Ground nut oil cake and rice bran	Mukherjee and Datta, 2000
	Liza parsia		100-110gm (Initial size: 4-6cm)		

(Table Contd...)

(1)	(2)	(3)	(4)	(5)	(6)
6.	*Mugil cephalus*	180 days	92.29 ± 4.36gm	Low cost pellet feed comprising mustard cake, rice bran, wheat flour, fish meal	Biswas *et al.*, 2012
	Liza tade		80.40 ± 4.02gm		
	Liza parsia		54.02 ± 2.11gm		
7.	*Liza macrolepis*	60 days	3.43±1.90gm (6.1±0.22cm) (Initial size: 1.49±0.07cm)	No feed neither fertilizer	Mondal *et al.*, 2016
		9 months (Feb to Nov)	130±3.30gm (19.1± 0.12cm)		
8.	*Liza tade*	18 months	250-265gm (Initial size: 5gm)	-	Bhowmick *et al.*, 1990
9.	*Liza tade*	9 months	260.41±10.50gm (Initial size: 4.24±0.76gm)	No feed neither fertilizer	Mondal *et al.*, 2016

Table 7.2: Particulars of early stages of mullets purchased by Sri M. Mondal for nursery rearing and subsequently grow-out culture

Sl. No.	Species (rice grain sized seeds)	Time of availability and procurement	Bought from (place)	Price
1.	*M. cephalus*	October-December and March-April	Dhamra port and Paradeep in Odisha	Rs 2000-2200/-/ 1000nos.
2.	*L. tade*	May-July	Namkhana and Kakdwip, Dist. South 24 Pgs	Rs 1800-2100/-/ 1000nos.
3.	*L. parsia*	December-February	Different places in Indian Sundarbans, South 24 Pgs	Rs 2200-2500/-/ kg
			Coastal Odisha	Rs 1200/-/kg
4.	*L. macrolepis*	December-February, April and July	Digha, Junput and Khejuri, Dist. East Midnapore and Diamond Harbour, South 24 Pgs	Rs 300-500/-/ 1000nos.

According to Sri Mondal, controlled management practices are followed in nursery mullet rearing chambers and extensive practices in gher. In gher, tidal influence persists and finfish production is largely dependent on natural fertility. Sri Mondal explained that a 'gher' is large dyked low-lying area characterized by an encirclement of land near the banks of tidal rivers/creeks. Dwarf earthen dykes and wooden sluice boxes/gates control the free entrance of saline water into the enclosed areas; where the practice of natural stocking is being progressively replaced by artificial stocking with only the young of specific, desired species of mullets. It is an extensive finfish polyculture gher-farming system. Ghers are occupied with unfiltered estuarine water (12-17ppt).

FISH SEEDS PROCURED BY SRI MONDAL AND REARING

Sri Mondal stated that the fish pearl spot and shrimp are compatible for culture with mullets in gher, but not milkfish and sea bass. Specifications of mullet seeds (8-14mm) procured separately for four species by Sri Mondal are specified in Table-2. The species *M. cephalus*, *L. tade*, *L. parsia* and *L. macrolepis* are termed as 'Aainsh bhangon', 'Gol bhangon', 'Disee parsey' and 'Aainsh parsey/Rupali parsey' respectively in Bengali vernacular in North and South 24 Pgs districts, WB. In seed containers of *L. parsia* and *L. macrolepis* brought from Sundarbans, 85-90% seeds consist of the desired species; rest consists of seeds of perch-like fishes, *Lutjanus* sp., *Terapon jarbua*, *Scatophagus argus* and other finfishes of less economic importance. About 50,000 *L. parsia* seeds weigh 1kg and at approx. 20-22mm stage, 12000-14000nos weigh 1kg. He improves soil fertility of his nursery ponds by applying 2 tonnes organic manure/ha in partial doses every month, and urea+SSP @ 250kg/ha/year. Seeds are counted in white porcelain dish and stocked @ 40,000-50,000nos./0.13ha area and reared for 100-120 days. Ponds are drained-off, sun-dried and raked after one crop. Fresh filtered tidal water is used. Slope region on four sides of nursery ponds are covered with mosquito net cloth from pond bottom till edge of embankment, and nets of large mesh set up overhead to repel away preying birds.

Mullet seeds brought are gradually acclimatized to lower salinity (from 17-18ppt to 4-6ppt) in rectangular cement cisterns. Low salinity in ponds favour good growth of fishes. Adequate zooplankton population in nurseries is very essential, Sri Mondal stated. He has earmarked his chambers for the four fishes separately. At fish seed wholesale markets at Madhukhali in Canning-I, Sonakhali in Basanti and Kelokhali in Gosaba Blocks in South 24 Pgs, *L. parsia* seeds 7-8mm are sold @ Rs 1500-2000/-/kg; those of *M. cephalus* and *L. tade* are sold @ Rs 5-7/-/piece (36-48mm). For every 1000 seeds, he uses 100-150gm of high quality wheat flour as feed daily for first three weeks, broadcasted over water surface. Thereafter 500gm is used everyday. Pulverized ground nut oil cake (@ 2.5kg/0.04ha) is used once in a week. From 10-14mm size, at harvest from nurseries, *L. tade* and *M. cephalus* reach 72mm size, *L. parsia* and *L. macrolepis* 36-48mm with 75-90% survivability. These are sold @ Rs 4-8/-/piece.

Sri Mondal explained some common identifying features of fishes at this fry/advanced fry stage:

- *M. cephalus*: Body is stout with broad head, and a dark black/purple spot at the base of pectoral fin on both sides is prominent. Its head is bigger in comparison to other mullet fry.
- *L. tade*: Body is slender, body colour is darker at dorsal half; a closed black lateral line extends from operculum to caudal base. Its dorsal profile is less convex than the ventral.
- *L. parsia*: Body colour is silvery white (slightly dull), a black straight lateral line is present extending from the operculum to the base of the caudal fin. Its dorsal and ventral profiles are equally convex. Its common size is 15cm and maximum 16cm.
- *L. macrolepis*: Body colour of large-scale mullet is bright silvery white and silvery grey in ventral region. Its common size is 25cm, maximum 60cm. Scales in *L. parsia* fry are small and more densely packed in comparison to *L. macrolepis*.

GHER FARMING SYSTEM

Sri Mondal stock fry/advanced fry of mullets in gher @ 7000-8000nos./ 0.13ha and rear in combination. The water column is 3-7 feet deep. Out of total area, 70% should comprise deep and 30% shallow zone and it is favourable for mullet growth. Natural plankton productivity is maintained in less-deep/shallow gher, whereas more supplementary feed has to be fed to growing fishes in deep ghers having less productivity, Sri Mondal stated. Natural planktonic food is brought into gher through 20-30% water exchange during lunar/moon cycles. Supplementary feed mix (maize powder/rice bran and oil cake) is used infrequently. They accept dry powdered feed. Sri Mondal harvests *M. cephalus* at 2000-2500gm body weight, *L. tade* 800-1000gm, *L. macrolepis* 100-200gm and *L. parsia* 40-80gm. Water in gher is influenced by high tide and low tide but that in well-managed 'chambers' remain stagnant. Presence of advanced fry/juveniles of *Lates calcarifer, Eleutheronema tetradactylum, Plotosus canius* in gher is dangerous for mullets, Sri Mondal warned.

Sri Nabin Barik, professional mullet farmer at Vill. Naskarpara, P.O. Rampur practices seed rearing of *L. macrolepis*. Large-scale mullet seeds 7-10mm are transported to his pond site from Kakdwip in aluminium Hundi loaded over Tata 407 Pick-up vehicle. An 18-inch Hundi holds 10000 seeds. He procures it @ Rs 250/-/1000nos and stock 1,00,000 seeds in each of his 0.12ha nursery pond. He applies 10kg good quality wheat flour as feed for every 1,00,000 seeds daily. At the end of six months, those reach 72-84mm each and such *L. macrolepis* advanced fry/juveniles (150kg harvested from each pond during March-April) are sold to gher owners @ Rs 350-450/-/ kg. In ghers, *L. macrolepis* attains 150-225gm body weight and harvested during July-August. Mixture of mustard oil cake and wheat flour is used. Advanced fry are again stocked in gher during July-August and August-September, marketable-sized *L. macrolepis* harvested and sold within mid-January. Sri Barik uses alum to clear colloidal clay particles in his brackishwater ponds.

MULLET SEED COLLECTION IN SUNDARBANS REGION

Owing to vast seed resource of cultivable finfishes, favourable tidal amplitudes and low cost of land in coastal areas (also mostly inexpensive labour), brackishwater finfish aquaculture in modified extensive method is making good progress in WB, Sri Mondal stated. During December to March, tiny stages 8-12mm of *L. parsia* are collected in good quantity in shooting nets or 'Behundi jaal' (also in shore seine) in Hooghly estuary in and around Kakdwip area, the net is dragged along edges of creeks. Mullet seeds are also collected at Mollakhali, Gosaba, Rangabelia, Bakkhali villages in South 24 Pgs. Seeds of *L. tade* 10-20mm can be collected in the Hooghly estuarine system around Sundarbans from June. About 1 lakh people in Sundarbans region earns a living by collecting 90 crores of brackishwater shrimp and finfish seeds every year, of which 40% comprise seeds of cultivable finfishes. Mullet seeds 10-20mm if kept @ 10-12nos/lit in Hundi, it can be transported for 5 hours duration and supplied to fish farmers. In oxygen-packed polythene bags (50cm x 75cm; 18lit capacity), 200nos of *L. parsia* seeds 8-14mm size or 50nos *L. tade* 50-60mm size are kept in each and transported safely for 6 hours.

FEED FOR MULLETS

The flat-head/stripped mullet *M. cephalus,* for being herbivorous fish, a fish meal-free supplementary feed can be prepared for it. In farm ponds, *M. cephalus* and others feed on natural planktonic food and on the by-products of grain mills and rice polishing plants. The gold spot mullet *L. parsia* is easily cultivable in shrimp growing areas with other mullets; planktonic algae is its dominant food item. According to Sri N. Barik, *L. parsia* 7-12mm attain 36mm in 30-40 days of nursery phase; these if stocked @ 10000-15000nos/0.4ha in gher will grow upto 50-60gm (9.6-14.4cm) in next 100 days of culture and harvested in June-July. It may reach 90-100gm with provision of good feed.

Scientists at ICAR-Central Institute of Brackishwater Aquaculture, Kakdwip, South 24 Pgs have prepared a formulated feed for *L. parsia* for grow-out culture; it comprise fish meal 40%, soyabean oil cake 7%, mustard oil cake 10%, wheat flour 20%, rice bran 20%, Mineral mix 1%, Vitamin mix

0.50% and Guar gum powder 1.50% (Source: 'Brackishwater shrimp, crab and finfish culture', ICAR-CIBA Bull. No. 25, Year 2006). In middle-east Asian countries, rice bran is used as feed in grow-out mullet farming ponds in first two months and a mixture of rice bran and peanut oil cake thereafter till end of culture. A brackishwater farmer at Gosaba Block stated that species like *M. rosenbergii*, mud crab *Scylla serrata* and mullets feed well on by-product of Kolkata leather complex (Rs 12/-/kg), which comprise only the thick skin (with thin layer of flesh) and ears of slaughter animals. The rigid mass is applied into ponds @ 10-12kg/33 decimal once in 14 days, which gets softened in next 15-18 hours and devoured by the fishes and shellfishes.

PROSPECTS OF MULLET FARMING

Sri M. Mondal has to stay for 2-4 days period at Muipith, Najat (known to be repository of *L. parsia* seeds) and other places in Indian Sundarbans; Khejuri and Junput in East Midnapore and even at Paradeep in Odisha to place order for good quality mullet seeds for his ponds in advance and to ensure it in desired quantity in proper time. In his absence, his younger brother and only son takes care of his ponds, both chambers and gher. Sri Mondal is disheartened about environmental perturbation and declining seed availability of mullets. He suffered great loss in mullet farming due to occurrence of the severe cyclonic storm 'Aila' in May 2009 and prolonged period thereafter. Due to steady degradation of natural aquatic ecosystem, 60-80 tonnes of *L. parsia* and *L. macrolepis* seeds could be captured from Bakkhali and Kumirmari in South and North 24 Pgs respectively in all in each season (2-3 months during winter) till 2006, but in 2011-2012, it has drastically reduced to 2-4 tonnes. *L. parsia* seeds were available @ Rs 400/-/kg during 2003-2004; now the price has increased to Rs 2500/-/kg. Salinity of rivers, creeks and also of culture systems has considerably increased after Aila; oil leakage from mechanized vessels operating in brackishwater rivers and in Hooghly-Matla estuary has contributed to declining resource of mullet seeds and gravid/matured fishes, Sri Mondal stated.

Fortunately, conditions have improved by now (2018), ill effects of Aila have been neutralized and original entity could be restored in brackishwater fish ponds. For development of brackishwater fish farming, Department of Fisheries, Government of WB has set up three Brackishwater Fish Farmers' Development Agencies for the coastal districts of North 24 Pgs, South 24 Pgs and East Midnapore. It is expected that commercial farming of mullets will persist as a sustainable source of income for hundreds of small- to medium-scale mullet farmers in the region between Sorberia and Dhamakhali in North 24 Pgs and other places in WB.

Fry of *Liza macrolepis* (45mm)

Fry of *Liza parsia* (25mm)

Fry of *Liza tade* (72mm)

A well-managed nursery pond for mullets

Harvested *Liza tade* 350gm

Mullet seeds captured here after high tide

Nursery chamber for rearing mullet seeds

Harvested *Liza macrolepis* (100gm)

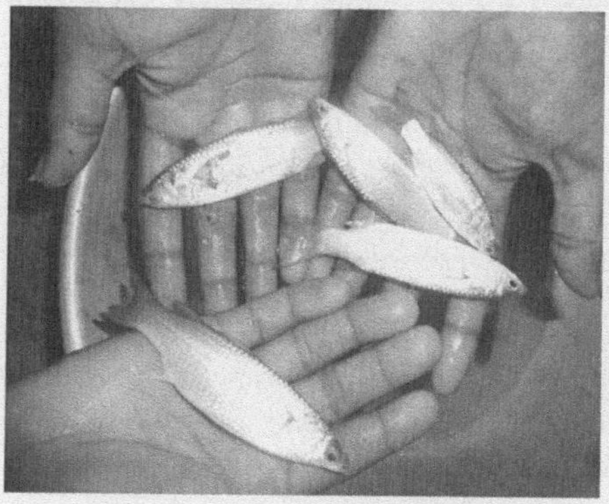

Growing *Liza* species in pond

Author (right) with Sri Monoranjan Mondal

REFERENCES

Bhattacharyya, S.B., Purkait, S., Mandal, S., Chakravorty, D. and Mitra, A. (2016): Studies on Growth, Food and Feeding Ecology, Prey Selection of Large Scale Mullet, *Liza macrolepis* in Extensive Brackishwater Farming System, *Trends in Fisheries Research*, 5(2): 14-28.

Bhowmik, M.L., Chakraborti, R.K., Das, N.K. and Mondal, S.K. (1990): On the Mixed Culture of *Liza tade* and *L. parsia* in Brackishwater with Reference to Pond Ecology, In. *Impacts of Environment on Animals and Aquaculture* (Ed. G.K. Manna and B.B. Jana): pp. 187-193.

Biswas, G., De, D., Ananda Raja, R and Ponniah, A.G. (2012): Evaluation of Productions and Economic Returns from two Brackishwater Polyculture Systems in Tide-fed Ponds, *Journal of Applied Ichthyology*, 28(1): 116-122.

Chakrabarti, P.K. (1998): Scope and Prospects of Fisheries in Estuarine Wetlands of West Bengal, *Meenbarta Wetland Issue*, Government of West Bengal: pp. 66-68.

Chand, B.K., Trivedi, R.K., Dubey, S.K., Rout, S.K., Beg, M.M. and Das, U.K. (2015): Effect of Salinity on Survival and Growth of Giant Freshwater Prawn *Macrobrachium rosenbergii* (de Man), *Aquaculture Reports*, 2: 26-33.

Gain, D., Md. Sarower, M., Mistri, M.A. and Md. Sohag, S.H. (2015): A Comparative Study on Freshwater Prawn (*Macrobrachium rosenbergii*) Farming using Wild Source and Hatchery produced Post larvae (PL), *International Journal of Fisheries and Aquatic Studies*, 2(5): 137-141.

Ghosh, S. (2012): Brackishwater Aquaculture in Context of Rural Livelihood and Food Security, In. A.P. Sharma *et.al.*, Ed. *Management Issues in Inland Fisheries and Aquaculture*, Narendra Publishing House: pp. 103-109.

Joseph, S. (2015): Different Species used for Coastal Pond Farming in India. In. *Winter School on Technological Advances in Mariculture for Production Enhancement and Sustainability*, ICAR-CMFRI Publication: pp. 231-239.

Mahapatra, B.K., Saha, D., Chattopadhyay, P. and Datta, N. C. (1995): Bounteous Potentiality of Scampi seed (*Macrobrachium rosenbergii*) resources in Sundarbans, West Bengal with a note on their Culture prospects, *J. Freshwater Biol.*, 7(2): 137-142.

Mondal, A., Sundaray, J.K., Bhattacharyya, S.B., Pramanick, P., Zaman, S. and Mitra, A. (2017): Feeding Ecology, Prey Selection and Growth Performances of Gold Spot Mullet, *Liza parsia* in Extensive Brackish Water Farming System of Indian Sundarbans, *International Journal of Marine Biology and Research*, 2(1): 1-7.

Mondal, A., Bhattacharyya, S.B., Mandal, S., Purkait, S., Chakravarty, D. and Mitra, A. (2016): Growth Performances, Feeding Ecology and Prey Preferences of *Liza tade* in Extensive Brackishwater Farming System, *International Journal of Fisheries and Aquatic Studies*, 4(3): 436-443.

Mukherjee, M. and Datta, S.K. (2000): Polyculture is the only Solution to Million Problems. In. *Antidote to Combat WSD of Shrimp in Culture Ponds*, GoWB Publication: pp. 9-18.

Pillai, V.N. and Menon, N.G. (2000): A Review of Marine Finfish Culture Experiments in India. ICAR-Central Marine Fisheries Research Institute, Tatapuram, Cochin: 682014.

Rajyalakshmi, T. (1980): Experiments on Mullet Culture at Kakdwip and Bakkhali Fish Farm, West Bengal. In. *Manual on Brackishwater Aquaculture in India*, ICAR-CIFRI Publication: pp. 141.

Tripathi, S.D. 2003. Inland Fisheries in India. *In. Proc. Fish for All – National Launch*, MSSRF Publication, Chennai: pp 33-57.

Pages: 135-155

Animal Biodiversity and Fisheries

Edited by: **Dr. Rashmi Tripathi; Dr. Vijay Sharma & Dr. Pawan Kumar 'Bharti'**

ISBN: 978-93-88854-06-1

Edition: **2019**

Published by: **Discovery Publishing House Pvt. Ltd., New Delhi (India)**

8 Poisonous and Venomous Fishes

Shraddha Dwivedi

INTRODUCTION

Poisonous (Venomous) animals can generally be correlated with the snakes, scorpions and spiders. We rarely hear about fishes that are poisonous or venomous, but in reality there are number of fishes that are fatal to others by the virtue of their ability to either bite, sting or contain toxic substances within their flesh, blood etc (Spanier 1987; Russell 1996). From last few decades, researchers have shown interest in gathering information about toxicity caused by fishes, as only fishes constitute almost half the number of vertebrates on earth, with approximately 22000 species in some 50 orders and 445 families (Church and Hodgson, 2002). More than 2,000 species of fish are poisonous among total 22,000 species of fishes, which causes more than 50,000 injuries annually (Blaszczak-Boxe, 2016). Current article explores different aspects related to fish toxicity *i.e.,* distribution of toxic fishes, conditions governing their toxicity and chemical nature of fish toxin termed as Ichthyotoxin. The information thus collect will not only helpful to assess the usefulness of particular fish as food source at particular conditions but also vital to develop antidotes. It also explores the idea of extracting new therapeutically active biological active chemicals against certain medical conditions.

Before discussing different aspects of related to toxic fish toxicity, we must go through the comprehensive classification system of toxic fishes given by Halstead (1965). Halstead differentiated toxic fishes into two major classes, poisonous and venomous fishes (Table 8.1).

A. Poisonous fishes

These fishes deliver its toxin in human after ingestion. These fishes are subdivided into:

Ph.D (Zoology) University of Lucknow, Lucknow -226 007, (India)

Table 8.1: Poisonous fishes verses venomous fishes

S.No.	Poisonous fishes	Venomous fishes
1.	Fishes containing poisons that affect humans after ingestion of the fishes.	Fishes Capable of producing poisons in highly developed secretary glands or group of cells.
2.	No mechanism or structure for delivery of poisons	Delivery of poisons through biting or stinging
3.	Poisonous fishes can't be eaten their poison affect the human after ingestion.	Venomous fishes are safe to eat, but they may give a fatal sting.

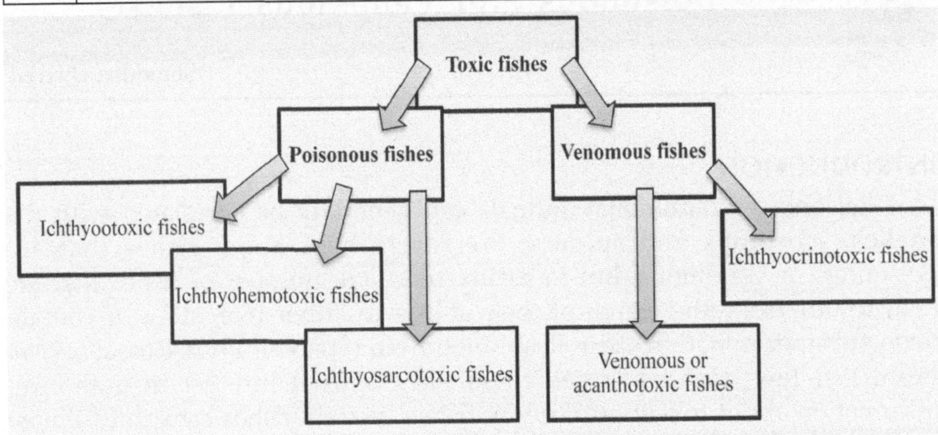

Fig. 8.1: Classification of Toxic fishes

A.1. Ichthyosarcotoxic fishes

These fishes contain poison in their musculature, viscera, etc which on ingestion by human produces toxicity. The ichthyosarcotoxic fishes are further subdivided into:

A.1.1 Ciguatoxic fishes

Ciguatera poisoning creates global health concern and many scientific papers were written about ciguatera poisoning and ciguatoxic fishes (Boydron-Le Garrec *et al.* 2005; Caillaud *et al.* 2010; Laurent *et al.* 2008; Munir *et al.* 2011). It is caused by ingestion of fish that harboured dinoflagellate, *Gambierdiscus toxicus* having ciguatoxins. After ingestion ciguatoxin targets the neuronal transmission by increasing the release of neurotransmitters (Molgo´ *et al.* 1990), intracellular calcium (Molgo´ *et al.* 1993), and blockage of voltage potassium channels (Hidalgo *et al.* 2002).

A.1.2 Fugo poisoning/Tetrodotoxin

Toxicity caused by tetraodontiformes fishes *i.e.*, puffers, ocean sunfishes, and porcupine fishes.

Table 8.2: Detailed analysis of Poisonous fishes

		Causative fishes	Poisons (Storage organ)	Responsible organism	Toxin
(1)	(2)	(3)	(4)	(5)	(6)
A.1.	**Icthyosarcotoxism: {Musculature, viscera, (excluding poisons due to bacterial action)}**				
A.1.1	Ciguatera	Certain tropical reef and pelagic marine species Eg-Barracudas, Groupers, Sea Bbasses, Snappers, Surgeon Fishes, Parrot Fishes, Jjacks Wrasses, and Eels	Liver, Viscera and Muscles (Vernou *et al*. 1985)	Dinoflagellate, *Gambierdiscus toxicus* (Yasumoto *et al*., 1977)	Ciguatoxin (Caillaud *et al*. 2010) Maitotoxin Scaritoxin
A.1.2	Fugo poisoning/ Tetrodotoxin	Puffers, Ocean Sunfishes, and Porcupine fishes	Mostly in ovaries and liver, lesser amount in intestine and skin, very small amounts in body musculature and blood	Bacteria – Listonella, Alteromones and shewanella	Tetrodotoxin
A.1.3	Scombroid poisoning	Tuna, Bonito, Mackerel, and Albacore	Toxic flesh	Histamin is formed by action of enzyme and bacteria or released by bacterial action after death of fish	Histamine, Saurine (named derived from saury, a japanese dried fish delicacy that often causes poisoning)
A.1.4	Cyclostomes poisoning	Lampreys and hagfishes	Slime and flesh of fishes	No specific organism is related	No specific toxin
A.1.5	Elsmobranch poisoning	Sharks, rays	Liver and Musculature in some cases	Somniosus microcephalus, Carcharhinus melanopterus, Heptranchias perlo, Hexanchus grisseus, Carcharodon carcharias, Sphyrna zygaena.	Carchatoxin-A and -B (Liposoluble toxin) (Boisier *et al*. 1995)

(Table Contd...)

(1)	(2)	(3)	(4)	(5)	(6)
A.1.6	Hallucinatory Fish poisoning	*Mugil cephalus, Neomyxus chaptalli, Paraupeneus chryserydros* and *Upeneus arge* of Tropical Indian and Pacific Oceans	Central nervous system and gastrointestinal system	Certain mullets, surmullet eg., mugil cephalus, Neomyxus chaptalli and Upeneus arge	No specific toxin
B.	**Ichthyootoxic**				
		Scorpaenichthys marmoratus	Reproductive organs and their products are poisonous	No specific organism is related	No specific toxin
C.	**Ichthyohemotoxic fishes**				
		Fresh, brackish and sea water in warm and temperate zones eg - Anguilla and Muraena.	Blood	No specific organism is related	Heat-labile toxins are present in the blood. Practically nothing is known about these toxins

Table 8.3: Detailed analysis of treatment of Poisonous fishes

		Mode of action	Symptomatology	Diagnosis	Treatment
(1)	(2)	(3)	(4)	(5)	(6)
A.1.	**Icthyosarcotoxism**				
A.1.1	Ciguatera	Sodium permeability increases causing depolarization (Molgo´ *et al.* 1990), Produces change in rate and force of heart contraction.	**In animal** – Salivation, Lacrimation, Lethargy, Respiratory difficulties, Cyanosis, Ataxia and Prostration **Human**- Nausea, Vomiting, Abdominal pain, Diarrhea, Hypoactive Reflexes and Bradycardia (Friedman *et al.* 2008)	ELISA, RIA	Intravenous mannitol (0.5–1.0 g/kg body weight) (Schnorf *et al.* 2002; Bagnis *et al.* 1992). This injection recommended to be given within 48–72 h of ingestion of toxic fish The leaf extract of *Argusia argentea* is also helpful in treatment (Benoit *et al.* 2000).
A.1.2	Fugo poisoning/ Tetrodotoxin	Effect ionic permeability of nerves, respiratory system, block skeleton muscle membrane	Weakness, Pallor, Dizziness, Paresthesia (tingling) around lips, tongue and throat.	Autopsy material by gas chromatography	Oxygen, intravenous fluids, atropine and if appropriate, activated charcoal, saline catharses, and nasoepigastric suctioning.

(Table Contd…)

(1)	(2)	(3)	(4)	(5)	(6)
A.1.3	Scombroid poisoning	Inadequate refrigeration allows marine bacteria to interact with the histidine in flesh of the fish and turn it into histamine and saurine, these chemical are heat stable so cooking won't destroy the toxin.	Intense Headache, Dizziness, Pain or Difficulty Swallowing and Abdominal Pain, Nausea, vomiting (Arnoldand Brown 1978; Gilbert *et al*. 1980; Taylor 1989)	No specific technique	H1 type Antihistamines, such as Chlorpheniramine (Chlortrimeton), Diphenhydramine (Benadryl), Dimenhydrinate (Dramamine) & Promethazine (phenergan) (Lerke et al. 1978; Blakesley 1983; Guss 1998). Antihistamine will work the best if they are injected. Possibly beneficial would be the H2 blockers such as Tagamet, Zantac, Pepcid and Axid. If swelling threatening the victim's airway, or wheezing then an injection of epinephrine (Adrenalin), & steroids such as prednisone should be given. Asthma inhalers such as albuterol are also useful.
A.1.4	Cyclostomes poisoning	No specific mode of action	Gastrointestinal signs and symptoms	No specific technique	Symptomatic treatment preferred
A.1.5	Elsmobranch poisoning	Poisoning is due to Hypervitaminosis A (Bouder *et al*., 1962)	Symptoms usually develop within 30 min. Nausea, Vomiting Diarrhea, Abdominal pain, Headache weak pulse, Burning Sensation of tongue, throat and Oesophagous (Symptoms progresses and neurological and other symptoms became more prominent)	No specific technique	Symptomatic treatment preferred

(Table Contd...)

(1)	(2)	(3)	(4)	(5)	(6)
A.1.6	Hallucinatory fish poisoning	No specific mode of action	Dizziness, loss of equilibrium, lack of motor coordination, hallucinations & mental depression. Sensation of tight constriction around the chest. Terror, nightmares. Itching, burning of the throat, muscular weakness, rarely abdominal distress (De Haro and Pommier 2006).	No specific technique	Stomach evacuation should be immediatelySymptomatic treatment is preferred
B.	**Ichthyootoxic**				
		Toxic phospholipids have been found in the roe of individual fish, it is still not certain whether the toxins are produced by the fish themselves or are ingested by the fish via the food chain.	Abdominal pain, Nausea, vomiting, Diarrhoea, Headache, Fever, Bitter taste in the mouth, Dryness of the mouth, Intense thirst, a sensation of constriction of the chest, Cold sweats, Irregular pulse, Low blood pressure, Cyanosis, Pupil Dilation, Syncope, Chills, Dysphagia and tinnitus. In severe cases there may be muscle cramps, paralysis, coma and even death.	No specific technique	The consumption of roe (fish eggs) is particularly dangerous. The presence of toxins appears to correlate with the reproductive season. Avoid eating Roe of fish especially in reproductive period.cooking is said to destroy most ichthyootoxins.
C.	**Ichthyohemotoxic fishes**				
		No specific Mode of action	Diarrhoea, Bloody stools, Nausea, Vomiting, Hypersalivation, skin eruptions, Cyanosis, Apathy, Irregular Pulse, Weakness, paraesthesias, Paralysis, Respiratory distress and possibly death. Ocular contact is said to invoke a severe burning sensation and redness of the conjunctivae, lacrimation and swelling of the eyelids.	No specific technique	Avoid uncooked blood; The toxins are inactivated by boiling or frying.

A.1.3 Scombroid poisoning

Scombroid poisoning is also known as histamine poisoning. Histamine is naturally present in humans and is not toxic but presence of some related toxic substances enhance its effect, which is harmful (Kawataba, 1962). Symptoms of scombroid poisoning appears within 10 min to 1h after consumption (Ansdell 2015). Patient will usually recover within 24 h, but can also last for days depending upon sensitivity of individual (Taylor 1986).

A.1.4 Cyclostomes poisoning

The slime and flesh of certain lampreys and hagfishes appear to contain a toxin that may produce gastrointestinal signs and symptoms.

A.1.5 Elasmobranch fish poisoning

The work on elasmobranch fish poisoning were firstly reported by Coutand (1879) although it has been known since centuries (De Sauvages, 1770). The studies were further elaborated by Macht and Spencer (1941) and Bouder *et al.* (1962). The poisoning can be prevented by cleaning fish meat with boiled water (Fabricius 1780).

A.1.6 Hallucinatory fish poisoning

Hallucinogenic is a less common fish poisoning. The causative agent of fish poisoning is still not known but it was reported that toxicity can occur after eating head or flesh of the fish. (Helfrich and Banner 1960; Chevaldonne 1990). Symptoms develop 2 h after eating.

A.2 Ichthyootoxic fishes

In ichthyootoxic fish, it is the reproductive organs and their products that are poisonous and musculature and other parts are edible. Thus poisoning occurs in breeding season so such fishes are prohibited from sale during the reproductive season (Meyer-Ahrens 1855).

A.3 Ichthyohemotoxic fishes

Toxic substances are found in the blood of certain fishes, e.g. Anguilla and Muraena. Consumption of fresh blood of eels will cause severe poisoning and can lead to death (Yoshida *et al.* 2008).

B. Venomous fishes

B.1 Ichthyocrinotoxic fishes

These fishes lack venomous apparatus such as spines and stings, but they do have poisonous glands by which they directly secrete their poisons into water. The discharge of poison is for defence. The poisonous gland has same basic structure with slight modification. Poisonous glands are present in several locations in the mouth region of the boxfish, in the lips, in the epithelial lining of the buccal cavity and the oesophagus. The poisonous secretions are located in the epidermis layers that are connected with the poisonous gland. When fish is disturbed the stomach expands by taking in air or water. This result in stretching of the epidermis along with the tissues of poisonous gland located deep inside and the poison expelled out. In toadfish, have two types of poisonous glands, a pectoral and axillary (Collette, 1966) at the time of excitement, the pectoral fin expands and the pore of gland opens wide so the poisonous content is easily expelled out.

Table 8.4: Detailed analysis of crinotoxic fish poisoning

		Causative fishes	Poisons (Storage organ)	Responsible Organism	Toxin
B	Crinotoxic fishes				
		Marine representatives, Petromyzontidae also in freshwater in the Northern Hemisphere	Skin (fish produce toxic secretions in their epidermal glands)	No specific organism is related	Ostracitoxin and Pahutoxin

B.2 Venomous or acanthotoxic fishes

These fishes have specialised glands associated with spines and stings to inject their toxin (Atkinson *et al.* 2006). Antivenom in unavailable for these toxins but in some countries traditional medicines are used to cure the patients like vinegar, fig juice, boiled cactus, heated stones, hot water, and ice (Auerbach 1991). In the stingray, the venomous apparatus consists of caudal appendages, spine and venomous gland. The venomous structures may differ in different species of stingrays. In catfishes venomous apparatus located on the dorsal spine and on the spines of the pectoral fins (Singletary *et al.* 2005).

DISTRIBUTION AND CHARACTERISTICS OF POISONS

Poisonous fishes are largely circumtropical in distribution, but on occasion occur in temperate waters. Large populations of poisonous fishes are occurring in central Indo- pacific area and in the West Indies. They are more common near inland than along continental shores.

Edible fishes cannot easily distinguishable from poisonous one but they have following common characteristics:

- Most live in shallow water around reefs or lagoons.
- Many have boxy or round bodies
- Hard shell-like skins covered with bony plates or spines
- Usually large specimens of jacks (Caranx spp.), grouper (Epinephelus spp.) and barracuda (Sphyraena spp.) are more likely to be toxic than smaller specimens. This has not been found to be necessarily true in other species.

ORIGIN OF THE POISON

Most of fish poisons are derived from the food which the fish eats. Toxic substances and their precursors are obtained directly from marine littoral algae. Stomach content analyses have revealed that algae are more frequently present in poisonous fishes than any other types of food. Controlled laboratory feeding tests demonstrate that it is possible to induce toxicity in carnivorous species, without evidence of detrimental effect on the fish, by feeding them toxic fish flesh. It is clear, with a single exception of scombroid poison, the poisons are not bacterial in origin, putrefactions and radioactive substances also do not play any role in production of fish poison.

DISTRIBUTION OF POISON IN BODY

If a fish is toxic, musculature will be found to be toxic in 50 percent of specimens, and viscera in about 90 percent or more. However distribution of poison may vary individual to individual species.

FACTORS AFFECTING POISONOUS BEHAVIOR OF FISH

Food Habit

Any marine fishes can under certain circumstances became poisonous as a result of its food habits. A species may be toxic in one part of island, but edible in another.

Seasonal Fluctuation

Toxin content of some fishes is greatest just prior to spawning for instances puffers, spawning takes place during late spring or early summer. Toxin content is lowest during fall and winter, barracuda (*Sphyraena* spp.) may follow similar but less pronounced, seasonal pattern. There are no other evidences of seasonal fluctuation in most other species.

Pollution

Pesticides, heavy metals, and various organic compounds used in agriculture and manufacturing practices they accumulate in fish to the point that fishes become poisons, *e.g.*, DDT. DDT have accumulated in fishes in that extent that advisories were issued, concerning the danger of eating the fatter portion of fish from the Great Lakes (Foren *et al.*,1989).

TREATMENT OF FISH POISONING THROUGH DRUGS

- **Calcium gluconate**: - given intravenously, has given prompt relief, in some cases.
- **Paraldehyde and ether inhalations**: - useful in controlling the convulsions.
- **Nikethamide**: useful in respiratory depression.
- **Antihistamic drugs**: useful in the treatment of scombroid poisoning.
- **Opiates (morphine)**: given in small divided doses will probably be required.

TREATMENT OF FISH POISONING

- Oxygen by inhalation and intravenous administration of fluids supplemented with vitamins given parenterally are usually beneficial.
- If the laryngeal spasm is present, intubation and tracheotomy may be necessary.

- Cool shower have been found to be effective in relieving, severe itching.

PREVENTION OF FISH POISONING

- Fishes should be promptly refrigerated or eaten soon after capture. As Geiger found that histamine content of the flesh of the Pacific mackerel, *Pneumatophorus diego*, increases when kept at room temperature (20 to 25) for about 10 hours.
- Scomboid meat having sharp or peppery taste should be discarded.
- If full fish is available gills should be examined, it should be bright red and without evidence of off-odor.
- Eliminate all of the visceral organs and skin from the diet regardless of the species.
- Ordinary cooking does not inactivate the toxin. Poison can be inactivated chemically by cooking the meat in a strong solution of sodium bicarbonate, ordinary baking soda, for prolonged period of time. This technique may destroy the flavor of fish and render it useless for consumption.
- Unknown Fish must be eviscerated promptly and only musculature be used.
- Meat should be cut or torn into small bits and soaked in water for a minimum of 3-4 hours. During this process the flesh should be kneaded while in the water, and water changed at frequent intervals. The toxin is water soluble and leaching will effectively.

Table 8.5: List of Poisonous fishes

Common name	Surgeon fish
Scientific name	*Acanthurus coeruleus*
Distribution	Indo-Pacific North East Pacific North Pacific, North West Atlantic
Type of poisoning	Ciguatera
Class	Actinopterygii
Order	Perciformes
Family	Acanthuridae

Source: http://upload.wikimedia.org/wikipedia/commons/9/9a/Blue_Tang.jpg

Common name	Bone fish
Scientific name	*Albula vulpes*
Distribution	Worldwide in warm seas
Type of poisoning	Ciguatera
Class	Actinopterygii
Order	Albuliformes
Family	Albulidae

Source: http://upload.wikimedia.org/wikipedia/commons/f/f4/Bonefish.png

Common name	Gray trigger fish
Scientific name	*Balistes carolinensis*
Distribution	Atlantic, Gulf of Mexico
Type of poisoning	Ciguatera
Class	Actinopterygii
Order	Tetraodontiformes
Family	Balistidae

Source: http://www.flmnh.ufl.edu/fish/Gallery/Descript/graytriggerfish/graytriggerfish.html

Common name	Saucereye porgy
Scientific name	*Calamus calamus*
Distribution	Western Atlantic
Type of poisoning	Ciguatera
Class	Actinopterygii
Order	Perciformes
Family	Sparidae

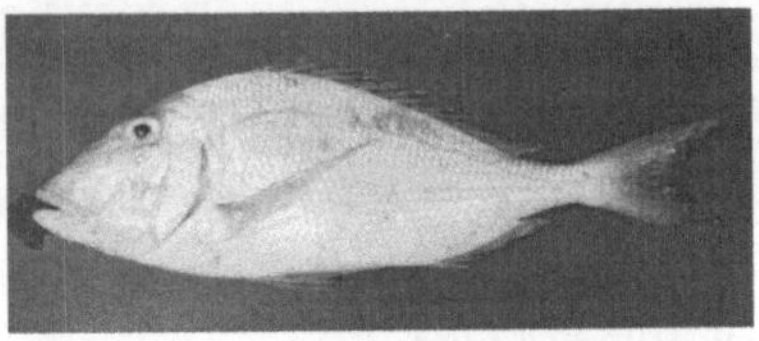

Source: http://en.wikipedia.org/wiki/File:Calamus_calamus.jpg

Common name	Horse-eye jack
Scientific name	*Caranx latus*
Distribution	Atlantic
Type of poisoning	Ciguatera
Class	Actinopterygii
Order	Perciformes
Family	Carangidae

Source: http://www.robertosozzani.it/Cuba2/carangide01.html

Common name	White tip shark
Scientific name	*Carcharhinus longimanus*
Distribution	Worldwide
Type of poisoning	Ciguatera
Class	Chondrichthyes
Order	Carcharhiniformes
Family	Carcharhinidae

Source: http://upload.wikimedia.org/wikipedia/commons/2/24/Oceanic_Whitetip_Shark.png

Common name	Humphead wrasse
Scientific name	*Cheilinus undulatus*
Distribution	Indo-Pacific
Type of poisoning	Ciguatera
Class	Actinopterygii
Order	Perciformes
Family	Labridae

Source: http://upload.wikimedia.org/wikipedia/commons/4/49/Humphead_ wrasse_ melb_aquarium.jpg

Common name	Heavy beak parrot fish
Scientific name	*Chlorurus gibbus*
Distribution	Indo-Pacific
Type of poisoning	Ciguatera
Class	Actinopterygii
Order	Perciformes
Family	Labridae

Source: http://www.fishbase.org/Photos/PicturesSummary.php?StartRow=1&ID=4979&what=species&TotRec=11

Common name	Red grouper
Scientific name	*Epinephelus morio*
Distribution	Western-Atlantic
Type of poisoning	Ciguatera
Class	Actinopterygii
Order	Perciformes
Family	Serranidae

Source: http://www.arkive.org/red-grouper/epinephelus-morio/

Common name	Giant moray
Scientific name	*Gymnothorax javanicus*
Distribution	Indo-Pacific
Type of poisoning	Ciguatera
Class	Actinopterygii
Order	Anguilliformes
Family	Muraenidae

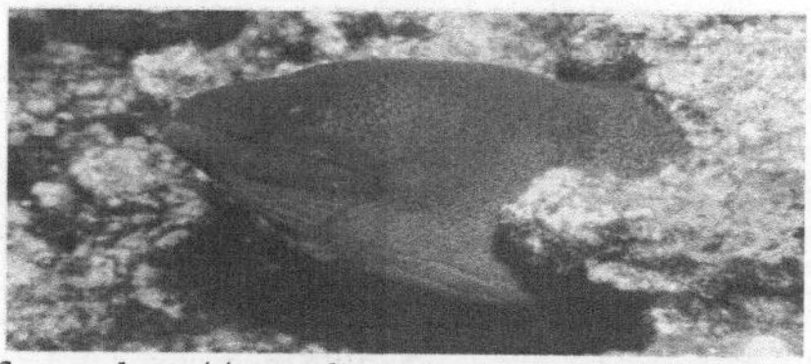

Source: http://australianmuseum.net.au/Uploads/Images/22115/gjavanicus_big.jpg

Common name	Hogfish
Scientific name	*Lachnolaimus maximus*
Distribution	Western Atlantic
Type of poisoning	Ciguatera
Class	Actinopterygii
Order	Perciformes
Family	Labridae

Source: http://www.arkive.org/hogfish/lachnolaimus-maximus/

Common name	Northern red snapper
Scientific name	*Lutjanus campechanus*
Distribution	Western Atlantic, Gulf of Mexico
Type of poisoning	Ciguatera
Class	Actinopterygii
Order	Perciformes
Family	Lutjanidae

Source: http://upload.wikimedia.org/wikipedia/commons/8/8b/Lutjanus_campechanus.png

Common name	Gray snapper
Scientific name	*Lutjanus griseus*
Distribution	Western Atlantic: Massachusetts, USA and Bermuda southward to Rio de Janeiro, Brazil, including West Indies (Anderson, pers. comm.), Gulf of Mexico and Caribbean Sea
Type of poisoning	Ciguatera
Class	Actinopterygii
Order	Perciformes
Family	Lutjanidae

Source: http://upload.wikimedia.org/wikipedia/commons/thumb/6/6b/Grey_snapper_-_Lutjanus_griseus.jpg/250px-Grey_snapper_-_Lutjanus_griseus.jpg

Common name	Blue parrotfish
Scientific name	*Scarus coeruleus*
Distribution	Western Atlantic
Type of poisoning	Ciguatera
Class	Actinopterygii
Order	Perciformes
Family	Scaridae

Source: http://reefguide.org/pix/blueparrot1.jpg

Common name	Spanish mackerel
Scientific name	*Scomberomorus maculates*
Distribution	Western Atlantic
Type of poisoning	Ciguatera
Class	Actinopterygii
Order	Perciformes
Family	Scombridae

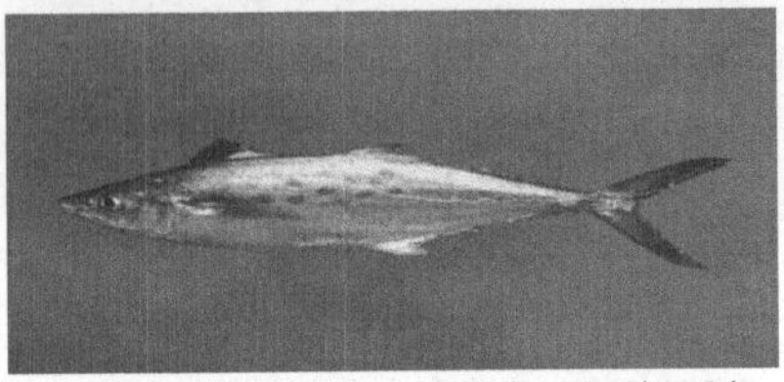

Source: http://www.dnr.sc.gov/marine/mrri/SEAMAP/species/img/smacul.jpg

Common name	Lesser amberjack
Scientific name	*Seriola fasciata*
Distribution	Western Atlantic
Type of poisoning	Ciguatera / Scombroid
Class	Actinopterygii
Order	Perciformes
Family	Carangidae

Source: http://www.safmc.net/Portals/6/images/fish/lesser_amberjack.jpg

Common name	Great barracuda
Scientific name	*Sphyraena barracuda*
Distribution	Indo-Pacific, Western Atlantic
Type of poisoning	Ciguatera
Class	Actinopterygii
Order	Perciformes
Family	Sphyraenidae

Source: http://upload.wikimedia.org/wikipedia/commons/e/eb/Barracuda_laban.jpg

Common name	Chinaman fish
Scientific name	*Symphorus nematophorus*
Distribution	Western Pacific
Type of poisoning	Ciguatera
Class	Actinopterygii
Order	Perciformes
Family	Lutjanidae

Source: http://www.fishbase.us/images/thumbnails/jpg/tn_Synem_u3.jpg

Common name	Swordfish
Scientific name	*Xiphias gladius*
Distribution	Atlantic, Indo-Pacific, Mediterranean
Type of poisoning	Ciguatera
Class	Actinopterygii
Order	Perciformes
Family	Xiphiidae

Source: http://upload.wikimedia.org/wikipedia/commons/9/98/Xiphias_gladius1.jpg

Common name	Mahi Mahi
Scientific name	*Coryphaena hippurus*
Distribution	temperate, tropical and subtropical waters worldwide
Type of poisoning	Scombroid
Class	Actinopterygii
Order	Perciformes
Family	Coryphaenidae

Source: http://upload.wikimedia.org/wikipedia/commons/d/d2/Coryphaena_hippurus.png

Common name	Blue fish
Scientific name	*Pomatomus saltatrix*
Distribution	Eastern America, Africa, the Mediterranean and Black Seas
Type of poisoning	Scombroid
Class	Actinopterygii
Order	Perciformes
Family	Pomatomidae

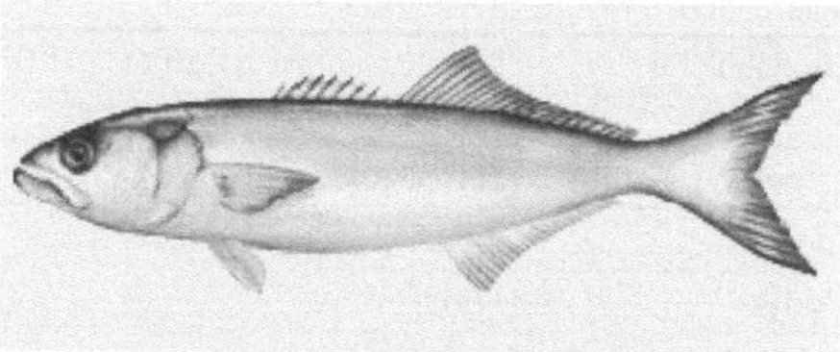

Source: http://upload.wikimedia.org/wikipedia/commons/d/de/Pomatomus_saltatrix.png

Common name	Blue trunk fish
Scientific name	*Ostracion lentiginosus*
Distribution	Africa, Hawaii,
Type of poisoning	Crinotoxic
Class	Actinopterygii
Order	Tetraodontiformes
Family	Ostraciidae

Source: http://animalkingdom.su/books/item/f00/s00/z0000020/pic/000874.jpg

Common name	Red Sea Moses sole
Scientific name	*Pardachirus marmoratus*
Distribution	Red Sea
Type of poisoning	Crinotoxic
Class	Actinopterygii
Order	Pleuronectiformes
Family	Soleidae

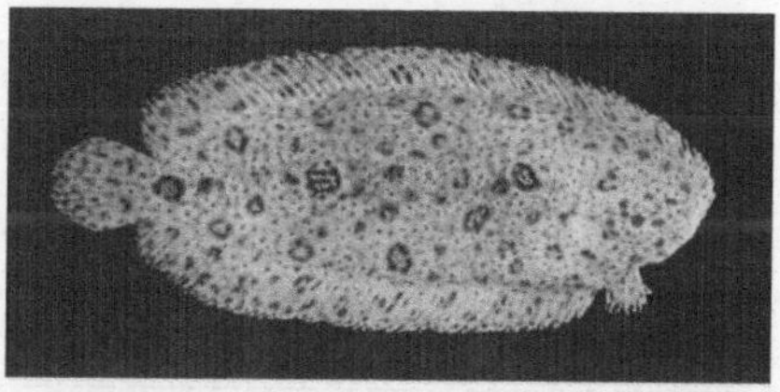

Source: http://www.dafni.com/fish/TN_Pamar_u1.jpg

Common name	Cabezon
Scientific name	*Scorpaenichthys marmoratus*
Distribution	British Columbia, Southern California
Type of poisoning	Ichthyootoxic (roe is poisonous)
Class	Actinopterygii
Order	Scorpaeniformes
Family	Cottidae

Source: http://angelinos.narod.ru/cabezong.jpg

Common name	Pufferfish/Blowfish/ Globefish/Toadfish
Scientific name	*Diodon holocanthus*
Distribution	Pacific Ocean, Baja California coast
Type of poisoning	Tetrodotoxin
Class	Actinopterygii
Order	Tetraodontiformes
Family	Tetraodontidae

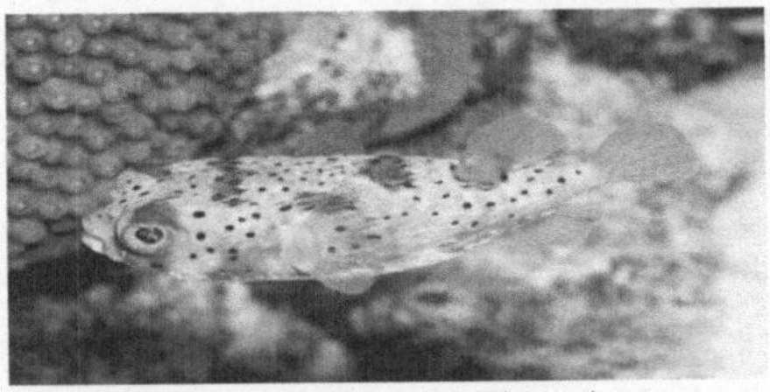

Source: http://www.fishbase.org/Photos/PicturesSummary.php?StartRow=0&ID=4659&what=species&TotRec=18

Common name	Atlantic horse mackerel
Scientific name	*Trachurus trachurus*
Distribution	North-eastern Atlantic, Mediterranean, Black Sea.
Type of poisoning	Scombroid
Class	Actinopterygii
Order	Perciformes
Family	Carangidae

Source: http://upload.wikimedia.org/wikipedia/commons/7/7d/Atlantic_Horse_Mackerel.jpg

Common name	Sturgeon fish
Scientific name	Acipenser sturio
Distribution	most coasts of Europe
Type of poisoning	icthyootoxic
Class	Actinopterygii
Order	Acipenseriformes
Family	Acipenseridae

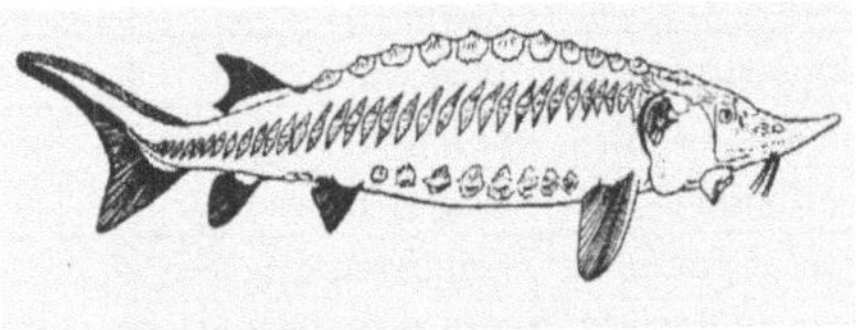

Source: The Poisonous Fishes Of The Croatianadriatic, Draga, 1994

Common name	Adriatic Sturgeon
Scientific name	Accippenser nacarii
Distribution	Adriatic Sea
Type of poisoning	icthyootoxic
Class	Actinopterygii
Order	Acipenseriformes
Family	Acipenseridae

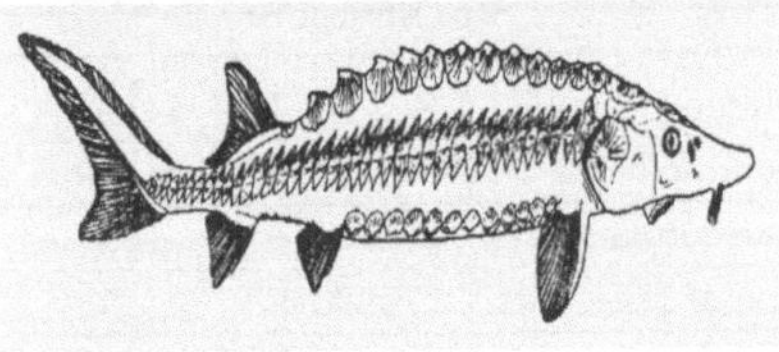

Source: The Poisonous Fishes Of The Croatianadriatic, Draga, 1994

Common name	Europaean Eel
Scientific name	Anguilla Anguilla
Distribution	North Atlantic, Baltic and Mediterranean Seas,
Type of poisoning	Ichthyohemotoxic
Class	Actinopterygii
Order	Anguilliformes
Family	Anguillidae

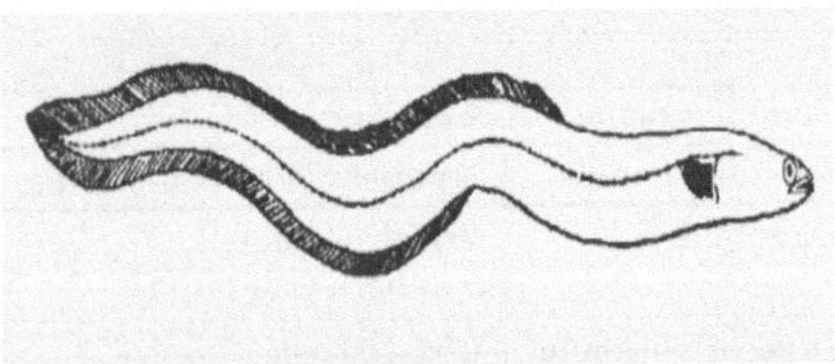

Source: The Poisonous Fishes of The Croatianadriatic, Draga, 1994

Common name	Gray Triggerfish
Scientific name	Balistes carolinensis
Distribution	western Atlantic
Type of poisoning	Tetrodotoxin
Class	Actinopterygii
Order	Tetraodontiformes
Family	Balistidae

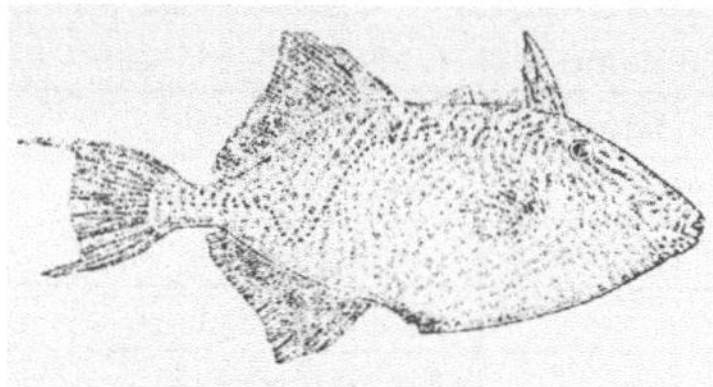

Source: The Poisonous Fishes Of The Croatianadriatic, Draga, 1994

Common name	Garfish, Flat Needlefish
Scientific name	*Belone belone*
Distribution	Baltic Sea, Mediterranean Sea, Eastern Atlantic
Type of poisoning	Scombroid
Class	Actinopterygii
Order	Beloniformes
Family	Belonidae

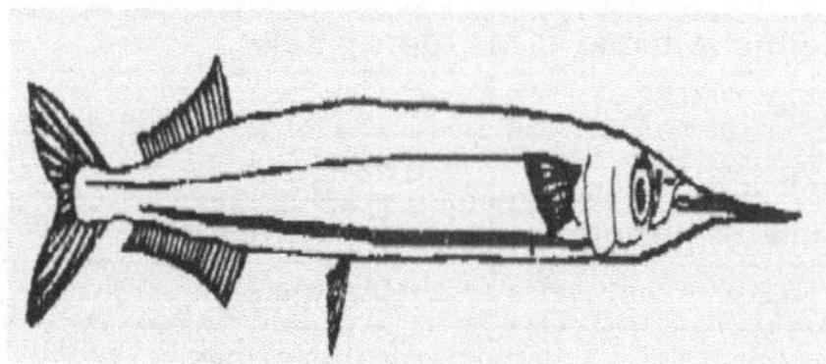

Source: The Poisonous Fishes Of The Croatianadriatic, Draga, 1994

Common name	Conger Eel
Scientific name	*Conger conger*
Distribution	Mediterranean Sea
Type of poisoning	Ichthyohemotoxic
Class	Actinopterygii
Order	Anguilliformes
Family	Congridae

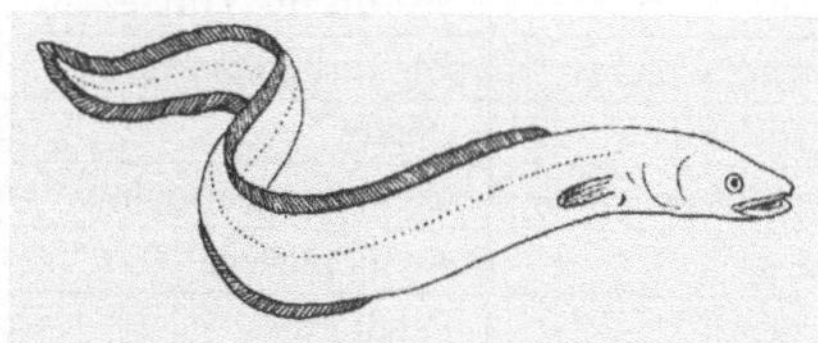

Source: The Poisonous Fishes Of The Croatianadriatic, Draga, 1994

Common name	Bluntnose, Six-gilled Shark
Scientific name	*Hexanchus griseus*
Distribution	Indian ocean, Atlantic ocean Pacific ocean, Mediterranean sea
Type of poisoning	Elsmobranch poisoning
Class	Chondrichthyes
Order	Hexanchiformes
Family	Hexanchidae

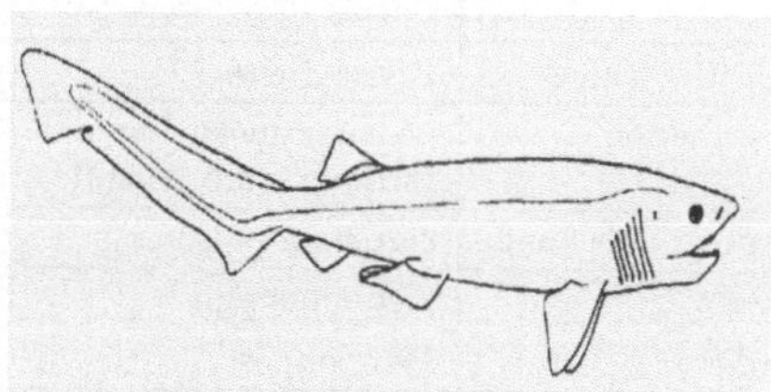

Source: The Poisonous Fishes Of The Croatianadriatic, Draga, 1994

Common name	Sunfish, Moonfish
Scientific name	*Mola mola*
Distribution	part of Pacific
Type of poisoning	Tetrodotoxin
Class	Actinopterygii
Order	Tetraodontiformes
Family	Molidae

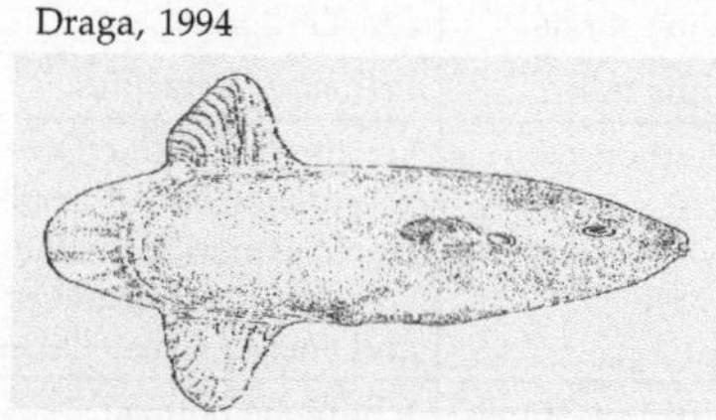

Source: The Poisonous Fishes Of The Croatianadriatic, Draga, 1994

Common name	Gray Mullet
Scientific name	*Mugil cephalus*
Distribution	Gila River region
Type of poisoning	Hallucinations
Class	Actinopterygii
Order	Mugiliformes
Family	Mugilidae

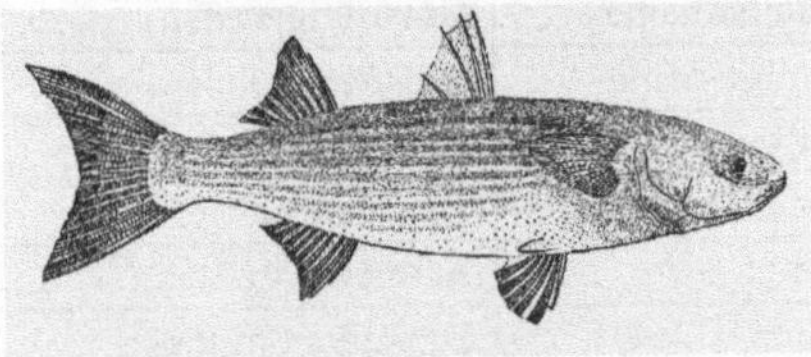

Source: The Poisonous Fishes Of The Croatianadriatic, Draga, 1994

Common name	Moray Eel
Scientific name	*Muraena helena*
Distribution	Adriatic fish
Type of poisoning	Ichthyohemotoxic
Class	Actinopterygii
Order	Anguilliformes
Family	Muraenidae

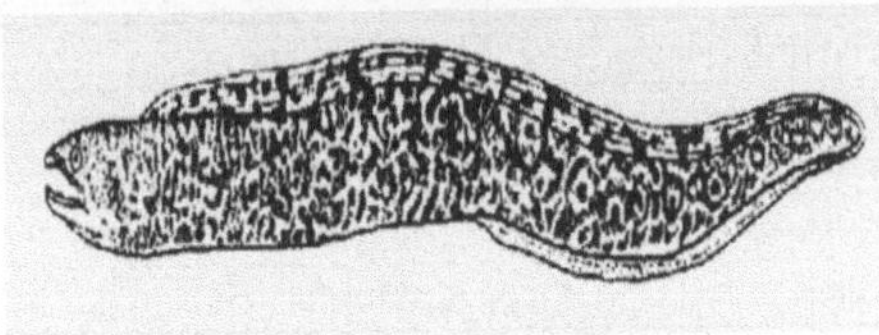

Source: The Poisonous Fishes Of The Croatianadriatic, Draga,

Common name	Sea bream, Porgie
Scientific name	*Pagellus erythrinus*
Distribution	tropics
Type of poisoning	Ciguatera poisoning
Class	Actinopterygii
Order	Perciformes
Family	Sparidae

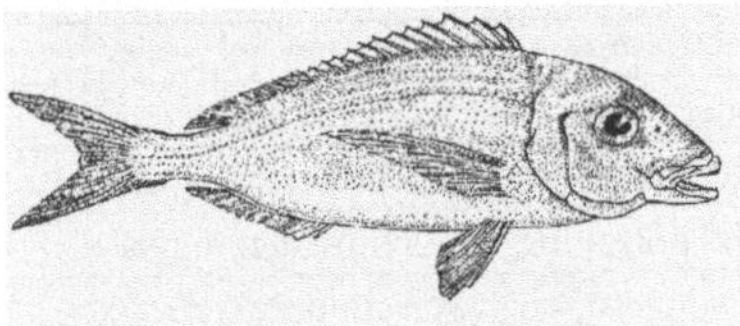

Source: The Poisonous Fishes Of The Croatianadriatic, Draga, 1994

Common name	Common sea bream, Porgie
Scientific name	*Pagrus pagrus*
Distribution	Mediterranean Sea and in the eastern Atlantic
Type of poisoning	ciguatera poisoning
Class	Actinopterygii
Order	Perciformes
Family	Sparidae

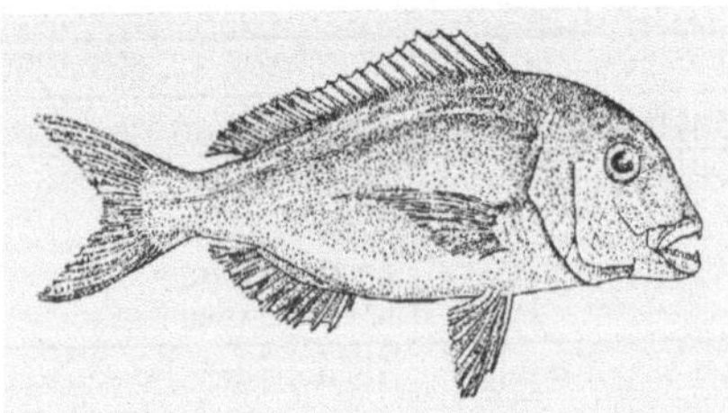

Source: The Poisonous Fishes Of The Croatianadriatic, Draga, 1994

Common name	Sea Lamprey
Scientific name	*Petromyzon marinus*
Distribution	Northern Atlantic Ocean along shores of Europe and North America, in the western Mediterranean Sea, and in the Great Lakes.
Type of poisoning	Ichthyohemotoxic
Class	Petromyzontida
Order	Petromyzontiformes
Family	Petromyzontidae

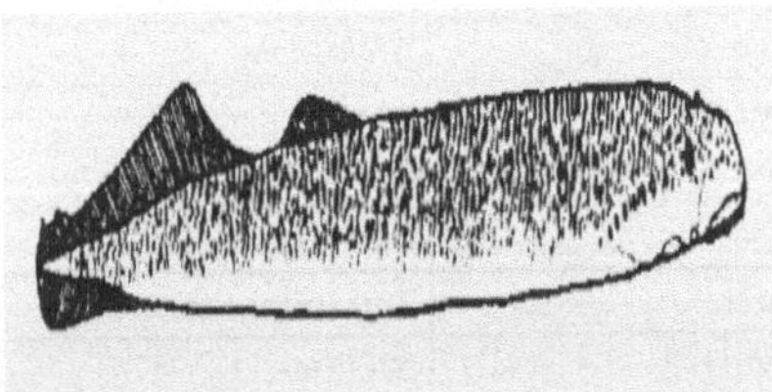

Source: The Poisonous Fishes Of The Croatianadriatic, Draga, 1994

Common name	Spanish Mackerel
Scientific name	*Scomber japonicus*
Distribution	Indo-Pacific
Type of poisoning	Scombroid
Class	Actinopterygii
Order	Perciformes
Family	Scombridae

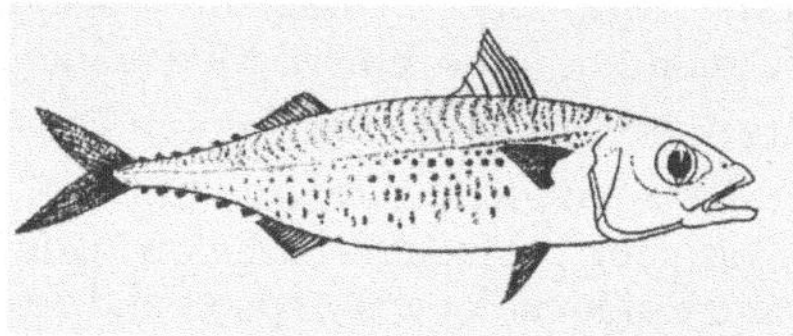

Source: The Poisonous Fishes Of The Croatianadriatic, Draga, 1994

Common name	Atlantic Mackerel
Scientific name	*Scomber scomber*
Distribution	North Atlantic
Type of poisoning	Scombroid
Class	Actinopterygii
Order	Perciformes
Family	Scombridae

Source: The Poisonous Fishes Of The Croatianadriatic, Draga, 1994

Common name	Atlantic bluefinTuna
Scientific name	*Thunnus thynnus*
Distribution	western and eastern Atlantic Ocean
Type of poisoning	Scombroid,
Class	Actinopterygii
Order	Perciformes
Family	Scombridae

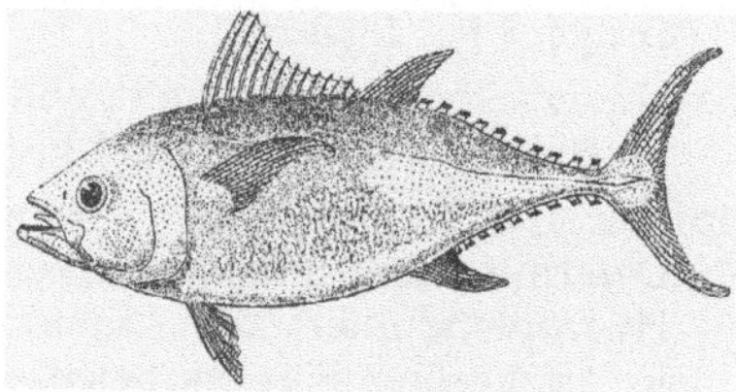

Source: The Poisonous Fishes Of The Croatianadriatic, Draga, 1994

Table 8.6: Example of Venomous fish

Common name	Bleeker's whipray
Scientific name	*Himantura bleekeri*
Distribution	Indo-Pacific region
Order	Myliobatiformes
Family	Dasyatidae

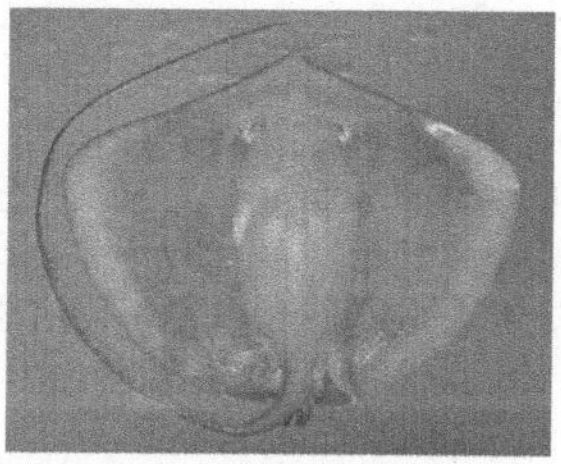

REFERENCES

Ansdell VE; 2015. Food Poisoning from Marine Toxins. CDC Health Inf Int Travel 2016. 100(8): 91.

Arnold SH, Brown WD; 1978. Histamine (?) Toxicity from Fish Products. Adv Food Res. 24: 113-54.

Atkinson PRT, Boyle D, Hartin D, Mcauley D; 2006. Is Hot Water Immersion an Effective Treatment for Marine Envenomation? Emerg Med J. 23: 503-8.

Auerbach PS; 1984. Hazardous Marine Animals. Emerg Med Clin North Am. 2: 531-44.

Bagnis R, Spiegel A, Boutin JP, Burucoa C, Nguyen L, Cartel JL, Capdevielle P, Imbert P, Prigent D, Gras C; 1992. Evaluation of the Efficacy of Mannitol in the Treatment of Ciguatera in French Polynesia. Med Trop. 52: 67-73.

Baumann F, Bourrat MB, Pauillac S, 2010. Prevalence, Symptoms and Chronicity of Ciguatera in New Caledonia: Results from an Adult Population Survey Conducted in Noumea during 2005. Toxicon, 56: 662-667.

Blakesley ML; 1983. Scombroid Poisoning: Prompt Resolution of Symptoms with Cimetidine. Ann Emerg Med. 12(2): 104-6.

Blaszczak-Boxe A; 2016. Fish Venom Unveiled: Toxins Evolved Many Times. Livescience.

Boisier P, Ranaivoson G, Rasolofonirina N, Roux J, Chanteau S, Takeshi Y; 1995. Fatal Mass Poisoning in Madagascar following Ingestion of a Shark (Carcharhinus leucas): Clinical and Epidemiological Aspects and Isolation of Toxins. Toxicon. 33 (10): 1359-64.

Bouder H, Cavallo A, Bouder MJ; 1962. Poissons Veneneux et ichryosarcotoxisme. Monaco: Bull. de l'Ins tit. Ocean. p. 66.

Bouder H, Cavallo A, Bouder MJ; 1962. Poissons veneneux et ichryosarcotoxisme. Monaco: Bull. de l'Ins tit. Ocean;. p. 66.

Boydron-Le Garrec R, Benoit E, Sauviat MP, Lewis RJ, Molgo´ J, Laurent D; 2005. Ability of some plant extracts, traditionally used to treat ciguatera fish poisoning, to prevent the in vitro neurotoxicity produced by sodium channel activators. Toxicon. 46(6):625–34.

Caillaud A, De la Iglesia P, Darius HT, Pauillac S, Aligizaki K, Fraga S, Chinain M, Dioge'ne J; 2010. Update on Methodologies Available for Ciguatoxin Determination: Perspectives to Confront the onset of Ciguatera Fish Poisoning in Europe. Mar Drugs. 8 (6): 1838-907.

Chevaldonne P; 1990. Ciguatera and the Saupe, Sarpa Salpa, in the Mediterranean: A Possible Misinterpretation. J Fish Biol. 37: 503-4.

Cho HE, Ahn SY, Son IS, In S, Hong RS, Kim DW, Woo SH, Moon DC, Kim S, 2012. Determination and Validation of Tetrodotoxin in Human whole Blood using Hydrophilic Interaction Liquid Chromatography–tandem Mass Spectroscopy and its Application. Forensic Science International, 217: 76-80.

Church JE, Hodgson WC; 2002. The Pharmacological Activity of Fish Venoms. Toxicon 40: 1083-1093.

Collette BB; 1966. A Review of the Venomous Toadfishes, Subfamily Thalassophryninae. Copeia. 4: 846-64.

Coutand H; 1879. Observations sur sept cas d'empoisonnement par le fois de requin a l'Ile des Pins (Nouvelle- Caledonie) en 1878. These, Faculte de Medecine, Universite´ de Montpellier.

De Haro L, Pommier P; 2006. Hallucinatory Fish Poisoning (ichthyoallyeinotoxism): Two Case Reports from the Western Mediterranean and Literature Review. Clin Toxicol. 44(2): 185 8.

De Sauvages FB; 1770. Les chefs-d'oeuvres de monsieur de Savages, vol. 2. V. Reguilliat: Lyon;. p. 212.

Fabricius O; 1780. Fauna Groenlandica, Systematice Sistens, Animalia Groenlandiae Occidentalis. Leipzig: Copenhagen.

Friedman MA, Fleming LE, Fernandez M, Bienfang P, Schrank K, Dickey R, Bottein MY, Backer L, Ayyar R, Weisman R, Watkins S; 2008. Ciguatera Fish Poisoning: Treatment, Prevention and Management. Mar Drugs. 6(3): 456-79.

Gilbert RJ, Hoeas G, Murnwy CK, Cruickshank JG, Young SEJ; 1980. Scombrotoxic Fish Poisoning: Features of the First SO Incidents to be Reported in Britain (1976- 79). Br Med J. 281:71.

Guss DA; 1998. Scombroid Fish Poisoning: Successful Treatment with Cimetidine. Undersea Hyperb Med. 25 (2): 123.

Halstead BW, Schall DW; 1956. A Report on the Poisonous Fishes Captured during the Woodrow G. Krieger Expedition to Cocos Island. Pacific Science, VoL X, January.

Halstead BW; 1965. Poisonous and Venomous Marine Animals of the World, Invertebrates, Vol. 1. Washington, DC: US Government Printing Office.

Halstead BW; 2001. Fish Toxins. In: Foodborne Disease: Handbook: Seafood and Environmental Toxins. 2nd ed. Y.H. Hui, D. Kitts and P.S. Stanfield (Eds), Marcek Dekker, New York, 4, 23-50.

Haro LD, and Pommier P, Hallucinatory Fish Poisoning (Ichthyoallyeinotoxism): Two Case Reports from the Western Mediterranean and Literature Review. Clinical Toxicology, 44:185-188, 2006.

Helfrich P, Banner A; 1960. Hallucinatory Mullet Poisoning. J Trop Med Hyg. 63: 86-9.

Kawataba T; 1962. Problems involved in the Research on Fish and Shellfish Poisonings. Jpn J Med Sci Biol. 15: 141-3.

Laurent D, Kerbrat AS, Darius HT, Girard E, Golubic S, Benoit E, Sauviat MP, Chinain M, Molgo J, Pauillac S; 2008. Are Cyanobacteria involved in Ciguatera Fish Poisoning-like Outbreaks in New Caledonia? Harmful Algae. 7(6): 827-38.

Lerke PA, Werner SB, Taylor SL, Guthertz LS; 1978. Scombroid Poisoning. Report of an outbreak. West J Med. 129: 381-6.

Macht DI, Spencer EC; 1941. Physiological and Toxicological Effects of some Fish Muscle Extracts. Proc Soc Exp Biol Med. 46(2): 228-33.

Meyer-Ahrens KM; 1855. Von den giftigen fischen. Schweiz Z Med Chir Geburtsh. 3: 188-230.

Ministry of Agriculture and Forestry www.foodsafety.govt.nz/science/research-projects/reports-projects/ 2010, Research of relevance to histamine poisoning in New Zealand A review.

Molgo´ J, Comella J, Legrand A; 1990. Ciguatoxin Enhances Quantal Transmitter Release from Frog Motor Nerve Terminals. Br J Pharmacol. 99: 695.

Molgo´ J, Shimahara T, Legrand A; 1993. Ciguatoxin, Extracted from Poisonous Morays eels, Causes Sodium Dependent Calcium Mobilization in NG108-15 Neuroblastoma Glioma Hybrid Cells. Neurosci Lett. 158: 147-50.

Munday PL, Schubert M, Baggio JA, Jones GP, Caley MJ and Grutter AS; 2003. Skin Toxins and External Parasitism of Coral-dwelling Gobies. Journal of Fish Biology, 62, 976-981.

Munir S, Siddiqui PJA, Morton SL; 2011. The Occurrence of the Ciguatera Fish Poisoning Producing Dinoflagellate genus Gambierdiscus in Pakistan Waters. Algae. 26(4): 317-25.

Russell FE; 1996. The Venomous and Poisonous Marine Invertebrates of the Indian Ocean. Enfield, NH: Science Publishers. p. 1-14.

Schnorf H, Taurarii M, Cundy T; 2002. Ciguatera Fish Poisoning: A Double-blind Randomized Trial of Mannitol Therapy. Neurology. 58: 873-80.

Singletary EM, Rochman AS, Bodmer JCA, Holstege CP; 2005. Envenomations. Med Clin North Am. 89:1195–224.

Spanier E; 1987. Dangerous Marine Organisms in the Coastal Waters. In: Nezer Y, Epstein Y, Editors. The Way out, the Skill to Survive. Tel Aviv: Israel Ministry of Defense Publishing Office. p. 235-74. (In Hebrew).

Taylor SL, 1986. Histamine Food Poisoning: Toxicology and Clinical Aspects. CRC Critical Reviews in Toxicology, 17, 91 (2).

The Poisonous Fishes of The Croatianadriatic Draga, 1994. ISBN 953-96204-2-2

Yasumoto T, Yasumura D, Yotsu M, Michishita T, Endo A, Kotaki Y; 1986. Bacterial Production of Tetrodotoxin and Anhydrotetrodotoxin. Agric Biol Chem. 50: 793-5.

Yoshida M, Sone S, Shiomi K; 2008. Purification and Characterization of a Proteinaceous Toxin from the Serum of Japanese eel Anguilla japonica. Protein J. 27 (7-8): 450-4.

Pages: 156-176

Animal Biodiversity and Fisheries
Edited by: Dr. Rashmi Tripathi; Dr. Vijay Sharma & Dr. Pawan Kumar 'Bharti'
ISBN: 978-93-88854-06-1
Edition: 2019
Published by: Discovery Publishing House Pvt. Ltd., New Delhi (India)

9

State-of-the-art of Seed Production of Pangas Catfish, Grow-out Farming of Major Carps and Contributions of a Renowned Fishery Scientist

Subrato Ghosh

ABSTRACT

In this communication we will discuss about the seed (fry, advanced fry) production practices of pangas catfish *Pangasianodon hypophthalmus* and achievements of fish breeder Sri Babul Majumdar, production technology of big-sized Indian major carps in grow-out ponds followed by exemplary fish farmer Sri Shyamapada Patra and contributions of eminent fishery scientist-cum-fish technologist Late Prof. Dr Arabindo Nath Bose. All these three persons belong to West Bengal and have achieved much fame at national level. Sri Majumdar and Sri Patra are national award-winning fish farmers and Prof. Bose had been Founder Director of ICAR-CIFT, Kochi. Author was fortunate to come in contact with these three persons at their home site; experiences gained *via* intimate conversation have been descriptively documented here. It is a modest endeavour to present the skill, knowledge, manner of living of these three persons, which do have influence in our lives and who have contributed in development and prosperity of Indian fisheries and commercial aquaculture sector but are less-remembered. This communication will be of interest to readers.

Pangasianodon hypophthalmus - A Commercially Important Fish

In India, West Bengal (WB) is the leading fish seed producing state and North 24 Parganas district is the hub of production centre of fry stages of major carps and economically important cultivable catfishes. Recently greater thrust has been given to production of the pangas catfish *Pangasianodon hypophthalmus* (*Pangasius sutchi* is a synonym of *P. hypophthalmus*) fry by fish breeders in commercial scale hatcheries in this

Formerly Lecturer (Part-time), MSc Fisheries and Aquaculture Division, Utkal University, Bhubaneswar.

district. It grows to almost 1kg in four months and a minimum harvest of 12000kg/ha/year is achievable from culture ponds. According to National Fisheries Development Board (Govt. of India) estimates, its farming has increased since 2004 due to the commercial importance and there is growing interest among fish farming community in Krishna and West Godavari districts of Andhra Pradesh (AP) to take up its culture in a larger extent, thus paving way for demand for its seed. About 300-500 million *P. hypophthalmus* seed is produced every year in WB (Lakra and Singh, 2010). *P. hypophthalmus* exhibits remarkable growth rate even in semi-clean grow-out ponds relatively old in existence. Much enthusiasm has arisen among fish breeders in North 24 Pgs, WB for artificial spawning of *P. hypophthalmus.*

Exemplary and three-times national awardee fish breeder Sri Babul Majumdar in North 24 Pgs is producing *P. hypophthalmus* fry in a large scale since 2002. He was able to introduce this fish to AP and other parts of India after his 34 years struggle in fish breeding and seed rearing business. It has been found that there is a shift of culture practice from major carps to pangas catfish in considerable areas in AP. The culture production of *P. hypophthalmus* ranges from 7 tonnes/ha/year to 20 tonnes/ha/year and the average production is found to be higher than carp production in the same area. It is a promising candidate species for freshwater catfish culture (Chaturvedi *et al.*, 2015).

Sri Majumdar is a well-known name in the field of fish breeding, not only in North 24 Parganas district of WB but in the entire state. He has experienced that breeding and seed production of rupchanda *Piaractus brachypomus* and *Pangasianodon hypophthalmus* is more profitable than major carps. For the first time in India, fry stages of *P. brachypomus* were produced in his hatchery-cum-seed farm in 2007. Recently, on 30/6/2018, author was fortunate to have a glimpse of the different *P. hypophthalmus* nursery ponds at Sri Majumdar's farm, each of which contain either 2-days, 3-days or 6-days old growing spawn. Sri Majumdar was generous to spend some time with author in the midst of supervision and giving instructions to his employees. We will discuss about experiences of Sri Majumdar about artificial spawning and seed production of *P. hypophthalmus.*

BRIEF PROFILE OF SRI SHRI BABUL MAZUMDER

Sri Babul Majumdar, aged 64 years, is proprietor of Majumdar Fisheries at Vill. Sibdaspur, P.O. Salidaha, Block Barrackpore-I, PS Naihati (via Kanchrapara), Dist. North 24 Parganas, WB. Sri Majumdar is a successful progressive fish breeder, with expertise in pangas catfish and rupchanda and his biography is a lesson to those who desire to accept aquaculture as their profession for income generation to support livelihood (Chakrabarti *et al.*, 2012). He had to face poverty since his childhood days. After 1978, during his daily travel from one village to another for artificial insemination of cows, he used to observe regular fish catch in village and their sale. He was attracted towards fishery and influenced to accept this practice for his livelihood support. He received training in pisciculture from District-level fishery training centre at Barasat town in this district, visited different places in WB where scientific fish culture was in vogue extensively, went to Bankura district for learning fish breeding techniques, obtained training from Freshwater Fisheries Research Station, Kulia, Dist. Nadia, also necessary guidance from renowned fish breeder Late Nilu Ghosh in Naihati area. Gradually he started fish culture activity and got seriously involved in rearing and grow-out pond management practices.

Sri Majumdar initially purchased carp spawn from Lalgola in Murshidabad district and Bankura and reared them in his ponds. He planned for developing hatchery of his own for production of spawn. He initially started breeding fishes in hapa enclosures and produced spawn sufficient for stocking in his culture ponds. After continuing this activity upto two years, in 1985, he achieved considerable success of monetary benefit and started carp hatchery by learning the technique from Sri Ghosh. Today, in 2018, he has come up at a highly successful stage through his persistence and untiring efforts with a motto to achieve success in fish culture, which had been his source of inspiration. Presently, he is running fish seed production as a large scale business enterprise and has become a leading and reliable fish seed producer in India.

In July 2011, an article was published about Sri Babul Majumdar with the title 'Untiring efforts and never failing attitude made a poor farmer to reach a height of successful progressive fish farmer' in the booklet Aquaculture Innovators, brought out by ICAR-CIFA, Bhubaneswar. It was authored by experienced scientists of ICAR-CIFA Regional Centre, Kalyani. Sri Majumdar is undoubtedly a fish farm innovator, and his innovative ideas and management practices in freshwater aquaculture have been descriptively documented in this booklet. In total seed farm area of 60 bigha (1980 decimal) at Majumdar Fisheries, there are total 16 well-maintained fish ponds, with 12 nursery ponds and 4 brood stock ponds. Area of his fish culture ponds range from 8 decimal to 100 decimal. His rearing pond is located outside this hatchery-cum-nursery pond premises at a distance of 6km. Seventeen concrete circular egg hatching-cum-incubation pools (familiar Chinese model) and fifteen rectangular cement cisterns (with water exchange facilities, for temporary maintenance of brood stock and seed fishes) have been constructed here, which are all running efficiently. The entire fish seed production unit is equipped with modern technologies.

RECOGNITIONS RECEIVED

Sri Majumdar was felicitated by West Bengal University of Animal and Fishery Sciences in 2010. In addition to this, he received felicitation from ICAR-CIFA, Bhubaneswar on 10th July 2011 on National Fish Farmers' Day and Aquaculture Innovators Meet 'for successful adoption of freshwater aquaculture technologies for enhancing fish farm productivity and providing leadership to the farming community'; was felicitated by ICAR-CIFE Kolkata Centre on National Fish Farmers' Day 2013 for his commendable achievement in fisheries and aquaculture; received Certificate of Appreciation from ICAR-CIFA on 18th August, 2012 'for his meritorious contribution towards aquaculture productivity by adopting and popularizing Pabda *Ompak pabda* breeding and culture in West Bengal'; received ICAR-CIFRI Platinum Jubilee Award in March 2018 'for outstanding achievement in fish and fisheries and supporting livelihood to vast community, which is a step towards doubling income of farmers by 2012' and at the same time delivered Platinum Jubilee lecture; received felicitation from ICAR-CIFA on 10th July 2009 on National Fish Farmers' Day 'for his efforts in adopting CIFA technologies in the field of carp seed production for enhancing fish farm productivity'; received Young Fish Farmer Award from ICAR-CIFRI, Barrackpore on 10th July, 2002.

In March-April 2019, most likely Sri Majumdar will receive the prestigious Jag Jivan Ram Innovative Farmer Award from Ministry of Agriculture, Govt. of India. Sri Majumdar was invited to ICAR-NBFGR, Lucknow in November 2016 to discuss about the prospects, conditions of farming, merits and demerits of farming of *Piaractus brachypomus* in freshwater ponds, which he introduced in WB. He was also invited by Director of Tripura State Fisheries Department as an Advisor at Agartala to discuss about prospects of farming of *Pangasianodon hypophthalmus* and *Piaractus brachypomus*. Sri Majumdar was an invitee in the one-day Scientists-Fish entrepreneurs' workshop (interactive discussion-cum-awareness programme) organized at ICAR-CIFA Kalyani Centre on 17th July 2017.

Induced breeding of *P. hypophthalmus*

Presently, as seen in the end June during the visit, artificial spawning and seed production (fry and advanced fry) of *P. hypophthalmus* only is conducted in this farm. Sri Majumdar is concentrating on this fish heavily as there is great demand of its early stages outside WB. From March, brooders are maintained for two months prior to breeding operation. *P. hypophthalmus* attains sexual maturity and becomes ready for induced breeding at 4+ years of age. In broodstock ponds with high stocking density, fishes attain less weight at 4 years of age, but in ponds with comparatively lesser stocking density, fishes attain a higher body weight at this age. Normally 1500kg brooders can be maintained in every 8-9 decimal pond. It does not require much space.

For the *P. hypophthalmus* (and also for *P. brachypomus*) brooders, 250kg good quality whole dry yellow peas is boiled and fed to the fishes every morning. Ground nut oil cake is used at evening time. For every 1500kg broodstock of *P. hypophthalmus*, 25kg boiled dry yellow peas is used as feed every morning and 20kg GNOC every evening. Males weighing 1000-2000gm and females 2500-3000gm are considered suitable for induced breeding. For females, an interval of 4.5-5.0 hours is maintained in between first and second injection, pituitary extract is used as the inducing agent. The first and second doses of injection are 1mg/kg and 14mg/kg body weight respectively. The single dosage for male fish is 0.5mg/kg body weight, applied at the time of second dose to female. Stripping for release of gametes is conducted on the 6th hour of second injection to female at 38-40°C water temperature and in between 7.0-7.5 hours at 33-34°C temperature. Wet stripping method is followed both for *P. brachypomus* and *P. hypophthalmus*.

Injected male and female brooders are kept separately in cement tanks. During artificial spawning and stripping of *P. hypophthalmus*, milt of 2 males is used to fertilize ova obtained from 3 females in enamel tray. Even sufficient milt of one male does work efficiently. In order to remove adhesiveness of ova and ensure effective fertilization, the fertilized eggs are rinsed and washed with buffalo milk or a mixture of urea and tannic acid, Sri Majumdar stated. But normally the sieved yellow clayey soil obtained from Bankura district, devoid of sand completely, is used. At the beginning of the season, in March-April, a dosage of 1mg/kg body weight is applied to males. If hormonal injection dosage to males is increased, fluidity of milt increases (becomes thinner) which is undesirable. It will not be able to cause fertilization of ova. Fertilized eggs obtained from 5-6 females are kept in a single hatching-cum-incubation chamber. After 20 hours of incubation period, larvae hatch out. The 17-18 days old *P. hypophthalmus* fry are harvested from rearing pond and maintained in rectangular cement cisterns of dimension 15 feet x 20 feet. Those are reared for next 6-8 days and these attain saleable size by then.

SOME FEATURES OF POND MANAGEMENT

The cherry plum fruit chebulic myrobalan *Terminalia chebula* is used in *P. hypophthalmus* ponds. It destroys dense mass of green algae in fish ponds and also turbidity of ponds caused due to mud particles can be eliminated. Upon application of chebulic myrobalan, mud particles coagulate and settle at bottom of pond. When required, it is applied @ 20kg/33 decimal water body. A mixture of soap 'LifeBuoy' brand and mustard oil is used in *P. hypophthalmus* nursery ponds. Besides killing aquatic insects, since mustard oil has fat content, application of it enriches zooplankton population in ponds. Soap is first boiled in huge iron kadhai utensil over furnace, thereafter oil is added. A mixture of 5kg soap and 15 kg oil is applied in every 33 decimal pond, 48 hours prior to spawn (*P. hypophthalmus*) stocking. Depth of his nursery ponds is 3.0-3.5 feet.

After 2-3 crops, nursery ponds are sundried, dust Mohua oil cake @ 25kg/33 decimal is applied over the earth. On the same day, mohua oil cake soaked in water in previous night is sprayed over the dry pond earth. On the next morning, lime $CaCO_3$ solution is applied @ 20kg/33 decimal. The pond is allowed to remain in this condition the whole day, and water is filled in during evening. When water is let into nursery ponds, before spawn stocking, it is sieved through fine-meshed bolting silk cloth (hapa enclosure is constructed with such cloth at one end of the ponds and water is poured in here first); in this process larger zooplankton of Copepoda group (*Cyclops* sp., *Diaptomus* sp.) is trapped and are not allowed to enter into nurseries. Otherwise these will predate upon spawn after stocking.

Sri Majumdar stated that for *Labeo bata* and *Puntius javanicus,* spawn are stocked in earthen nurseries on 120th hour of second injection to females, but for *P. brachypomus*, *P. hypophthalmus* and *Ctenopharyngodon idella,* it is stocked on 96th hour. *P. hypophthalmus* spawn obtained from hatching-cum-incubation chambers is first kept in hapa enclosures in cement tanks for few hours, then stocked in nursery ponds. On 10th day, these small fry (advanced spawn) are harvested from nurseries and stocked in rearing pond. At the time when *P. hypophthalmus* fry weigh 250mg (4000 pieces/ kg), those are harvested from rearing pond and stocked in those rectangular cisterns, maintained for a brief period before sale. Four borewell submersible pumps are used here as water source. Drawn-out water is stored in one pond, oxygenation is provided here at a high rate and water is continuously agitated by traditional but effective aeration device. This water is allowed to flow into overhead tank, next it flows down into the hatching-cum-incubation units, used water finally flows into different ponds.

FEED FOR GROWING SPAWN

The 4-day old stage is stocked into nursery ponds @ 6-9 lakh/pond. On the 9-10th day of stocking, these are harvested from nurseries and stocked in rearing pond (bigger in size) @ 4-5 lakh/pond. From 9-10th day, liquefied form of GNOC is fed to the advanced spawn two times a day. An amount of 8kg GNOC is used for every 2,00,000 spawn (10-days stage) daily in rearing pond. From 10th day, dry rice polish (5-7kg in each pond) is fed to advanced spawn of *P. hypophthalmus*. For every 3000nos. of spawn (10-days stage), 10-15kg rice polish is used everyday.

For the first ten days after stocking, powdered milk suspension is used (@ 4kg/82 decimal pond everyday and 3kg in smaller nurseries) in morning and evening in nurseries where *P. hypophthalmus* spawn are stocked. From same time, minced tubifex worm is applied in the ponds @ 3kg/33 decimal pond. A mixture of GNOC (50kg), dust shrimp feed (Rs 95/-/kg; 40kg) and AgriMin. Feed supplement (40kg) is allowed to compost in cement cisterns; then it is applied @ 7-8kg/65 decimal pond. It is used considering the condition of pond water, not used routinewise. Transparent and thin extract of chebulic myrobalan is used in nursery ponds @ 60-70kg/65 decimal water body. Thicker extract of the same is used in *P. hypophthalmus* brooders' pond.

The 10-days stage is propagated in rearing pond for next 7-8 days, which is a large pond of 650 decimal located at a distance of 6km from this campus. In each of the large rectangular cement cisterns, before sale, the 17-18 days old fry are fed 30-35kg tubifex worms, 10kg pelleted shrimp feed and lumpfulls of dust-type commercial feed daily. In addition to tubifex worms, pelleted feed (1mm dia) is used. In each such cistern, 3-4 quintals of *P. hypophthalmus* fry are stocked. Seeds weighing 250-1000mg (22-24mm) are supplied to Andhra Pradesh by air and sold @ Re 0.40-0.50 / piece; larger ones of 45-48mm size are sold at renowned Rajendrapur-Battala fish seed market in North 24 Parganas @ Re 0.70-0.80 / piece.

END NOTE

Sri Babul Majumdar has been thoroughly trained by ICAR-CIFA, Kalyani in breeding and rearing of *O. pabda*. He is now capable of selling pabda seeds in the market @ Rs 3/-/piece. Deep-layer ground water is required for breeding and seed production of *O. pabda*, and it must be completely iron-free, Sri Majumdar opined. It attains 50-60gm in one year. In one of his brood stock pond of 2.5 bigha (82 decimal), he is maintaining 10-12 tonnes of brood fishes comprising Indian major carps and *P. brachypomus*. In one of his nursery pond of 3 bigha (100 decimal), he stocked 20,00,000nos. spawn of *P. hypophthalmus* and those were being maintained (9-10 days stage as on 30th June 2018) under proper condition. Every management aspect in each pond is cautiously and meticulously looked into by Sri Majumdar and his workforce. There are 35 male and 5 female workers in this seed farm. Since 2007, *P. brachypomus* seeds are produced here. According to Sri Majumdar, brooders and spawn of *P. brachypomus* cannot be reared in chebulic myrobalan extract treated water.

Sri Majumdar has installed closed-circuit television camera in different places in his farm. His residence is at Ramkrishna Colony, which is 2km away. He is working on seed production of economically-important cultivable freshwater fishes for the last 38 years. In last 14 years, many trainees and State Government officers from different parts of India, who come for weeklong training at ICAR-CIFA Kalyani Regional Centre, have visited this farm and undergone demonstration of different facets of induced breeding and fish seed production. Dignitaries including Dr S. Ayyappan, Former DG, ICAR; Dr P. Jayasankar, Former Director, ICAR-CIFA; Dr J. K. Sundaray, Director, ICAR-CIFA; Sri Kiranmoy Nanda, Former Minister of Fisheries, Government of WB; Minister of Fisheries, Government of Tripura; Scientists of ICAR-CIFA Kalyani and Rahara Regional Centres have visited Sri Babul Majumdar's hatchery. Author is truly grateful to Sri Babul Majumdar and Sri Jafar Ali, elderly farm employee for entertaining author at hatchery site and patiently explaining different activities pertaining to induced breeding and seed production of *P. hypophthalmus*. There exists a lot of scope for freshwater catfish (*O. pabda, P. hypophthalmus, Mystus vittatus, M. cavasius, Clarias batrachus, Heteropneustes fossilis*) seed production and farming in India for diversification of aquaculture and sustainable production. It is particularly suited to agro-climatic condition of Dist. North 24 Parganas and other places in WB.

A matured *Pangasianodon hypophthalmus*

Oxygenation method in pond

Maintenance of tubifex worms

Chebulic myrobalan treated brooders' pond

Normal broodstock pond

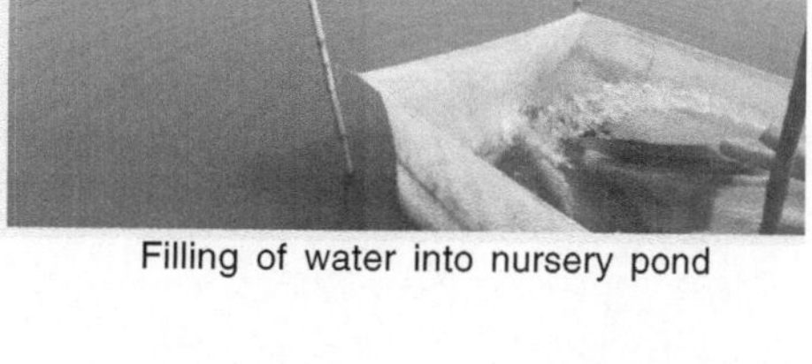

Filling of water into nursery pond

Hapa enclosures constructed in a tank

Egg hatching-cum-incubation pools

A rectangular cemented cistern

Nursery pond preparation in progress

Sri Babul Majumdar (on right)

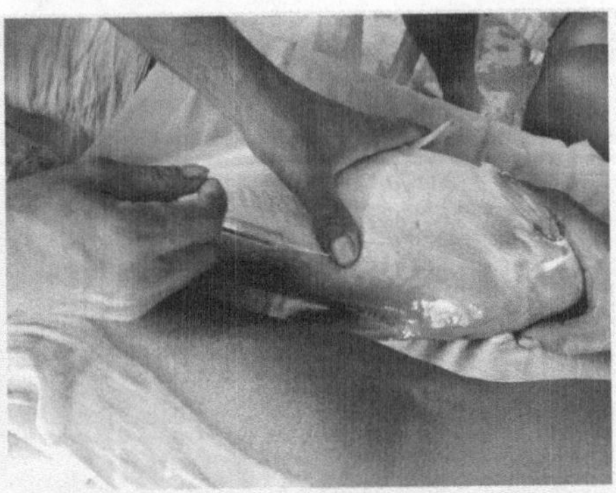

Pituitary extract injected to brood fish – 1

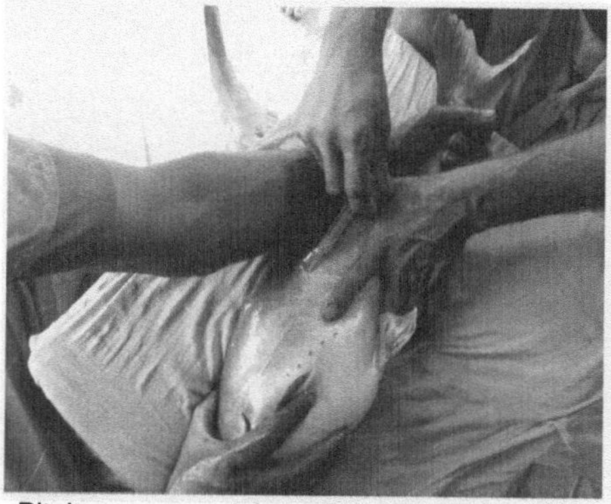

Pituitary extract injected to brooder – 2

Injected brood fish storage chambers

Preparation of powdered milk suspension

Preparing minced tubifex worms

Compost of GNOC and other ingredients

Tubifex fed to *P. hypophthalmus* fry

Advanced fry of *P. hypophthalmus*

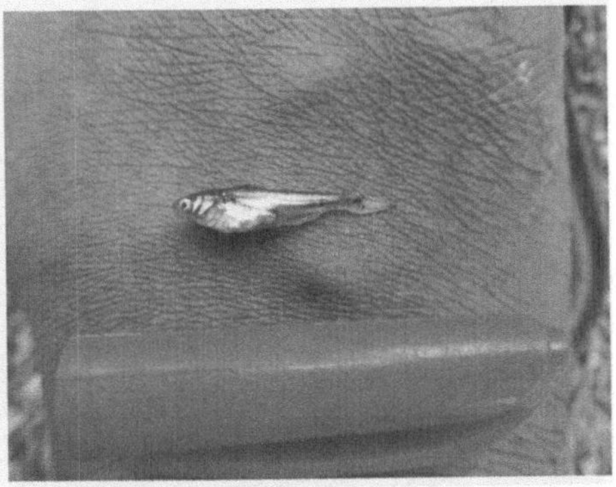

Normal pangas fry (24mm)

Mixing of milt and ova of *P. hypophthalmus*

Release of ova from female brooder

Stripping of female fish

Addition of water over mixed gametes

Mixing of stripped ova and milt

Pouring mixed gametes into Hundi

Mixing of gametes – another view

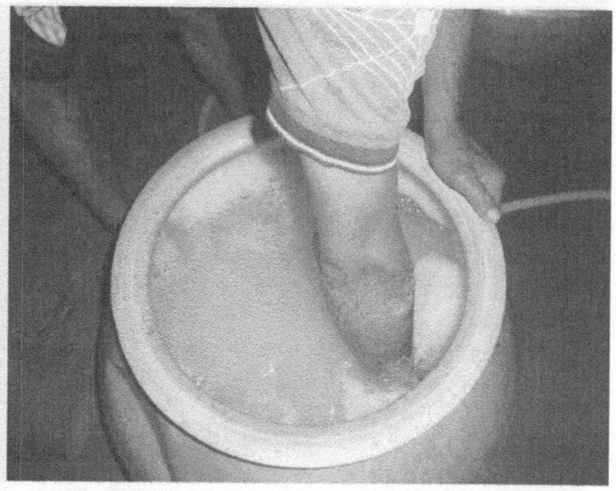

Mixing of dry clay soil with gametes

Addition of dry Bankura clay soil

Rinsing and washing of gametes

Pouring of gametes in hatching pool water

Stripping of male brood fish

Release of fertilized eggs in hatching pool

Thorough mixing of gametes and dry soil

SRI SHYAMAPADA PATRA AND HIS ACHIEVEMENTS

We will get an idea about a successful progressive fish farmer and big fish producer of Hooghly district of WB, Sri Shyamapada Patra, who grows larger major carps that are preferred by consumers in total 120 acre (306 bigha) water body. Author had a conversation with Sri Patra at his pond site on 5/5/2018. Since 2012, Hon'ble Chief Minister, West Bengal has been conferring 'Maati Samman Award' every year to the farmers who have done pioneering work in their respective fields (ARD, agriculture, horticulture, fisheries, agri-marketing). In 2017, Sri Shyamapada Patra (aged 48), a noted fish farmer and big fish producer from Hooghly district was the only awardee in fisheries sector; the award was conferred to him at Mati-Tirtha Krishi Katha Prangan, Burdwan on 9th January, 2017. His outstanding contribution to inland fisheries and aquaculture development was also duly acknowledged as conferred upon the 'Best Fish Farmer Award' in National Fish Farmers' Day programme by Hon'ble Director, ICAR-Central Inland Fisheries Research Institute, Barrackpore on 10th July, 2016 at ICAR-CIFRI. Sri Patra has set an example for those who desire to adopt aquaculture of major carps in ponds as the profession/vocation for income generation.

In 2007, Dr C. Mohankumaran Nair and Dr K. R. Salin had mentioned in their article 'Carp polyculture in India' that in Andhra Pradesh, 20% of fish farmers stock *Labeo rohita, Catla catla* and *Cirrhinus mrigala* and get an overall yield of 9000-11000kg/ha/year. Remaining 80% farmers stock *L. rohita* and *C. catla* and get an average production of 13000-15000kg/ha/year (Nair and Salin, 2007). In recent years, there has been a significant expansion in commercial pond carp culture in India. Remarkably Sri Patra has achieved a higher fish production in comparison to afore-mentioned production of AP farmers. With a production rate of 8000-9000kg/40 decimal water body/year in total 3-4 crops, he motivates all farmers to come into the fold of aquaculture of major carps. Sri Shyamapada Patra is a sincere, dedicated, hardworking and experienced fish farmer.

THE BEGINNING

Sri Shyamapada Patra, S/o Late Badal Chandra Patra has been practicing major carp culture in large freshwater bodies since 1995-1996. His residence is at: Vill and P.O. Hatbasantapur, Mayapur-II GP under Arambagh CD Block, PS Arambagh, Dist. Hooghly. Due to instable and impecunious economic condition of family, Sri Patra had his education only till VIIIth standard. His mother worked as maid-servant in nearby homes to support family income. Till 22 years of age, Sri Patra earned a living by selling fishes door-to-door in semi-urban and rural areas (Muthudanga, Balarampur, etc.) of Arambagh carrying on Hundi (40 litre rounded aluminium container) over shoulders, and working as temporary waged labour as and when called for netting operation for harvesting of pond-raised fishes. But income from this business was not sufficient to support his family. In 1995, Sri Patra decided to enter the fish farming business; took a large freshwater body on lease, 20 acre in area, for scientific fish farming at Vill. Uttar Narayanpur, P.O. Bhalia, Batanol GP under Arambagh Block by paying Rs 1,00,000/-. It was a distance of 5km from his residence. Successes that were achieved by private fish farmers in pond fish culture in the Kolleru lake region of AP (where 700000 tonnes of major carps is produced every year) encouraged Sri Patra to take up commercial fish farming. He understood that culture of fish is a scientific process and good management is essential.

Presently Sri Patra is producing table-sized fishes in total nine fish ponds ('macchher bheri' in local dialect) taken on lease for continuous term of five years; six of them each 800-1000 decimal (20-25 bigha) in area, two ponds each 2400 decimal (60 bigha) in area and one pond 1600 decimal (40 bigha). Depth of water is 5-7 feet. Most of these are located in Uttar Narayanpur village, others in Gorbari and Mayapur villages under Arambagh PS. He has engaged 8 regular/permanent employees who are elderly and experienced; in addition to this, more than 60 daily wage labourers find work from time to time. His fish ponds are well-managed and looked after by all of them. He has to pay lease amount of Rs 12,00,000/- per year for a 60 bigha water body. Hut-like night shelters are constructed at three places on pond embankment in each of the three large ponds.

MANAGEMENT PRACTICES

In India, Kolleru carp culture system is the dominant production model for IMC culture. Sri Patra tried to replicate this production system in his ponds and has been successful. His production scenario (on-going semi-intensive polyculture type) enables him to grow big fishes. Sri Patra stocks larger stunted yearlings of major carps 150-250gm in size. Since major carps are known to grow faster during their second year, now-a-days grow-out ponds are stocked with 8-12 month old stunted fishes or much large-sized fingerlings by progressive farmers, instead of normal fingerlings as practiced in the traditional system. At time of stocking, his *C. catla* weigh 250gm (procured at Rs 145/-/kg), *L. rohita* and *C. mrigala* 150-175gm each (*L. rohita* and *C. mrigala* are procured at Rs 138/-/kg and Rs 115/-/kg respectively). Such fishes are stocked at density of 850-900nos./40 decimal water area. Black carp *Mylopharyngodon piceus* and grass carp *Ctenopharyngodon idella* are also stocked in lesser numbers. Fish-eating birds are unable to prey upon those.

As supplementary feed, Sri Patra uses a dry, finely-ground mixture of de-oiled rice bran, groundnut oil cake, maize dust, soyabean meal, Vit.Min. mixture, molasses and common salt. Feeding to fishes is undertaken daily in the morning. Supposedly, for growing fishes in a 60 bigha pond, considering the main ingredients, daily feed contains 25 sacks of de-oiled rice bran, 4 sacks of GNOC, 2 sacks of maize dust, 1 sack of soyabean meal, 16kg molasses; each sack contains 60kg material. In terms of fish growth and economic returns, Sri Patra is satisfied with such mash feed that he is using. Ingredients are thoroughly mixed and loaded into feed bags, which are perforated fertilizer bags of 50kg capacity. Holes 8-10mm are drilled in each bag usually in 5-6 rows. Required quantity of mash is placed in bags. Sri Patra's workers transport feed-filled bags to middle areas of pond at feeding points with the help of tin-built boat (supported by iron plates), and the 'pole bag feeding' method is followed. Bags are tied individually to upright fixed feeding poles such that it remains completely submerged.

In a 60 bigha pond, 45 upright bamboo poles and 45 feeding bags are used every time. A set of 45 bags used on a day is replaced by another set next day; the previous used set of bags are washed, dried and meant to be used 'day after tomorrow'. In this way, two sets of 45 bags are used on every alternate day. Sri Patra is using 120 bags in all for such a pond. For a 60 bigha pond, he uses 300 sacks of mohua oil cake (18000kg) and 1000kg lime before fish stocking. In such pond, he applies 3.5-4.0 quintals of lime once in every month. Sri Patra uses diesel water pumps mounted in boats to aerate pond water and enhance dissolved oxygen content, uses recommended fish medicines and $KMnO_4$ solution in correct dosage. In all fish culture ponds, he has kept provision of submersible pumps (240 feet deep) to draw groundwater and maintain the ideal depth of water. He uses fish carrier containers (light in weight, semi-flexible, carried by two persons) for 150-250gm fishes as well as harvested big fishes; 60kg fishes can be given bath (prophylactic) treatment in 60lit $KMnO_4$ solution in such container.

Sri Patra harvest fishes in between 90th-100th day of stocking. In this three-month culture period, *C. catla* attains 1800-2000gm body weight, *L. rohita* 900-1000gm, *C. mrigala* 750-900gm. Fishes grow rapidly in enormous space in such big ponds and on good quality feed. Total annual production level, as mentioned earlier, is 8-9 tonnes/bigha [1 bigha = 40 decimal]. Purposefully healthy IMC 4 pieces weighing 1kg (for *C. catla*) and 6 pieces weighing 1kg (for *L. rohita, C. mrigala*) are stocked, which are brought from Pandua, Dasghara in Hooghly and other selected places. Harvested fishes are transported for sale to Arambagh town, distant places like Tarakeswar, Chawkbazar and Bandel in Hooghly district, Ukhra, Durgapur and Asansol in Burdwan district.

[*Note:* In a conversation with Sri Bijoy Pakhira, Secretary of Mudially Fishermen Cooperative Society Ltd. 'Nature Park' (renowned in West Bengal), Taratala Road in west Kolkata on 4/5/2018, author was informed that in each of large water bodies 1.5-2.0 hectare in area (located within FCS complex) taken on lease from Kolkata Port Trust authority for fish farming, which are very well-managed by FCS members, major carp fingerlings (35-40 pieces weighing 1kg) grow upto 250-300gm in 60-75 days period; such fishes grow upto 700-750gm in next 20-21 days and fishes of size 750gm attain 2500-3500gm in next 40 days. Good quality floating pelleted-type fish feed, supplied to them from Office of Asst. Director of Fisheries, South 24 Parganas, is provided to growing fishes in routine-wise manner. The earlier statement is applicable for Mudially FCS also: 'Fishes grow rapidly in high quality feed and in enormous space'. Mudially FCS was awarded on 10th July 2016 at ICAR-CIFRI for being the best managed FCS for big fish production in large water bodies].

END NOTE

Story of Sri Shyamapada Patra is quoted as an example of the success of a private fish farmer in WB. Unfortunately, few years earlier, he lost 10 tonnes of fish due to red ulcer disease. Now he has recovered from this setback. In addition to the afore-mentioned two awards conferred to him, Sri Patra earned the recognition of 'Kriti Krishak' from Office of the Asst.

Director of Agriculture, Arambagh Block in January 2016. During February 2015, he has successfully completed a four-day Block-level fishery training programme conducted by Office of the Asst. Director of Fisheries, Hooghly and organized at Arambagh Block office. He has acquainted himself with the particulars of scientific fish farming to improve his techniques and production. He has trained and encouraged his younger brother and others to grow more fish and is interested in new techniques and findings in fish farming.

Sri Patra expressed his gratefulness to Office of Assistant Director of Fisheries, Hooghly district for all kind of help and encouragement that were extended to him. In a four hour meet with Sri Patra, author has realized that Sri Patra takes keen interest and is cautious about every aspect of pond management practice. He is also owner of an auction stall/point at Muthudanga wholesale fish market in Arambagh town. Sri Patra is expected to contribute and bring a positive change in farmed freshwater fish production in Hooghly district, will motivate and inspire other fish farmers. Sri Patra entertained author at his home and pond sites. Sri Hironmoy Kundu and Sri Shyamsundar Malik, elderly employees at Sri Patra's fish ponds explained some important features in fish pond management practices to author.

A large fish pond of Sri Patra

Author with Sri Shyamapada Patra

Author, Sri Patra and Sri H. Kundu

Fish carrier container

Sri Patra applying fish feed in pond

Submersible pump in operation

Perforated fish feed bags used by Sri Patra

পশ্চিমবঙ্গ সরকার

মাটি সম্মান

শ্যামাপদ পাত্র

সুধী,

রাজ্যের মৎস্য চাষের সামগ্রিক উন্নয়নে ও উন্নত প্রযুক্তি সম্প্রসারণে আপনার অনন্য অবদানের স্বীকৃতিস্বরূপ আপনাকে মাটি সম্মান পুরস্কার প্রদান করে পশ্চিমবঙ্গ সরকার আনন্দিত ও গর্বিত।

নবান্ন, হাওড়া
১ ই জানুয়ারী, ২০১৭

মমতা বন্দ্যোপাধ্যায়
মুখ্যমন্ত্রী, পশ্চিমবঙ্গ

Letter of Appreciation from Hon'ble CM

CONTRIBUTIONS OF LATE PROF. A.N. BOSE

Renowned Indian fishery scientist and food technologist Prof. Dr A. N. Bose left this mortal world on 19th March, 2003 and year 2018 marks the 15th death anniversary of Dr Bose. We will recapitulate the life sketch and works of Dr Bose. Topics of some of his important research publications have been presented here and revisited, which may not be known to all readers. Those were published in an era when technology of fish processing in India was in its budding stage. Dr A. N. Bose's role in the development of finfish and shellfish post-harvest technology in India will be remembered for long. True to the values he lived by, he left his body to the Kolkata Medical College in cause of scientific study and research.

Dr A.N. Bose's contribution to Indian fisheries and aquaculture is less-remembered as his name is not linked with standardization/ development/refinement of any successful technology on freshwater pond aquaculture, neither did he contributed to livelihood development of rural fish farmers nor in basic science of ichthyology. But, at the same time, it must be mentioned that Dr A.N. Bose was a prominent figure in Indian scientific fraternity engaged in food research and development during late fifties and later on. Indian scientists like Dr M. S. Swaminathan (Former DG, ICAR), Dr V. Subrahmanian, Dr H. A. B. Parpia (both Former Directors of CSIR-CFTRI, Mysore), Dr A. Srinivasan (Former Director of Food Technology Department, BARC, Mumbai) and Dr A. N. Bose contributed by providing a firm base for fundamental research in food production, development of technology for conservation and processing of fish food and non-fish food products, human resource development for R & D and manufacturing industry, identification of R & D priorities.

Edible marine finfish and shellfish resources are perishable goods considerably affected by fishing and storage conditions. Development of fishery technologies supports food sustainability to achieve a steady supply of good quality fish and fishery products. In this connection, Dr A. N. Bose, the pioneering fish technologist and pioneer in research and education in food technology in India, gave new orientation to fish foods-related technology through his leadership at ICAR-Central Institute of Fisheries Technology, Cochin (Sen, 2005; Baisya, 2008). As a Bengalee scientist, Dr P. Das became the first Director of ICAR-National Bureau of Fish Genetic Resources, Lucknow in 1986. Similarly, much earlier, Late Dr A. N. Bose became the first and founder Director of another ICAR research institute on fisheries science and aquaculture, namely ICAR-CIFT in 1957.

A SHORT OBITUARY – DR E.G. SILAS

A man with great scientific versatility and visionary in academic and research activities in Indian fisheries and aquaculture, Dr Eric Godwin Silas, died on 27th April 2018 at 90 years of age at his home in Ernakulam town. Dr Silas has contributed much to our knowledge on the biology and populations of coastal and oceanic tunas (Perciformes : Scombridae) from the Indian Ocean, which are the fastest-swimming pelagic fish. By participating in expeditions (ocean-going cruises) in the oceanic waters, Dr Silas contributed wealth of information on the Scombroid resources. Right from college days, Dr Silas continued to study hill-stream fishes by identifying it systematically. After completing M.Sc studies, Dr Silas obtained Ph.D in 1954 and D.Sc. in 1972, all from University of Madras. Dr Silas registered for M.Sc through research under eminent personality Dr S. L. Hora. On completion of Ph.D, Dr Silas was selected to the position of Curator of the Bombay Natural History Society (BNHS) and the Natural History Section of the Prince of Wales Museum. After US visit, he rejoined BNHS as Registrar and worked there until 1959.

In 1948 and sometimes later, Dr Silas had sent hill-stream fish samples from the southern Western Ghats to Dr. S. L. Hora, the then Director at Zoological Survey of India (ZSI), Kolkata for research purpose. Following advice of Dr Hora at Calcutta in 1949, Dr Silas documented his observations and submitted it for publication. Dr E. G. Silas was a honourary research worker at ZSI during 1950-1955, and joined ICAR-CMFRI as honourary research worker in June 1959. He chose to work on tunas and tuna-like fishes of Scombridae family at Mandapam camp of ICAR-CMFRI. He also served as Pool Officer of CSIR here. Till 1953, Dr Silas often had to stay less comfortably with fishermen, collected fishes from Gujarat to Kanyakumari along the Western Ghats and studied the icthyofauna of hill streams, thereby contributed a wealth of knowledge on the species richness and diversity of Indian finfishes. During his Fulbright-cum-Rockefeller Post-Doctoral Fellowship in USA, Dr Silas had the privilege of working with Dr. Carl L. Hubbs and had contacts with scientists of the Inter-American Tropical Tuna Commission at San Diego. In 1963, Dr Silas got his first permanent job as marine biologist at ICAR-CMFRI.

Dr Silas served as Director of ICAR-Central Marine Fisheries Research Institute, Ernakulam during June 1975 - June 1985, he was founder Director of ICAR-Central Institute of Brackishwater Aquaculture, Chennai during November 1985 - July 1987, Hon'ble Vice-Chancellor of Kerala Agricultural University during August 1987 - June 1992. Dr Silas was also Chairman of Marine Products Exports Development Authority; founder Chairman of Salim Ali Centre for Ornithology and Natural History; Officer on Special Duty (for 18 months) for establishment of ICAR-Central Agricultural Research Institute, Port Blair; Chairman of Scientific and Technical Committee for planning the research programmes of FORV SAGAR SAMPADA; Chairman of Scientific Advisory Committees of Centre for Marine Living Resources and Ecology at Kochi, Rajiv Gandhi Centre for Aquaculture and that of Research Advisory Committee of ICAR-Central Institute of Fisheries Education, Mumbai.

The UNDP/FAO/ICAR Centre of Advanced Studies (CAS) in Mariculture at ICAR-CMFRI started under his leadership in 1978-1979; research students who joined for PhD under this programme have now rose to position of Principal Scientist in ICAR institutes, some heading the seafood industry in India today. All of them have augmented the scientific manpower strength in research institutions and the fisheries colleges of State Agricultural Universities and agricultural banks. They are heading several national and international aquaculture programmes. The proposal for CAS was prepared by Dr Silas and it was possible to get the approval from ICAR, FAO/UNDP. In the Mariculture programme, topics of research on open sea mussel farming, edible oyster culture, pearl oyster culture and pearl production, seaweed culture, etc were taken up. Dr Silas gave an impetus to Indian marine and brackishwater fisheries sector and was a guiding force behind fisheries research in India. He loved to be engaged in hard and purposeful work.

In the early 1970s, Dr Silas initiated the breeding programme of penaeid prawns at the Narakkal farm of ICAR-CMFRI. He was instrumental in getting the land and water areas for establishment of ICAR-CIBA and its 90 acre farm at Muttukadu, about 35km south of Chennai. He demonstrated that *Penaeus* sp. could be bred after four to six months of farming. At ICAR-CIBA, Dr Silas was able to breed and culture *Penaeus japonicus* and other penaeids. At ICAR-CMFRI, he gave emphasis on monitoring resource exploitation in capture fisheries at the national level and researching on biological and oceanographic factors influencing the fisheries. To meet one of his commitment that research results should reach the stakeholders and industry without delay, Dr Silas started publishing Marine Fisheries Information Service and CMFRI Newsletter.

Fishery scientists Dr G. N. Mitra and Dr T. V. R. Pillay died on 18/7/2006 and 9/2/2005 respectively. Since 2010 till date (May 2018), other eminent fishery and aquaculture scientists of India who have left for heavenly abode are Dr K. H. Alikunhi (died on 26/9/2010), Dr P. V. Dehadrai (died in June 2011), Dr S. N. Dwivedi (died on 26/4/2012), Dr M. C. Nandeesha (died on 27/12/2012), Dr Hiralal Chaudhuri (died on 12/9/2014), Dr J. V. H. Dixitulu (died on 29/5/2015), Dr H. P. C. Shetty (died on 11/11/2015), Dr Radheyshyam (died on 10/10/2017), Dr N. C. Datta (died on 19/3/2018). Most recently we have lost Dr E. G. Silas. Contributions of all of these great fishery scientists have left indelible footprints in growth of education and research in Indian fisheries and aquaculture sector. Dr Silas by his firm steps has evidently marked his footprints in his sphere of activities (Courtesy: Dr V. Kripa, Principal Scientist, ICAR-CMFRI, Kochi).

All photographs: Subrato Ghosh

REFERENCES

Baisya, R.K. (2008): Changing Face of Processed Food Industry in India, *Ane Books India*, New Delhi, pp: 224.

Chakrabarti, P.P., Mandal, S.C., Chattopadhyay, D.N., Mandal, R.N., Paul, B.N. and Jayasankar, P. (2012): Pabda Seed Production and Culture, *ICAR-CIFA Publication*, Bhubaneswar, pp: 29.

Chaturvedi, C.S., Lakra, W.S., Singh, R.K. and Pandey, A.K. (2005): Successful induced Breeding and Larval Rearing of *Pangasianodon hypophthalmus* under Controlled Conditions of Raipur (Chhattisgarh), Souvenir of UP State Biodiversity Board released on Occasion of International Day for Biological Diversity: 106-112.

Lakra, W.S. and Singh, A.K. (2010): Risk Analysis and Sustainability of *Pangasianodon hypophthalmus* Culture in India, *Aquaculture Asia*, XV(1): 34-37.

Nair, C. Mohankumaran and Salin, K.R. (2007): Carp Polyculture in India: Practices and Emerging Trends, *Global Aquaculture Advocate*: 55-57.

Sen, D.P. (2005): Advances in Fish Processing Technology, *Allied Publishers Pvt. Ltd.*, Mumbai, pp:xii.

Index

❑❑❑❑❑